The Implementation and Enforcement of European Union Law in Small Member States

Ivan Sammut • Jelena Agranovska
Editors

The Implementation and Enforcement of European Union Law in Small Member States

A Case Study of Malta

palgrave
macmillan

Editors
Ivan Sammut
University of Malta
Msida, Malta

Jelena Agranovska
University of Malta
Msida, Malta

ISBN 978-3-030-66114-4   ISBN 978-3-030-66115-1   (eBook)
https://doi.org/10.1007/978-3-030-66115-1

This Palgrave Macmillan imprint is published by the registered company Springer Nature Switzerland AG.
The registered company address is: Gewerbestrasse 11, 6330 Cham, Switzerland

Preface

This book is the result of an academic project to study the impact of EU law on Maltese law, undertaken by the Department of the European and Comparative Law within the Faculty of Laws of the University of Malta. The project was closed in October 2020 and does not take into account developments that occurred after this month. The main objective of this work is to examine how the legal order of Malta, which is the European Union's smallest Member State, manages to cope with the obligations of the EU's *acquis communautaire*. As far as the legal obligations are concerned, it does not make a difference whether you are from a Member State of around half a million or a Member State of over 80 million people. Smaller Member States have the same obligations as the largest Member States, yet they have to meet these same obligations with very fewer resources. This work looks at the marriage between Malta's legal order, which is a mixed legal order based mainly on the civil law tradition but heavily influenced by the common law tradition. It examines how the Maltese legal system manages to fulfil its obligations both in terms of the primacy of EU law, as well as how the substantive European Union law is transposed and implemented. It also examines on how Maltese courts look at EU law and how they manage or not manage to enforce it within the context of national law. The first chapter deals with the relationship between EU law and the Maltese constitutional order, which is mainly based upon the Westminster model. It then looks at how substantive EU law, mainly through directives, is implemented into Maltese law. This is followed by some case-studies dealing with specific examples on the implementation of substantive law into the Maltese legal system such as Consumer law, Company law or Criminal law, among others. This work can serve as a model to demonstrate how EU law is being implemented in the EU's smallest Member State and can serve as a basis to study the effectiveness of European Union law into the domestic law of its Member States in general.

Msida, Malta   Ivan Sammut
                                                    Jelena Agranovska

CONTENTS

NOTES ON CONTRIBUTORS

Jelena Agranovska is a Lecturer in European and Comparative Law within the Faculty of Laws, University of Malta. Before joining the University of Malta in 2016 she had read the degrees of PhD at King's College London, LL.M in European and International Law at London Metropolitan University and LL.B at the Moscow State University. Jelena's academic interests lie broadly in the areas of EU law, corporate law and the law of the Internal Market. Her research often takes a transnational, European or comparative perspective and applies an interdisciplinary approach to law. Dr Agranovska has published reports, articles and book chapters on various aspects of EU law. She has been elected as Associate of King's College. She is also a member of the UM Faculty of Laws Research Ethics Committee and a member of the Faculty Board.

Christopher P. Buttigieg is the Chief Officer Supervision at the Malta Financial Services Authority (MFSA) and sits on the Authority's Executive Committee. He is a member of the Board of Supervisors of the European Banking Authority and the European Securities and Markets Authority (ESMA). He is the Chair of the ESMA Data Standing Committee. Dr Buttigieg has a D.Phil. in Law Studies from the University of Sussex (UK) and is a Senior Lecturer in the Banking and Finance Department of University of Malta.

Joseph A. Cannataci is head of the Department of Information Policy & Governance at the Faculty of Media & Knowledge Sciences of the University of Malta. He was appointed as the first-ever UN Special Rapporteur on Privacy in 2015, UN mandate was renewed in 2018 until

July 2021. He continues as Co-director (on a part-time basis), of STeP, the Security, Technology & e-Privacy Research Group at the University of Groningen in the Netherlands, where he is Full Professor, holding the Chair of European Information Policy & Technology Law. A Fellow of the British Computer Society (FBCS) and UK Chartered Information Technology Professional (CITP), Full Professor (adjunct) at the Security Research Institute & School of Computer and Security Science, Edith Cowan University Australia, Senior Fellow and Associate Researcher at the CNAM Security-Defense-Intelligence Department in Paris, France. He has designed and led several EU-supported research projects, both as PI and overall scientific coordinator, since 1986. The Republic of France decorated him as *Officier de l'Ordre de Palmes Academiques* (2002).

Mireille M. Caruana is Senior Lecturer and Head of the Department of Media, Communications and Technology Law at the Faculty of Laws of the University of Malta. Previously she was employed within the same University as a research assistant for various research projects coordinated by the Department of Information Policy and Governance at the Faculty of Media and Knowledge Sciences. Her research interests span a set of topics that raises new political, social and ethical issues, and requires consideration of appropriate legal and regulatory approaches to tackling them, normally outside of traditional legal paradigms. She was awarded her PhD from the University of Bristol in 2014 based on her thesis on privacy and the differing European approaches to uses of personal data in the criminal justice sector. She graduated Doctor of Laws (LLD) from the University of Malta in 2002 and Magister Juris in European and Comparative Law in 2004. She was called to the bar (Advocate) in Malta in 2003. She specialised in Computer and Communications law at Queen Mary University of London (LLM 2008). She has written and published articles on various aspects of privacy and data protection law. She has been appointed as a member of the UM Board of the Centre for Distributed Ledger Technologies. She is also a member of the University Research Ethics Committee and its sub-committee on data protection.

David Fabri LL.D., PhD (Melit.) graduated in law from the University of Malta in 1979. For many years he headed the Department of Commercial Law at the University of Malta and coordinated the Master's programme in Financial Services. He has been lecturing at University since 1994, where his main areas of interest are company law, financial services legislation, consumer protection policy, whistle-blowing, regulation and business ethics, subjects on which he has written and lectured extensively. He has been involved in consumer protection since 1978 and was the official advisor on consumer law and policy to successive governments between 1990 and 2005. He led the official negotiations and transposition of the Consumer Protection Chapter throughout the EU Accession process between 1999 and 2004. He has served on the University Research Ethics Committee, the Cooperatives Board, the Consumer Affairs Council and the Financial Services Tribunal, and he is currently a member of the Administrative Review Tribunal. Between 1992 and 2015, he occupied senior regulatory positions with the Malta Financial Services Authority. He was a co-drafter of various laws, including the Consumer Affairs Act, the Product Safety Act, the Companies Act, the Malta Financial Services Authority Act and the Co-operative Societies Act.

Stefano Filletti graduated with a Bachelor of Laws, Diploma of Notary Public and Doctor of Laws from the University of Malta. He furthered his studies in international law and law of the seas at the International Maritime Law Institute (IMO) where he was awarded a Masters of Law Degree with distinction. As a Chevening Scholar, he read law at the University of Oxford where he was awarded a Masters of Law Degree in Criminal Law (M.Jur) with distinction. He was also awarded a Doctor of Philosophy (PhD) Degree from the University of Malta. He is a resident lecturer at the University of Malta in Criminal law and also a visiting lecturer at the International Maritime Law Institute (IMO). He is the co-editor of the New Journal of European Criminal law published by Intersentia, co-editor of the Mediterranean Journal of Human Rights published by the Faculty of Laws at the University of Malta, and co-editor of the journal Law and Practice published by the Chamber of Advocates (Malta). Filletti also acts as an advisor to both private and public entities and has held various posts. He Heads the Maltese Delegation to the Council of Europe—European Committee on Crime Problems. Filletti is also the Head of the Department of Criminal Law within the Faculty of Laws at the University of Malta.

Ivan Mifsud graduated LLD in 1999 and PhD in Administrative Law, in 2008. After thirteen years working for the Maltese Parliamentary Ombudsman (mainly investigating complaints related to planning, police and local councils), and three years chairing the Prison Board of Vistors, he joined the University of Malta as a resident academic as Senior Lecturer, in September 2013. He is currently Head of the Department of Public

Law, and Dean, Faculty of Laws. He has authored various contributions and in 2017 published a monograph called *Judicial Review of Administrative Action; An Examination of Article 469A COCP and Judicial Review in General.*

Jeanine Rizzo is a lawyer who graduated from the University of Malta who has furthered her studies in the fields of intellectual property law and art & antiquity law at Masters level at University College London. While in London she was researching the law of bailment and antiquity law. Upon her return to Malta, she built a practice in intellectual property law and art law at Fenech & Fenech Advocates for 11 years. She has now ventured forward with her own consultancy, RIZZO. Jeanine specialises in Copyright (both new and old media), trademarks, patents, design rights, entertainment law, music law and film law. Her experience has taken her into the depth of the creative industries with tailored legal expertise to all matters concerning the industry. She is also a lecturer and examiner at the University of Malta and at MCAST, is frequently published writing about the subject and is a former member of the Chamber of Commerce RTDI Committee.

Ivan Sammut is the Head of Department of European and Comparative Law at the Faculty of Laws of the University of Malta, where he has been a resident academic since 2005. He is currently the Deputy Dean of the Faculty of Laws. Before joining the University, as an academic, he practised law in Malta and acted as a consultant in EU law. He was also employed with the European Commission for two years. He also acts a freelance EU law consultant with various local law-firms and has authored several reports for the European Commission among others. As a practising lawyer in Malta, his practice specialises in EU law. He has been a Senior Lecturer and a coordinator of a Jean Monnet module dealing with EU legal drafting and translation since 2013. He has considerable experience in the translation of EU documents and also holds an MA in Translation Studies from the University of Birmingham in the UK. He graduated BA in Law and European Studies in 1999 and Doctor of Laws in 2002 from the University of Malta. He was called to the Maltese bar in 2003. Subsequently, he read for LL.M. in European Legal Studies from the College of Europe in Bruges (Belgium), and a Magister Juris in European & Comparative law from the University of Malta. In 2010 he successfully defended his PhD thesis, which is in the area of European private law, at the University of London. His teaching and research interests focus in particular on the EU Internal Market legislation, Justice and Home Affairs law, Competition law, European private law from a comparative perspective and European private international law. He has published various academic articles in international peer-reviewed journals such as the *European Private Law Review* among others. Dr Sammut is also the author of a monograph entitled *Constructing Modern European Private Law – A Hybrid System* published by CSP in the UK. He is also an Associate Research Fellow at the IALS, University of London.

Ruth Vella Falzon (LL.B.(Melit.), LL.D.(Melit.), M.Jur. (Melit.) graduated from the University of Malta in 2009 with a Doctor of Laws, and she holds a Magister Juris degree in European & Comparative Law. She was admitted to the bar in 2009. Ruth is a Senior Legal Executive within the Legal Office of the University of Malta. She lectures in the LL.M. in European & Comparative Law course at the Faculty of Laws. She also delivers lectures to several Faculties including an Intellectual Property course at the Edward Debono Institute and the Doctoral School. She is also an examiner and supervises several dissertations in the LL.B (Hons) and LL.M programmes at the University of Malta.

Abbreviations

AFCOS	Anti-Fraud Co-Coordinating Service
AFSJ	Area of Freedom Security & Justice
AG	Advocate General
AIF	Alternative Investment Funds
AIFMD	Alternative Investment Funds Managers Directive
AML/CFT	Anti-Money Laundering/Combating the Financing of Terrorism
APA	Approved Publication Arrangements
ARM	Approved Reporting Mechanisms
CCTV	Closed-circuit Television
CFI	Court of First Instance
CFREU	Charter of Fundamental Rights of the European Union
CFSP	Common Foreign & Security Policy
CJEU	Court of Justice of the European Union
CMLRev	Common Market Law Review
COCP	Code of Organisation and Civil Procedure
COREPER	Committee of Permanent Representatives in the EU
CSP	Cambridge Scholar Publishing
CTP	Consolidated Tape Provider
CUP	Cambridge University Press
DG	Directorate-General
DGT	Directorate-General for Translation
DPA	Data Protection Act
DSM	Digital Single Market
EAW	European Arrest Warrant
EBLR	European Business Law Review

EC	European Community
ECB	European Central Bank
ECHR	European Convention on Human Rights
ECJ	European Court of Justice
ECR	European Court Report
ECtHR	European Court of Human Rights
EEC	European Economic Community
EEIG	European Economic Interest Grouping
EFTA	European Free Trade Area
EJN	European Justice Network
ELJ	European Law Journal
ELRev	European Law Review
EMU	Economic Monetary Union
EP	European Parliament
EPC	European Patent Convention
EPO	European Patent Office
EPSO	European Personnel and Selection Office
ESMA	European Securities and Markets Authority
EU	European Union
EUI	European University Institute
EUIPO	European Union Patent Office
EUTM	European Union Trademark
FIAU	Internal Audit and Financial Investigations Unit
GDPR	General Data Protection Regulation
IAID	Internal Audit and Investigations Department
IALS	Institute of Advanced Legal Studies (London)
IATE	Interactive Terminology for Europe
IDPC	Information and Data Protection Commissioner
IP	Intellectual Property
IPRD	Industrial Property Registrations Directorate
IT	Information Technology
JIT	Joint Investigative Team
LN	Legal Notice
LTR	Long-Term Residence
MCCAA	Malta Competition and Consumer Affairs Authority
MCST	Malta Council for Science and Technology
MEP	Member of the European Parliament
MEUSAC	Malta EU Action Steering Committee
MiFID	Markets in Financial Instruments Directive
MJ	Maastricht Law Journal
MLR	Modern Law Review
MS	Member States

NAIFs	Notified Alternative Investment Funds
NEM	National Execution Measure
OHIM	Office for the Harmonisation of the Internal Market
OJ	Official Journal
OUP	Oxford University Press
PCT	Patents Cooperation Treaty
SCN	Supervisory Coordination Network
SE	*Societas Europeas*
SEA	Single European Act
SIFI	Systemically Important Financial Institutions
SL	Source Language
SMEs	Small & Medium-Sized Enterprises
TEC	Treaty European Community
TEU	Treaty European Union
TFEU	Treaty on the Functioning of the European Union
TL	Target Language
TRIPS	Trade-Related Aspects of Intellectual Property Rights
TRIS	Technical Regulation Information System
UCITSD	Undertaking for Collective Investment in Transferable Securities Directive
UK	United Kingdom
UN	United Nations
UPCA	Agreement on a Unified Patent Court
WIPO	World Intellectual Property Organisation
WTO	World Trade Organisation

LIST OF FIGURES

LIST OF TABLES

CHAPTER 1

Introduction—The Maltese Legal System and the EU

Ivan Sammut

The Republic of Malta or in Maltese *Repubblika ta' Malta* lies in the heart of the Mediterranean Sea, between Europe and North Africa. The island state is situated 90 km south of Sicily, Italy and 288 km east of Tunisia. The state comprises an archipelago—Malta, Gozo, and Comino and several smaller uninhabited islets. The combined area is 316 km², the larger island of Malta being 246 km² while Gozo, the second largest island is 67 km². The population is around half a million making Malta the most densely populated country in Europe, with well over 1300 inhabitants per square kilometer. Valletta, is the capital, the cultural, administrative and commercial centre of the country and the official languages are English and Maltese. Maltese is a language of Semitic origin written in Latin scripts.

Malta has experienced turbulent history marked by several invasions. The archipelago has been inhabited for 7000 years. In the ninth century

I. Sammut (✉)
University of Malta, Msida, Malta
e-mail: ivan.sammut@um.edu.mt

© The Author(s), under exclusive license to Springer Nature Switzerland AG 2021
I. Sammut, J. Agranovska (eds.), *The Implementation and Enforcement of European Union Law in Small Member States*,
https://doi.org/10.1007/978-3-030-66115-1_1

BC, the Phoenicians colonised the Maltese islands. A succession of other rulers followed notably Carthaginians, Romans, Byzantines Arabs and then Spanish. In 1530 Malta was ceded by the Emperor Charles V of Spain to the Knights of the Order of St John. During the next 250 years, Malta functioned as a *de facto* independent state ruled by the Knights. After the departure of the Order in 1798, the French forces briefly occupied Malta. Then at the request of the Maltese, the Maltese islands were placed under British protection in 1799 and formally became part of the British Empire from 1814 under the Treaty of Paris. Malta gained its independence on 21 September 1964 and became a democratic constitutional monarchy. The Constitution was amended on 13 December 1974 turning Malta into a Republic with a unicameral Parliament. The Maltese constitutional setup is based on the Westminster model with an election taking place not longer than five years from the previous one. The House of Representatives elects the President, who is the head of state with a two-thirds majority.[1] The President of the Republic appoints a Prime Minister who is the chief executive of the government and who commands a majority in the House of Representatives. In 2004, Malta joined the European Union after a process that took almost 15 years. In 2008, Malta joined the European Monetary Union with the Euro replacing the Maltese Lira and also joined the Schengen area.

The Maltese legal framework reflects its history. Malta has been a traditional Civil law country. The British introduced Common law, especially in the domain of public law. After independence, Malta became a hybrid jurisdiction keeping the traditional civil law notions in its private law but adopting modern common law influences, especially with regards to its commercial law. Public and administrative law remain mainly modelled on English law. In the run-up to the EU's accession and after, Maltese law became also heavily influenced by European Union law. The Maltese legal order is a microcosm of hybrid legal traditions.

A legal tradition has been defined as a set of 'deeply rooted historically conditioned attitudes about the nature of law, the role of law in the society and the political ideology, the organisation and operation of a legal system'.[2] Merryman goes on to suggest that whereas 'a legal system is an

---

[1] The President used to be elected by a simple majority of the House until the constitutional amendments of 2020.

[2] Merryman J. H., *The Civil Law Tradition: An Introduction to the Legal Systems of Western Europe and Latin America*, 2nd ed., Stanford, CA: Stanford University Press, 1985. pp. 19–25.

operating set of legal institutions, procedures and rules, ... a legal tradition puts the legal system into cultural perspective'.[3] Suppose one were to take on his arguments. In that case, it can be established that while each legal system, which very often can be attributed to a political unit, is independent, yet there may be common denominators with other independent legal systems. Together these independent legal systems may share history, culture or political ideology and can be described as legal tradition.

As far as the historical development is concerned de Cruz argues that on the one hand, it was widely accepted that the English common law development was reasonably clear-cut, wherein a large body of rules founded on unwritten customary law evolved and developed throughout the centuries with pragmatism, strong monarchs and unwritten Constitution.[4] On the other hand, non-common law European countries have a more chequered history, and this has led several writers to label the tradition as 'Roman-Germanic'.[5] This reflects the strong influence of Roman law as well as the influence of the French Civil Code, namely the Code Napoleon and the German Civil Code. The most significant influence is that Roman law introduced the notions of codification and systematisation of concepts into identifiable concepts. This is in stark contrast with common law whose principles developed in an *ad hoc* fashion mostly in response to dispute settlement. Therefore the significant historical fact is that common law was developed by the courts, giving judge-made law considerable 'weight' whereas civil law was formulated and compiled at universities.

Having highlighted the difference between civil law and common law jurisdictions, one may ask, but what about mixed jurisdictions? Legal systems are generally 'mixed' in the sense that a variety of other systems has influenced them. While not going into the argument at this stage as to whether 'mixed' implies a legal family in its own right, one can easily refer to jurisdictions which for various reasons in their development drew principles from both common law and civil law. One can mention the laws of Scotland, Québec, Louisiana, Malta, and differently, one can also mention the European Union legal order itself as examples.

---

[3] de Cruz P., *A Modern Approach to Comparative Law*, Kluwer, Deventer-Boston, 1993, p. 27.
[4] *Ibid* p. 30.
[5] *Ibid* p. 30.

The Maltese legal order is at the crossroads of civil law and common law. Malta has a long legal history tied to continental Europe, and this very strong connection strengthened, during the period of the Knights from 1530 to 1798 and continued well beyond the arrival of the British in 1800. When the Maltese Civil Code was first enacted in 1868,[6] the major source was the Code de Napoléon. As a result, Maltese substantive private law is based on the Roman/Civil law system. The British period which lasted more than a century and a half did leave a powerful impact on the Maltese legal order. British influence is mostly found in procedural and administrative law whereby the Maltese system is much closer to the British common law system than to the continental civil system.

Nevertheless, the Maltese legal system, unlike the common law system, is a codified system whereby even though the administrative and procedural law is based on common law, it is yet codified. The Maltese Code of Organisation and Civil Procedure (COCP) dates back to 1865.[7] Although the Laws of Malta include codes as their continental counterpart, common law influence can still be seen as codification is not complete. While a good part of private law is found in the Civil Code and Commercial Code, other laws of private law nature are scattered across various chapters of the more than 600 chapters of laws that make up Maltese law. While the courts adopt the adversarial system similar to common law, yet the doctrine of precedent, essential for a 'pure' common law system is absent from Malta. From a constitutional point of view, the Maltese Constitution follows the British model with one major difference. Under the British system, Parliament is supreme, and a Parliament can never bind a future Parliament. Under the Maltese Constitution, Parliament sovereignty is limited by the supremacy clause of the Maltese Constitution.[8]

---

[6] Laws of Malta, Chapter 16, http://www.justiceservices.gov.mt/LOM. aspx?pageid=27&mode=chrono accessed on 5 June 2020.
[7] Laws of Malta, Chapter 12, http://www.justiceservices.gov.mt/LOM. aspx?pageid=27&mode=chrono accessed on 5 June 2020.
[8] Article 66 of the Maltese Constitution, http://www.justiceservices.gov.mt/LOM. aspx?pageid=27&mode=chrono accessed on 5 June 2020.

The above can be appreciated in Maltese law as it belongs to a 'mixed' legal family where concepts from the two major legal families exist side by side. European law is also evolving on a 'mixed family' line. While as a system it originated on civil law grounds, given the fact that the original six countries were civil law jurisdictions, common law principles started leaving their marks following the UK's accession. An example would be the Second Company Directive.[9] In a way, the Maltese legal system could serve as a laboratory to prove how EU law could evolve, bearing in mind certain obvious variables such as that the Maltese legal order is a national legal order. In contrast, the EU legal order is a *sui generis* kind of legal order that exists side by side the national legal order.

Malta's independence from the UK in 1964 was marked by legal continuity at both constitutional and private law level. The advent of independence did not bring any significant changes. Malta opted to continue with the same legal regime it had before, and there was no attempt to shift back to a civil law system as it was before the British colonial period. The change over from monarchy to republic did not alter the *status quo* with regards private law and public law as well. Malta continued to follow the old civil law tradition with regards to pure civil law principles while procedure and new commercial law were modelled from common law traditions. Between 1987 and the beginning of negotiations on EU accession in 1998, Malta continued to come up with modern legal initiatives, particularly in the fields of commercial law and financial services law mainly drawing inspirations from common law traditions. One can mention the introduction of Trust legislation as an example.[10]

Following the EU's accession negotiations and subsequent accession in 2004, Malta seems to have lost the initiative to come up with local legal initiatives. Over the past decade, Malta has been busy transposing EU legislation, namely directives, across various chapters of the laws of Malta rather than through codification. The way transposition takes place is usually through the enactment of an Act of Parliament or subsidiary

---

[9] Second Council Directive 77/91/EEC of 13 December 1976 on coordination of safeguards which, for the protection of the interests of members and others, are required by Member States of companies within the meaning of the second paragraph of Article 58 of the Treaty, in respect of the formation of public limited liability companies and the maintenance and alteration of their capital, with a view to making such safeguards equivalent [1977] OJ L26/1.

[10] Laws   of   Malta,   Chapter   331,   http://www.justiceservices.gov.mt/LOM. aspx?pageid=27&mode=chrono accessed on 1 September 2020.

legislation without any thought as to the origins of the legal tradition of the EU legal instrument and as to how it would best suit the Maltese legal order. One can say that EU transposition is done in a way which is more convenient to satisfy the EU Commission rather than any local legal tradition. The result is that while Malta generally complies with the *acquis communautaire* and the EU Commission is generally satisfied with Malta, the Republic of Malta now has laws spread over more than 600 chapters, and by choice and for political convenience with its European obligations, it is a 'purely' hybrid system. 'Purely' because little thought is given as to how to create and respect local legal traditions, but the aim is to comply with EU law in the shortest possible time and to avoid EU infringement proceedings. Further to this, one could argue that over the past decades since its independence Malta created a mixed legal tradition were ideas can be drawn from various legal systems. Still, mainly the English system and legal tradition is easily adjusted to the local scenario. Basically one can say that it is very difficult to experience legal 'irritants' as it is easy to accept legal 'transplant'.

Malta's legal system is a synthesis of the various legal cultures which exerted influence on it during long years of colonial rule. Though British rule was officialised in 1814, the British refrained from imposing common law in Malta. The Code de Rohan which had been promulgated in the dying days of the long rule of the Knights of Malta was substituted by a local version of the Code de Napoléon in 1852. Other codes were enacted in the same period, most notably the Code of Organization and Civil Procedure, the Criminal Code and the Code of Criminal Procedure. A Maltese legal luminary, Sir Adrian Dingli, was instrumental in the promulgation of these codes, which though extensively amended over the years, still form the backbone of Maltese legislation. He drew extensively from continental codes, such as those of the Italian city-states and the Two Sicilies. However, the Code of Criminal Procedure departed somehow from the continental models, and the accused were given rights which were already prevalent in the United Kingdom, and trial by jury was also introduced.

Over the long years of British colonial rule, British legal influence came increasingly to bear. Fiscal and company legislation follows the British model closely. Since independence in 1964, UK legislation is often mirrored in legislation enacted by the House of Representatives, which is run on rules followed by Westminster. The Maltese Constitution, enacted in 1964, reflects closely British constitutional principles. Still, it also promulgated a bill of fundamental rights which was very much influenced by the European Convention on Human Rights.

The European Convention on Human Rights was subsequently incorporated in domestic legislation in 1987. Since Malta's accession to the European Union in 2004, the *acquis communitaire* and future EU regulations prevail over domestic legislation, and EU directives have to be incorporated in domestic legislation.

The Maltese judicial system is basically a two-tier system comprising a Court of First Instance presided over by a judge or a magistrate, and a Court of Appeal. The Court of Appeal in its superior jurisdiction is composed of three judges and hears appeals from a Court of First Instance presided over by a judge. The Court of Appeal in its inferior jurisdiction is presided over by a single judge and hears appeals from a Court of First Instance presided over by a magistrate. There are also various tribunals which deal with specific areas of law and have varying degrees of competence. The Court hears the majority of appeals from decisions awarded by any of these Tribunals of Appeal in its Inferior Jurisdiction. In contrast, others are heard by the Court of Appeal in its Superior Jurisdiction.

The Director-General (courts), who is appointed by the Prime Minister, is responsible for the administration of the courts. He or she is assisted by the Registrar, Civil Courts and Tribunals, the Registrar Criminal Courts and Tribunals, the Registrar (Gozo Courts and Tribunals), and the Director (Support Services).

The Director-General (courts) is responsible for the management and administration of the Courts of Justice Division, including the registries, archives and other services, and also heads the Courts of Justice Division. All court executive officers performing duties in the Courts of Justice Division take their instructions from and are answerable to, the Director-General (Courts).

The Court of Appeal	Second instance Appellate	The court of appeal hears appeals from the civil courts in both their superior and inferior jurisdiction. (i) this court hears appeals from the first hall of the civil court and the civil court (family section). (ii) appeals from the court of magistrates in its civil jurisdiction, the small claims tribunal and the administrative tribunals are also heard by this court.	(i) Composed of three judges. (ii) composed of one judge.
The Court of Criminal Appeal	Second instance Appellate	This court, in its superior jurisdiction, hears appeals by persons convicted by the criminal court. This court, in its inferior jurisdiction, hears appeals in respect of cases decided by the court of magistrates sitting as a court of criminal judicature.	Composed of three judges Composed of one judge
The Criminal Court	First instance	This court sits as a criminal court and hears criminal cases exceeding the competence of the court of magistrates.	Presided over by a judge who sits with a jury of nine persons
The Civil Court: The first hall of the civil court Civil Court (voluntary jurisdiction section) The Civil Court (family section)	First instance	The first hall of the civil court hears all cases of a civil and/or a commercial nature exceeding the jurisdiction of the court of magistrates. In its constitutional jurisdiction, it also hears cases relating to violations of the constitutionally protected human rights and fundamental freedoms protected by the European Convention of Human Rights and Fundamental Freedoms. The civil court (voluntary jurisdiction section) is a voluntary jurisdiction court. It is responsible for the interdiction or incapacitation of persons of unsound mind, the nomination of tutors for same persons, the opening of successions and the confirmation of testamentary executors. It is also a repository for secret wills. This court hears all cases relating to family matters such as marriage annulment, personal separation, divorce, maintenance and custody of children.	Presided over by a judge Presided over by a judge Presided over by a judge

(*continued*)

(continued)

The Court of Magistrates	First instance	In the civil field, the court of magistrates only has an inferior jurisdiction of first instance, in general, limited to claims not exceeding €11,646.87. In the criminal field, the court has a twofold jurisdiction: as a court of criminal judicature in respect of cases falling within its jurisdiction, and as a court of criminal inquiry in respect of offences falling within the jurisdiction of the criminal court. (i) Court of criminal judicature—this court is competent to try all offences punishable by a term of up to six months' imprisonment. (ii) Court of inquiry—this court conducts the preliminary inquiry in respect of indictable offences and transmits the relevant records to the attorney general. Suppose there is no objection from the accused. In that case, the attorney general may refer cases punishable with a sentence of up to ten years' imprisonment back to the court of magistrates as a court of criminal judicature to hear and decide the case.	Presided over by a magistrate
The Court of Magistrates for Gozo	First instance	In the civil field, the court of magistrates for Gozo has a two-fold jurisdiction: (i) an inferior jurisdiction comparable to that exercised by its counterpart court in Malta; and (ii) a superior jurisdiction, with the same competence as the first hall of the civil court, excluding its constitutional jurisdiction, and the civil court (voluntary jurisdiction section) in Malta. In the criminal field, the court of magistrates for Gozo has the same competence as the court of magistrates as a court of criminal inquiry and as a court of criminal judicature in Malta.	Presided over by a magistrate
The Juvenile Court	First instance	The juvenile court hears charges against, and holds other proceedings relating to minors under the age of 16 years and may make care orders.	Presided over by a magistrate and two members
Small Claims Tribunal	First instance	The tribunal summarily decides, on principles of equity and law, money claims of less than €3,494.06.	Presided over by an adjudicator

The next chapter analyses the relationship between the European and Maltese legal orders. This is then followed by a number of chapters dealing with the way how the Maltese legal order absorbed European Union law from judicial protection and administrative point of view. This is then followed by several chapters dealing with certain specific substantive areas of law.

CHAPTER 2

EU Law and Maltese Law—An Integration or Legal Irritants

Ivan Sammut

1 Introduction

The accession of Malta to the European Union followed a very turbulent political process that witnessed various twists and turns.[1] Before joining the EU Malta had been associated with the European Community for over 30 years. An association agreement was signed already in 1970 and entered into force on 1 April 1971.[2] It provided for an ambitious plan of creating a customs union over ten years (divided into two phases), however, this objective—due to political circumstances—was never achieved under the association framework. A formal application for the

---

[1] For a detailed account see, inter alia, R.C. Caruana, 'The accession of Malta to the EU', in G. Vassiliou, ed., The Accession Story. The EU from 15 to 25 Countries (Oxford, Oxford University Press 2007) pp. 259–296.

[2] Agreement establishing an association between the European Economic Community and Malta, OJ 1971 L 61/2.

I. Sammut (✉)
University of Malta, Msida, Malta
e-mail: ivan.sammut@um.edu.mt

I. Sammut, J. Agranovska (eds.), *The Implementation and Enforcement of European Union Law in Small Member States*, https://doi.org/10.1007/978-3-030-66115-1_2

11

membership in the European Communities was submitted on 16 July 1990. Avis of the European Commission followed in 1993.[3] For several reasons—mainly economic—the opinion was negative. The membership application was frozen in 1996 as a result of changing domestic political climate and reactivated following parliamentary elections in 1998. A subsequent positive opinion of the European Commission permitted Malta to join the second group of countries negotiating the terms of accession and—following the negotiations—allowed it to become a part of the significant bang enlargement of 2004. It is a rule of thumb that membership in the European Union has far-reaching consequences for a national legal order of any Member State. Malta is no exception in this respect.

This chapter seeks to examine the relationship between the EU legal order and the Maltese one and to see how and to what extent the EU legal order has integrated into the Maltese one. The kick-off point is a brief analysis of the constitutional implications of Malta's EU accession, drawing upon the inspiration of the major source of Maltese public law: the British Constitutional and Administrative law. Following a constitutional analysis, the chapter examines how the two legal orders effectively work side by side in day-to-day matters. This is analysed through a brief study of the impact and application of the direct effect of EU legal instruments in the Maltese legal system. The third section of the chapter looks at the way EU substantive law has managed to penetrate Maltese law as a mixed legal system. The examples chosen are indicative of how other legal concepts can be integrated, and the study is by no means an exhaustive exercise. It also helps to analyse how much the Maltese legal system is ready to face new challenges such as that presented by the DCFR (Draft Common Frame of Reference). Finally, the chapter concludes with the effectiveness of EU law from the Maltese experience.

2   THE EU LEGAL ORDER AND ITS IMPLICATIONS FOR MALTESE CONSTITUTIONAL LAW

2.1   *The EU and National Legal Order*

National law derives its validity from the fact that the state that enacts the law is sovereign and is capable of enforcing it in its national territory. Maltese law derives its validity from the Maltese Constitution as the basis

---

[3] Commission Opinion on Malta's Application for Membership, COM (93) 312 final.

of Maltese sovereignty which was recognised internationally when Malta achieved independence in 1964. National law is separate from any other national or international system. A sovereign country is free to sign international treaties. Treaty obligations must be respected, but this merely means that the state could not invoke national law as an excuse for failing to perform its obligations under the Treaties which it has signed towards other contracting parties. States are left to their own devices for finding the most appropriate domestic arrangements for fulfilling their international obligations. So one can say there is *internal supremacy* as opposed to *international supremacy* of treaties and other aspects of their domestic status are a matter of national law.[4] As a result, two theories evolved to demonstrate the relationship between domestic law and international treaties. The monist view, as expressed for instance, by Kelsen, is that national legal orders are 'creatures' of international law. The dualist view, as exposed by Treipel[5] and Anzilotti[6] is somewhat more convincing where they show that national legal orders are separate legal orders, able to resist the penetration of international norms.

Monism and dualism become alternative doctrines when taken in a narrow sense of comparing the actual attitude taken towards international law within each constitutional system. Dualist countries are those countries where the attitude took is that international treaties cannot as such display legal effects in the municipal sphere. This means that their norms must be 'transplanted' into national law before they become operational there. Malta and the United Kingdom are such countries. A good example is the transposition of the European Convention on Human Rights into Maltese Law. For it to be enforceable in the Maltese courts, Parliament had to enact the European Convention Act, and therefore one can plead the provisions of the said Convention as part of Maltese law.[7] Monist countries then are those where the view prevails that international norms are, upon their ratification and publication, 'received' within the national legal orders while preserving their nature of international law.

What are now the consequences of these two different worlds vis-à-vis European Law? Is European Union law a branch of International law? It

---

[4] See F.G. Jacobs & S. Roberts (eds), *The Effect of Treaties in Domestic Law* (Sweet & Maxwell, 1987).
[5] H. Treipel, 'Les rapports entre le droit interne et le droit international' (1923) *Hague Recueil* 77.
[6] D. Anzilotti, *Il diritto internazionale nei giudizi interni* (1905).
[7] Act XIV of 1987.

makes sense to answer first the latter question as opposed to the former. The answer is not found in the Treaties but the landmark judgement of the Court of Justice of the European Union (CJEU)[8] of *Van Gend en Loos*.[9] The CJEU said:

> The objective of the EEC Treaty,[10] which is to establish a Common Market, the functioning of which is the direct concern to the interested parties in the Community, implies that this Treaty is more than an agreement which merely creates mutual obligations between contracting states … It is also confirmed more specifically by the establishment of institutions endowed with sovereign rights …

> The conclusion to be drawn from this is that the Community constitutes a new legal order of international law for the benefit of which the states have limited their sovereign rights, albeit within limited fields, and the subjects of which comprise not only Member States but also their nationals.

The CJEU established that EU law is a separate legal order from that of the Member States. Also, EU law is derived from international law. In this case, the relevant international law is found in the EC Treaty and following Maastricht also in the EU Treaty. From this and subsequent judgments of the CJEU, the doctrines of direct effect and supremacy of EU law have developed. Direct effect can be defined as the capacity of a norm of EU law to be applied in domestic court proceedings. Supremacy or primacy of EU law implies the capacity of that norm of EU law to overrule inconsistent norms of national law in domestic court proceedings. These two principles are closely linked and could be considered in conjunction with each other. However, it could be argued that the principle of supremacy has a much broader implication than direct effect as it could mean the setting aside of national laws to give way to EU law.

Back to the first question posed earlier on, about countries adhering to a monist doctrine, the above does not pose any significant problems. As far

---

[8] The European Court of Justice (ECJ) has been renamed Court of Justice of the European Union (CJEU) by the Lisbon amending Treaty which came into force on 1st December 2009.

[9] Case 26/62 NV *Algemene Transporten Expeditie Onderneming van Gend en Loos v Nederlandse Administratie der Belastingen* [1963] ECR 1.

[10] The European Economic Community Treaty (EEC) of 1957 has been renamed European Community Treaty (EC) in 1993 by the Maastricht Treaty and renamed again as Treaty on the Functioning of the European Union (TFEU) by the Lisbon Treaty amendments which came into force in December 2009.

as the attitude of the dualist doctrine is concerned, it is likely to be more problematic towards EU law, particularly with the issue of supremacy. The relationship between a norm of international origin and a purely national norm becomes, through the transformation of the former, a matter of the internal cohesion of the domestic legal order, and conflicts are to be solved according to the ordinary conflict rules applying within that order. For treaties to take preference over national administrative practices they have to be transformed by an act of the legislator and, in case of conflict, the *lex posterior derogat priori* rule would prevail.

The position as to the extent the application, and not the interpretation, of the Treaty on the Functioning of the EU (TFEU), is a matter of the CJEU and not a national court has been an issue of controversy especially in the early years of European Union law. This was the main reason why the Governments of Belgium and the Netherlands intervened in the *Van Gend en Loos* proceedings in front of the CJEU.[11] In their view, the State Parties to the TFEU had not intended to lay down any obligations concerning the domestic effect of its provisions, so that this matter was left for determination by national authorities and courts according to their respective constitutional rules or judicial traditions. The Advocate General concurred with the three governments and advised the court to declare the question inadmissible. However, despite the impressive barrage of opinions, the CJEU decided that this matter could not be left to the national legal systems themselves but that the TFEU had a direct effect and is therefore applicable in the national courts.

The novelty of this case is not the discovery that European law could have a direct effect. This is because in the case of a Regulation, as an example, it is stated in Article 288 TFEU that a Regulation is capable of having a direct effect. As for the provision of the TFEU itself, they could be perfectly suitable for judicial enforcement in the same way as other international agreements. The crucial contribution of the judgement was instead the question that specific provisions of the Treaty (and later also secondary legislation) had a direct effect was to be decided centrally by the CJEU, rather than by the various national courts each in their way and style. The result of this judgement is that the EEC Treaty, now renamed the TFEU is capable of conferring rights upon individuals which become

---

[11] Case 26/62 *NV Algemene Transportem Expeditie Onderneming van Gend en Loos v Nederlandse Administratie der Belastingen* [1963] ECR 1.

part of their legal heritage and therefore they would be able to be raised in domestic proceedings before the domestic court.

Despite the very close link between direct effect and supremacy, the issue was not dealt with in *Van Gend en Loos* as the referring Dutch Court did not raise the issue. The close link has been examined in a subsequent judgement of the CJEU in *Costa v ENEL*.[12] In the Netherlands whose juridical system is more of a monist than a dualist one, under Dutch Constitutional law, an international treaty is self-executing, and it would prevail over conflicting national law; thus the issue of supremacy was less problematic than that of direct effect.[13] The second occasion for the CJEU to reaffirm the principle of supremacy of Community law came from a Member State that adopts the dualistic approach vis-à-vis international law—Italy. The case concerned the payment of electricity bills to the state company ENEL that has been nationalised contrary to the provisions of the TFEU. The national court was asked to set aside a national law (that nationalised the electricity company) as a result of breaching the TFEU, at that time the EEC Treaty. The Italian Government intervened in the case arguing that the reference by the national court was 'inadmissible', as the national court which referred had no power, under EU law and under national law, to set aside the Italian municipal law. The Government argued that a question on interpretation could not serve a useful purpose.

The CJEU's task in the latter case is much more delicate than the former. Whereas the definition of the conditions of direct effect may easily be considered, under the canons of international law, as an inherent part of the interpretation function of the CJEU, the same cannot be said about supremacy. It is indeed an established principle of international law that international treaties prevail over domestic law when it is applied to relations between powers.[14] However, the issue in *Costa v ENEL* is about internal supremacy of EU law. This is the duty of national courts to enforce an international treaty when it conflicts with national legislation. Such a duty has never been considered as part of international law. However, the failure of international courts could be a contributory factor in the establishment of State responsibility under international law.

---

[12] Case 6/64 *Flaminio Costa v ENEL* [1964] ECR 585, 593.

[13] Article 66 of the Dutch Constitution. Following a renumbering this Article is now Article 94.

[14] See the case of Greco-Bulgarian Communities, Advisory Opinion, 1930 P.C.I.J. (ser. B) No. 17 (July 31).

Wyatt explains that in *Costa*, the preliminary reference mechanism allowed the CJEU to 'stop the clock'.[15] Instead of letting national judges commit what would be a breach of EU law to be sanctioned under Article 258 TFEU, the CJEU seized the opportunity provided by Article 267 TFEU and decided to make EU law prevail over conflicting national norms. The special feature of the TFEU under Article 267 is that it, unlike other treaties, provided for the ingenious judicial mechanism which allowed the CJEU to state its supreme doctrine and to request national courts to follow suit. In the CJEU's own words:[16]

> It follows from all these observations that the law stemming from the Treaty, an independent source of law, could not, because of its special and original nature, be overridden by domestic legal provisions, however framed, without being deprived of its character as Community law and without the legal basis of the Community itself being called into question.

> The transfer by the states from their domestic legal system to the Community legal system of the rights and obligations arising under the Treaty carries with it a permanent limitation of their sovereign rights, against which a subsequent unilateral act incompatible with the concept of the Community cannot prevail.

2.2   The Constitution of Malta

The Constitution serves as the basis of Maltese sovereignty which was recognised internationally when Malta achieved independence in 1964. Before pre-accession reforms of fundamentals of the Maltese legal order, there had been no constitutional provisions dealing with international law and membership in the European Union. The approach of Maltese legal order to international law is a textbook example of dualism, meaning that as long as an international treaty is not formally incorporated into the national law, it remains outside the ambit of the Maltese law. According to the Ratification of Treaties Act 1983,[17] 'no provision of a treaty shall become, or be enforceable as part of the law of Malta expect by or under an Act of Parliament.' This *modus operandi* was employed to incorporate

---

[15] D. Wyatt, 'New Legal Order, or Old?' (1982) 7147, 153.
[16] Case 6/64 *Flaminio Costa v ENEL* [1964] ECR 585, 593.
[17] Ratification of Treaties Act; Act V of 1983; Chapter 304 of the Laws of Malta; text available at http://docs.justice.gov.mt/lom/legislation/english/leg/vol_6/chapt304.pdf

the European Convention for the Protection of Human Rights and Fundamental Freedoms into Maltese law. To make ECHR domestically enforceable the national Parliament had to enact the European Convention Act 1987[18] allowing individuals to plead based on the ECHR as part of Maltese law. In this respect, the system is quite similar to the one known from the United Kingdom. Bearing in mind the experience of the latter with an opening—in the dualist environment—of its domestic legal orders to EU law a very similar modus operandi was employed in Malta. On 16 July 2003 a tailor-made European Union Act the Maltese House of Representatives passed 2003.[19] It entered into force on 1 May 2004—the day of accession to the European Union. The Act facilitated the ratification of the Accession Treaty 2003[20] as well as the opening of the domestic legal system to EU law and amendment of Article 65 of the Maltese Constitution.

2.3   The European Union Act

Having discussed *Van Gen den Loos* and *Costa v Enel*, EU law is, therefore, a separate legal order which has to be distinguished from international law and national law. However, unlike a national legal order, it does not exist independently. Still, its existence is a complement to a national legal order that is the national legal order of each particular Member State for its enforcement. The acceptance of the above vis-à-vis Maltese law could

[18] European Convention Act; Act XIV of 1987, as amended by Acts XXI of 2002, IX of 2006 and Legal Notice 424 of 2007; Chapter 319 of the Laws of Malta; text available at http://docs.justice.gov.mt/lom/legislation/english/leg/vol_7/chapt319.pdf

[19] European Union Act; Act V of 2003, as amended by Act III of 2006 and Legal Notice 427 of 2007 Chapter 460 of the Laws of Malta. Text available at http://www.commonlii.org/mt/legis/consol_act/eua176.pdf

[20] Treaty between the Kingdom of Belgium, the Kingdom of Denmark, the Federal Republic of Germany, the Hellenic Republic, the Kingdom of Spain, the French Republic, Ireland, the Italian Republic, the Grand Duchy of Luxembourg, the Kingdom of the Netherlands, the Republic of Austria, the Portuguese Republic, the Republic of Finland, the Kingdom of Sweden, the United Kingdom of Great Britain and Northern Ireland (Member States of the European Union) and the Czech Republic, the Republic of Estonia, the Republic of Cyprus, the Republic of Latvia, the Republic of Lithuania, the Republic of Hungary, the Republic of Malta, the Republic of Poland, the Republic of Slovenia, the Slovak Republic, concerning the accession of the Czech Republic, the Republic of Estonia, the Republic of Cyprus, the Republic of Latvia, the Republic of Lithuania, the Republic of Hungary, the Republic of Malta, the Republic of Poland, the Republic of Slovenia and the Slovak Republic to the European Union, OJ 2003 L 236/17.

appear to be problematic. First of all, because Malta adopts the dualistic approach and secondly, more important than this for Malta is the issue of the supranationality of its Constitution. Article 6 of the Maltese Constitution provides that:

> Subject to the provisions of sub-articles (7) and (9) of Article 47 and of Article 66 of this Constitution, if any other law is inconsistent with this Constitution, this Constitution shall prevail and the other law shall, to the extent of the inconsistency, be void.

One can get the impression that as a result of this clause, the doctrine of supremacy, as explained in *Costa*, could prove to be problematic. If an EU Treaty or an EU Regulation was to conflict with ordinary Maltese law, it could somehow be accepted, but what if it conflicts with the Constitution?

Malta was not alone in facing such problems at the time of accession. The acceptance of supremacy in the United Kingdom has been even more problematic. Since the British Constitution is mainly unwritten, it is even challenging to conceive amending the Constitution. The main problem is that Parliament is deemed to be supreme. This means that the Parliament has the power to do anything except bind itself in the future. Such a position clearly would make it difficult to transfer power permanently to the European Union as is the spirit in *Costa*. The UK also adopts the dualistic approach.

The UK, after signing and ratifying its Accession Treaty in 1972, decided to give internal legal effect to Community Law, now EU law, through an Act of Parliament: The European Communities Act 1972. Malta followed the UK example by enacting the European Union Act[21] which came into force on accession on 1 May 2004. The aim of this Act is that it incorporates into Maltese law the *acquis communautaire*. This means that by the power of the Act, the *acquis* would have the power of law as Maltese law. This solves the dualistic approach. As far as Maltese law is concerned, a similar instance occurred in 1987 when the European Convention on Human Rights of the Council of Europe, which had been signed and ratified before by Malta, was incorporated into Maltese law through Act XIV of 1987. Also, it is worth mentioning that for this discussion, there is no need to refer to the Brexit process, as Malta has no intention of exiting the EU. Should ever Malta decide to exit the EU, the

---

[21] Chapter 460 of the Laws of Malta.

legal process would probably involve similar legal procedures as the Brexit process in 2019 and 2020.

As far as supremacy is concerned, the issue remains more problematic. In the UK, Parliament is sovereign, and the traditional constitutional principle is that the previous law could never bound it. This means that if Westminster were to enact legislation which conflicts with the EC Treaty after 1972, that law would prevail in terms of British law. According to the doctrine of implied repeal, the courts would be obliged to give effect to the latest expression of Parliament's legislative will and to treat the earlier Act as having been implicitly repealed. As far as Malta is concerned, the problem would appear to be similar, though more limited to the provisions of the Constitution.

So what happens if a British Act of Parliament or the Maltese Constitution were to conflict with European Union law before Brexit? When the UK and Malta signed their accession Treaty, they have accepted an international obligation to comply with EU law. If national legislation were to conflict with EU law, this would mean that the respective Member State would be in breach of the Treaty obligations. If this were to happen theoretically, sanctions could range from a simple Article 258 TFEU procedure to political sanctions and eventual exclusion from the Union. However, this is unlikely ever to happen in good faith. Membership of the Union is voluntary, and a country could, in theory, withdraw from the Union.[22] In practice, it is highly unlikely that a Member State would ever be in a position where its fundamental law would conflict with the principles enshrined in EU law. In fact in *Hauer v. Land Rheinland-Pfatz*, the Court of Justice of the EU argued that it would accept as a fundamental right a rule of law that is protected in the constitutions of some of the Member States.[23] Suppose the right in question would be generally accepted throughout the Union and does not prejudice fundamental Union aims. In that case, the CJEU would probably, as a matter of policy, accept it as a fundamental right under European Union law, even if it is constitutionally protected in one Member State. If the right were a controversial one, it would probably be unlikely that the CJEU would seek to

---

[22] Greenland which became part of the then EEC as part of Denmark in 1973 withdrew from the Community in 1985 after obtaining autonomy from Denmark and negotiated a withdrawal. Then 2020 brought Brexit.

[23] Case 44/79, [1979] ECR 3727.

impose the will of the majority on those Member States who would consider such a right to be fundamental.

Going back to the European Union Act, the primary provision, Article 4(1) provides that:

> All such rights, powers, liabilities, obligations and restrictions from time to time created or arising by or under the Treaty, and all such remedies and procedures from time to time provided for by or under the Treaty, that in accordance with the Treaty are without further enactment to be given legal effect or used in Malta, shall be recognised and available in Law, and be enforced, allowed and followed accordingly.

This is merely a reproduction of Section 2(1) of the British European Communities Act, which proves that Malta attempts to adopt the British approach as regards the legal framework of the adoption of the *acquis*. Section 2(2) of the British Act provides for the implementation of Community obligations even when they are intended to replace national legislation and Acts of Parliament through Order in Council or statutory instrument rather than by primary legislation.

The Maltese Act in Article 3 provides that from 1 May 2004, the Treaty and existing and future acts adopted by the European Union shall be binding on Malta and shall be part of the domestic law thereof under the conditions laid down in the Treaty. Any provision of any law which from the said date is incompatible with Malta's obligations under the Treaty or which derogates from any right, given to any person by or under the Treaty shall to the extent that such law is incompatible with such obligations or to the extent that it derogates from such rights be without effect and unenforceable. From here it emerges that the supremacy of EU law over Maltese law emanates from Article 3 of the said Act. To what extent this would apply if there is a potential conflict with the provisions of the Constitution is debatable. Parallelism can be drawn to the theoretical[24] scenario of having the European Convention of Human Right as enacted in conflict with the Maltese Constitution. The same clout afforded to the European Convention by the Maltese Courts would probably be afforded to the European Union Act. However, given the unique nature of EU law and the rights and obligations that it entails, the fact that Malta voluntarily accepted to join the club should be enough to convince any Maltese Court

---

[24] Theoretical because in practice it is difficult, if not impossible to happen.

that should this theoretical scenario happen in reality, as long as Malta wants to be part of the Union, EU law is supreme. It should prevail even if there were to be a conflict with the Constitution. The sharing of sovereignty is voluntary and unlike a federation, if a country feels that it should no longer share its sovereignty with the other Member States, then legally speaking either opt-out or withdrawal from the Union should be negotiated. Unlike a federation, the EU does not compel the Member States to stay in the Union by force, and in theory, a Member State does not give up any sovereignty, but simply shares it with the rest of the Member States.

To give effect to the provisions of Article 3, the Prime Minister or/and any designated Minister or Authority may by order provide for the implementation of any obligation of Malta, or enable any such obligation to be implemented. Any right enjoyed or to be enjoyed in Malta under or by the Treaty has to be exercised. The same authorities shall also provide for the implementation of any necessary legislation to deal with matters arising out of or related to any such obligation or right or the coming into force, or the operation from time to time of sub-article 4(1) of the Act.

Article 4(1) of the European Union Act aims to make the concept of direct effect part of the Maltese legal system. It deems law which under the EU Treaties is to be given immediate legal effect to be directly enforceable in Malta. Accordingly, Maltese courts, which on the orthodox domestic approach to international law may not directly enforce a provision of an international treaty or a measure passed thereunder, are directed by this Article to enforce any directly effective EU measure. There is no need for a new act of incorporation to enable Malta to enforce each EU Treaty provision, regulation or directive which, according to EU law, has direct effect. Just as in the cases of France, Germany and Italy, the supremacy of EU law is recognised in Malta by a domestic legal process and legal theory—through an Act of Parliament.

The European Union Act also provides for any international treaty concluded by the European Union through its external relations powers. The procedure laid down in Article 4 concern streaties and international conventions which Malta may accede to as Member State of the European Union. Treaties and international conventions which Malta is bound to ratify in its name or on behalf of the European Union by its membership within the European Union shall come into force one month following their being submitted to be discussed by the Standing Committee on Foreign and European Affairs. Also, any financial obligations arising out of the Treaty obligations are to be a charge against the Consolidated Fund.

As for the relationship between the Maltese courts and those of the European Union, the European Union Act provides that for any proceedings before any court or other adjudicating authority in Malta, any question as to the meaning or effect of the Treaty, or as to the validity, meaning or effect of any instruments arising from there or thereunder, shall be treated as a question of law. If the issue is not referred to the CJEU, it must be determined as such by the principles laid down by, and any relevant decision of, the CJEU or any court attached to it. This allows the preliminary reference procedure under Article 267 TFEU from Maltese law. As for the judgments handed down by the Maltese courts, judicial notice must be taken of the Treaty, of the Official Journal of the European Union and of any decision of, or expression of opinion by, the CJEU or any court attached to it on any such question as aforesaid, and the Official Journal shall be admissible as evidence of any instrument or any other act thereby communicated by any institution of the European Union.

To facilitate the implementation to the European Union Act, Act V of 2003 amended Article 65(1) of the Maltese Constitution as follows:

> Subject to the provisions of this Constitution, Parliament may make laws for the peace, order and good Government of Malta in conformity with full respect for human rights, generally accepted principles of international law and Malta's international and regional obligations in particular those assumed by the treaty of accession to the European Union signed in Athens on the 16 April 2003.

In the above provision, the Constitution is complementing the European Union Act in ensuring that all legislation passed in Malta is in line with the EU legal order. The inclusion of this provision ensures that even in the fundamental law of the land, it is provided that all legislation enacted in Malta has to be in line with EU legislation. This makes it easier for the Maltese courts to give priority to EU law in case of conflicting legislation. However, it is worth mentioning that Article 65(1) is not entrenched in Article 66 of the said Constitution. Article 66 provides for special procedures such as a two-thirds majority of the House of Representatives to amend certain parts of the Constitution. Article 65(1) is not included, and thus it can be amended like any other provision of the law. This makes it constitutionally possible for a government to amend the Constitution and to ensure that national law would be supreme over EU law in terms of the Maltese Constitution. However, the very fact that a Constitutional amendment would be necessary would make it clear politically that the Government of the day would like to withdraw from the Union and therefore national law cannot overrule EU accidentally. Withdrawal from the Union is technically possible as Malta is sharing its sovereignty with the other Member States and it has not lost it.

Maltese courts have not yet had enough opportunities to rule on how the EU legal order has been incorporated into the Maltese legal order. However, a look at some British cases could offer some hint as to how the Maltese courts should view the above. Initially, British courts were hesitant in applying the above principles.[25] However, Lord Denning in *Shields v E Coomes (Holdings) Ltd* seemed willing to accept the principle of supremacy of Community law, declaring that Parliament intended, when it enacted the European Communities Act in 1972, to abide by the principles of direct effect and supremacy.[26] As a consequence, in his view, national courts should resolve any ambiguity or inconsistency with EU law in national statutes to give primacy to EU law. He avoided the problem of implied repeal by giving such weight to the 1972 Act, and to Parliament's presumed intention in enacting it. He argued that a UK court should not enforce a later conflicting Act of Parliament if the domestic statute is ambiguous or if it is inconsistent with EU law. However, he did not expressly state that EC law, now EU law, should be given primacy. In Lord Denning's own words:

> In construing our statute, we are entitled to look to the EC Treaty as an aid to its construction; but not only as an aid but as an overriding force. If on close investigation it should appear that our legislation is deficient or is inconsistent with Community law by some oversight of our draftsmen then it is our bounded duty to give priority to Community law ...

> Thus far I have assumed that our Parliament, whenever it passes legislation, intends to fulfil its obligations under the Treaty. If the time should come when our Parliament deliberately passes an Act with the intention of repudiating the Treaty or any provision in it or intentionally of acting inconsis-

---

[25] See *Felixstowe Dock and Railway Company v British Transport and Docks Board* [1976] 2 CMLR 655.
[26] *Shields v E Coomes (Holdings) Ltd.* [1979] 1 ALL ER 456, 461.

tently with it and says so in express terms then I should have thought that it would be the duty of our courts to follow the statute of our Parliament.[27]

Here one can see the judicial reconciliation of Parliament sovereignty with the supremacy of EU law. Suppose a domestic provision of law appears to contravene the EU Treaty or any EU subsidiary legislation. In that case, this is presumed to be an accidental contravention, and in such circumstances, the nation's courts should give effect to the doctrine of the direct effect of EU law if it is the case. So, EU law would prevail over conflicting domestic law. Such overriding is to be viewed as the fulfilment of a real parliamentary intention that the European Communities Act should prevail in case of conflicting legislation. If it is clear that domestic law should prevail, then it must do so.[28]

Lord Denning's overview gives a good idea of how EU law became accepted as a legal order working side by side the English legal order. He explains the position in a nutshell and any further analysis on this point is beyond the scope of this chapter.[29] Naturally, Lord Denning's explanation can be extended to the Maltese legal order. If one were to apply his explanation to the Maltese system, it would mean as follows: if Parliament enacts any law that happens to conflict with the EU obligations, Maltese courts should ensure that the EU Treaties would prevail. However, given the fact that the CJEU has developed the doctrine of supremacy and direct effect, the author of this article would dare to interpret the European Union Act as prevailing over any Maltese legislation and the Maltese Constitution for two important reasons. The Act itself provides for the CJEU's judgments to prevail in case of conflict. This would also mean that if the CJEU says that its ruling should prevail over the Constitution that that will be the case. Secondly, as long as there is the intention to remain in the Union, there is no place for any domestic legislation to conflict with the *acquis*. If a Maltese Act of Parliament were to be enacted to conflict with the *acquis*, then that cannot prevail as long as Malta is in the Union. Once a Community obligation has been legally implemented in terms of the *acquis* and Malta did not negotiate any derogations or opt-outs, Europe is not *à la carte*, and so EU law prevails over any Maltese law.

---

[27] *Macarthys Ltd v Smith* [1979] 23 All ER 325, 329.
[28] For a more detailed debate on this issue see T. Allan, 'Parliamentary Sovereignty: Lord Denning's Dexterous Revolution' (1983) 3 OJLS 22.
[29] ibid. 22.

Does this mean that Malta has lost its sovereignty? No, it has not. By signing the Treaty of Accession of 2003, Malta has accepted voluntarily to take all measures implemented by the Union, to which Malta is now part of the decision-making process, or withdraw from the Union. Malta has pooled some of its sovereignty, and as long as it remains pooled sovereignty is limited. If Malta were to wish no longer to abide with its EU's obligations, then as Brexit was the answer to the UK's wishes, Mexit would be the answer to Malta's.

Could it be argued that the European Union Act amended the Constitution? The answer is no. First of all, nothing in the *acquis* is presumed to conflict with the Constitution. Secondly, the EU Treaties do not provide for any requirement whatsoever in the organisation of the state. A Member State is free to choose and maintain whatever form of Government or legal system it prefers. Thirdly, as far as fundamental rights are concerned, the CJEU has said that it will also draw its inspiration from the constitutions of the Member States.[30] Thus, the European Union Act by making EU law supreme over Maltese law is in no way contravening the provisions of the Maltese Constitution. Any new human rights legislation is likely to be implemented in order to further the protection of, rather than being a threat to, the fundamental rights as enshrined in our Constitution.

Foreseeable problems could be envisaged if 'new human rights' are introduced at European level, which could conflict with principles of the majority of Maltese such as the right to abortion or the right to divorce. As for the first case, this could never affect Malta against its will as it is provided for in the Accession Treaty.[31] As for the latter, it is not a constitutional right in Malta, so if it was introduced as a right, Malta might be bound. However, suppose Malta was to provide against such a right in its Constitution. In that case, likely, European law would not force such a right upon Malta as it is a general principle of EU law not to conflict with the fundamental rights enshrined in the Constitution of its Member States.[32] Thus, a conflict between the European Union Act and the Maltese Constitution is unlikely to exist both in theory and practice.

Naturally, Malta can amend its Constitution in a way as to conflict with EU law. In this case, the Maltese courts should rule that EU law would

[30] See Case 44/79 *Hauer v. Land Rheinland-Pfatz* [1979] ECR 3727.
[31] See Article 50 TEU as amended by the Lisbon Treaty
[32] See Case C-159/90 *SPUC v. Grogan*, [1991] ECR I-4685.

prevail as long as the political intention is to stay within the Union. Malta can get back its full sovereignty if it chooses to withdraw from the EU.

3   The Application of EU Law and the Doctrine of the Direct Effect of EU Law in Maltese Courts

Following Malta's accession, EU law became directly applicable, but this did not result in having a lot of cases dealing with issues of EU law on accession. Lawyers somehow needed time to get accustomed to the idea that now EU law is not foreign law but local law as well. As a result, there have been very few judgments dealing with issues of EU law in the first few months. However, the trend is slowly changing. The number of judgments dealing with EU law has increased and would continue to increase in the future. A good number of the most relevant case law of the Maltese courts dealing with EU law concerns the application of Regulation No 44/2001 and Regulation 1215/2012 concerning the enforcement of judgments delivered by the courts of other Member State.[33]

One of the first cases in this regard is *Opateckan v Ciantar* decided by the First Hall of the Civil Court on 30 June 2005 and confirmed by the Court of Appeal on 27 June 2006.[34] The case is an order of maintenance by a Polish court against a Maltese citizen resident in Malta. The courts of both instances accepted the direct applicability of the above regulation as part of Maltese law. This was one of the first opportunities whereby Maltese courts had the opportunity to accept the direct applicability of an EU Regulation. As a result, the Maltese courts found no difficulties in enforcing the Polish judgment in Malta.

Another case in this regard is *Refalo v Garden of Eden Limited*.[35] This case is about the enforcement of a judgement delivered by the Central London County Court on 14 December 2005 concerning damages as a result of a traffic accident suffered by the plaintiffs against the defendant while on holiday in Malta. The Court of Appeal confirmed the judgement

---

[33] Council Regulation (EC) No 44/2001 of 22 December 2000 on jurisdiction and the recognition and enforcement of judgments in civil and commercial matters [2001] *OJ L12/1; Council Regulation (EU) No 1212/2012* of the European Parliament and of the Council of 12 December 2012 on jurisdiction and the recognition and enforcement of judgments in civil and commercial matters (recast) OJ L 351, 20.12.2012, p. 1

[34] Application number 303/2005 decided on 30/6/2005 and Civil Appeal 303/205/1 decided on 27/1/2006.

[35] Civil Appeal 305/2006/1 decided by the Court of Appeal on 13/03/2007.

of the lower court ordering the enforcement of the English judgement in Malta. The court accepted that the English Court had jurisdiction over the case as the facts arose out of a package tour contract signed in England and based on Article 6 of the said Regulation,

[a] person domiciled in a Member State may also be sued ... where he is one of a number of defendants, in the courts of the place where any of them is domiciled, provided that the claims are so closely connected that it is expedient to hear and determine them together to avoid the risk of irreconcilable judgments resulting from separate proceedings.

While the above case proves that the Maltese highest court is ready to enforce EU law and enforce judgments from the other EU Member States, the Court of Appeal ensures that this is only done after careful analysis that the case falls under the Brussels Regulation. In *GIE (PMU) v Zeturf Ltd*[36] the Court of Appeal revoked a judgment of the lower court enforcing a judgment of the Court of Appeal of Paris. The Maltese Court of Appeal refused to enforce the French judgment because the French Court based its judgement on the grounds of public policy as interpreted by French law. The Maltese Superior Court noted that the French provisions on which the judgement is based do not have an economic objective and are simply intended to protect French public policy. The Maltese Court rightly concluded that the French Court based its judgement on French public law rather than French private law in civil and commercial matters. The Brussels I Regulation expressly excludes the former, so the court concluded that the regulation does not apply to the facts of the case. Another example which one can mention is *RS Software Ltd v. G-T-P Group*[37], where the Court of Appeal dealt with the issue of domicile under the Brussels I Regulation.

While the above case law centred on the application of EU law, there have also been instances where the Maltese Courts had to rule about which law should prevail in case of conflict between EU law and domestic law. In *Sansone v Comptroller of Industrial Property*, the Court of Appeal recognised the hierarchal superiority of an EU regulation over domestic law in case of conflict.[38] Therefore, Maltese courts have no problem in

---

[36] Civil Appeal 92/2006/1 decided by the Court of Appeal on 3/1/2007.
[37] Civil Appeal 147/2006/1 decided by the Court of Appeal on 27/11/2009.
[38] Application 15/20 of 2005 Court of Appeal decided on 22/3/2006.

accepting the superiority of EU law. However, sometimes things do go wrong, and the Maltese Courts do make mistakes in the application of EU law. A typical example is the case of *Izola Bank Ltd v Commissioner of VAT*.[39]

The above case is about the discrepancy between the domestic VAT law[40] and the Schedule under Article 9 of the Sixth VAT Directive.[41] Upon membership, the state had failed to introduce an item taxable under the directive but not taxable under the Maltese VAT law as was implemented. In other words, the state had failed to introduce the tax required under the directive but not under Maltese law as it was enacted. The Court of Appeal quoting *Marleasing*,[42] came to the conclusion that the concept of the direct effect of directives as laid down by the CJEU in *Marleasing* is similar to that of a Regulation. Referring to the earlier *Sansone* judgment delivered by the same court, it ruled that the directive is superior to the Maltese VAT law as it stood. Therefore, the taxpayer had to pay tax based on the non-implemented directive as opposed to the basis of the transposing legislation.

While the above is another proof that the Maltese Courts have no problem in enforcing EU law as such, mistakes are also made. In the above case, the Maltese Court seems to be making the mistake that directives are identical to regulations. While directives could be capable of a direct effect, this does not mean that they are directly applicable. In this case, the Maltese Court is treating a directive as if it is directly applicable. Another mistake made by the Maltese Court is that it ignored the difference between two private parties and the state and individual. In *Marleasing*, although the case was against a private party, another company, it was the Spanish state that was ultimately responsible for the transposition of the

---

[39] Application 18/2006 Court of Appeal decided on 9/5/2007.

[40] Value Added Tax Act, Chapter 406 of the Laws of Malta.

[41] Council Directive 77/388/EC, OJ L 145, 13.6.1977, p. 1

[42] Case C-106/899 *Marleasing SA v. La Commercial Internacionale de Alimetacion SA* [1990] ECR I-4135: 'In applying national law, whether the provisions in question were adopted before or after the directive, the national court called upon to interpret it is required to do so, as far as possible, in the light of the wording and the purpose of the directive in order to achieve the result pursued by the latter and thereby comply with the third paragraph of article 189 of the Treaty.' See also Case C-456/98 *Centrosteel v. Adipol* [2000] ECR I-6007 & C-240-244/98 *Océano Grupo Editorial v. Rocio Murciano Quintero* Case [2000] ECR I-4491.

company law directive into the Spanish Civil Code. The issue here was that the state had failed to transpose a directive which was conferring rights on the individual.

In the local case, it is the Maltese state that is claiming a right against an individual which the state had failed to implement. Thus, the situation of *Marleasing* is inversed. The Maltese Court of Appeal ignored the *Ratti* judgment[43] which is not referred to in its judgement, where the CJEU held that a Member State which has not adopted the implementing measures required by a directive at issue might not rely on, vis-à-vis individuals, on its failure to perform the obligation which the directive entails. It has been reiterated in other CJEU's cases such as *Faccini Dori*,[44] where the CJEU maintained that its case-law on the direct effect of directives seeks to prevent the state from using its failure to comply with EU law and thus depriving individuals of the benefit of the rights which directives may confer on them. Prechal argues that doctrine declared the so-called principle of estoppel to be the ultimate rationale of the direct effect of directives.[45] The Maltese Court of Appeal in the *Izola Bank* case has failed to recognise this. A preliminary reference would probably have been a more cautious approach to clarify matters.

3.1   References for Preliminary Ruling

While the application of EU law is generally satisfactory, surprisingly, there have been very few attempts where the Maltese courts felt the need to explore the possibility of making a preliminary reference under Article 267 TFEU. In fact, during the first five years of membership, no questions were referred to the CJEU under the said procedure. More than 15 years later only four have been referred, an average of one every four years! One of the lowest averages in terms of referrals to the CJEU in the EU.

The most significant attempt in the period between 1 May 2004 and 1 May 2009 which is worth mentioning is the judgement passed by the Court of Appeal on the 26 June 2007 in *GIE Pari Mutuel Urbain (PMU) v. Bell Med Ltd & Computer-Aided Technologies Ltd.*[46] This case is about

[43] Case 148/78 [1979] ECR 1629.
[44] Case C-91/92 [1994] ECR-3325.
[45] S. Prechal *Directives in EC Law* (Oxford, 2004) 258.
[46] Civil Appeal 224/2006/1 GIE Pari Mutuel Urbain (PMU) v. Bell Med Ltd. & Computer Aided Technologies Ltd. decided by the Court of Appeal on 26th June 2007 (text on file with the Author).

the enforcement of a judgement delivered by the French Tribunal de Grande Instance under the Brussels Regulation.[47] The dispute was about the applicability of the Brussels Regulation to the facts of the case. The regulation applies to civil and commercial matters while the French court delivering the judgement was an administrative court.[48] In passing judgment, the Maltese Court of Appeal gave a well-studied analysis of why it should decline to refer. The national court accepted that concerning issues of interpretation of a Community law provision, the said court is obliged to refer to the CJEU. Thus, here the Maltese Court of Appeal is stating clearly that it accepts its duty to refer if the conditions of Article 267 TFEU are satisfied. As regards the interpretation of civil and commercial matters, the court said there are several jurisprudences of the CJEU dealing with this issue. The court refers to authoritative textbooks as proof.[49] However, the court went on to say that the dispute before it was not an issue of interpretation but more of an issue of application. While referring to P. Craig and G. de Bùrca,[50] the Court of Appeal acknowledged that the distinction between interpretation and application is meant to be one of the characteristic features of the division of authority between the CJEU and the national courts, the former interprets EU law while the latter applies it. In this case, the national court felt that there was no need to seek a reference on this point.

The above judgment shows that the Maltese courts are occasionally ready to examine issues concerning points seriously and will not hesitate to refer if it is needed. One can mention Case C-221/09 *AJD Tuna Limited v Direttur tal-Agrikoltura u s-Sajd u Avukat Ġenerali*. This is the first preliminary reference from a Maltese Court, and the First Hall made it of the Civil Court.[51] The Maltese Court referred ten questions about the interpretation of Commission Regulation (EC) No 530/2008 of 12 June

---

[47] Council Regulation (EC) No 44/2001 of 22 December 2000 on jurisdiction and the recognition and enforcement of judgments in civil and commercial matters, *OJ* 2001 L 12/1.

[48] Article 1.1 of the Regulation reads: 'This Regulation shall apply in civil and commercial matters whatever the nature of the court or tribunal. It shall not extend, in particular, to revenue, customs or administrative matters'.

[49] A. Layton and H. Mercer, European Civil Practice *Vol. 1*, 2nd ed., (London, Sweet & Maxwell 2004) pp. 336–349; A. Briggs and P. Rees, Civil Jurisdiction and Judgments, 5th ed., (London LLP 2005) pp. 46–51.

[50] P. Craig and G. de Bùrca, EU Law—Texts, Cases and Materials, 3rd ed., (Oxford, Oxford University Press 2002) pp. 472–473.

[51] OJ 2009/C 205/41.

2008 establishing emergency measures as regards purse seiners fishing for bluefin tuna in the Atlantic Ocean, east of longitude 45 °W, and in the Mediterranean Sea,[52] Council Regulation (EC) No 2371/2002 of 20 December 2002 on the conservation and sustainable exploitation of fisheries resources under the Common Fisheries Policy[53] and Commission Regulation (EC) No 446/2008 of 22 May 2008 adapting specific bluefin tuna quotas in 2008 according to Article 21(4) of Council Regulation (EEC) No 2847/93 establishing a control system applicable to the Common Fisheries Policy.[54]

In this case, the CJEU ruled that:

1. Examination of the questions referred has disclosed no factor of such a kind as to affect the validity of Commission Regulation (EC) No 530/2008 of 12 June 2008 establishing emergency measures as regards purse seiners fishing for bluefin tuna in the Atlantic Ocean, east of longitude 45°W, and in the Mediterranean Sea or of Article 7(2) of Council Regulation (EC) No 2371/2002 of 20 December 2002 on the conservation and sustainable exploitation of fisheries resources under the Common Fisheries Policy as regards the adversarial principle and the principle of effective judicial protection.

2. Examination of the questions referred has disclosed no factor of such a kind as to affect the validity of Regulation No 530/2008 as regards the requirement to state reasons laid down in Article 296(2) TFEU, the principle of the protection of legitimate expectations and the principle of proportionality.

3. Regulation No 530/2008 is invalid in so far as, having been adopted based on Article 7(1) of Regulation No 2371/2002, the prohibitions it contains, took effect from 23 June 2008 for purse seiners flying the flag of or registered in Spain and Community operators who had concluded contracts with them. In contrast, those prohibitions took effect from 16 June 2008 for purse seiners flying the flag of or registered in Malta, Greece, France, Italy and Cyprus and Community operators who had concluded contracts with them, without such difference in the treatment is objectively justified.

---

[52] [2008] OJ L155/9.
[53] [2002] OJ L358/59.
[54] [2008] OJ L134/11.

The second preliminary reference from Malta was made in 2012 in Case C-71/12 *Vodafone Malta Ltd., Mobisle Communications Ltd, v Avukat Generali* et al.[55] This related to a case before the Maltese courts filed by Vodafone Malta Limited and Mobisle Communications Limited against the Attorney General, the Comptroller of Customs, the Minister of Finance and the Malta Communications Authority whereby plaintiffs are contesting the legality of 3% excise tax levied by Government on the use of mobile telephony services arguing that this tax is in breach of EU law—specifically Articles 12 and 13 of Directive 2002/20/EC known as the 'Authorisation Directive'. The European Court in response to the reference made to it decided that Article 12 must be interpreted as not precluding the legislation of a Member State such as the legislation at issue in the main proceedings, under which operators providing mobile telephony services are liable to pay 'excise' duty, calculated as a percentage of the charges paid to them by the users of those services, provided the trigger for that duty is not linked to the general authorisation procedure for access to the electronic communications services market but to the use of mobile telephony services provided by the operators and the duty is ultimately borne by the user of those services, which is a matter for the national court to verify.

The third preliminary reference from Malta was Case C-125/16 *Malta Dental Technologists Association and John Salomone Reynaud v Superintendent tas-Saħħa Pubblika and Kunsill tal-Professjonijiet Kumplimentari għall-Mediċina.*[56] The case is about the recognition of professional qualifications under Directive 2005/36/EC dealing with the conditions governing the practice of the profession in the host Member State. It also dealt with the requirements for the compulsory intermediation of dental practitioner/clinical dental technologists pursuing their profession in the home Member state. The CJEU decided that: Article 49 TFEU, and Article 4(1) and the first subparagraph of Article 13(1) of Directive 2005/36/EC of the European Parliament and of the Council of 7 September 2005 on the recognition of professional qualifications, as amended by Directive 2013/55/EU of the European Parliament and of the Council of 20 November 2013, must be interpreted to the effect that they do not preclude legislation of a Member State, such as that at issue in the main proceedings, which stipulates that the activities of a dental

[55] Decided on 27 June 2013
[56] Decided on 21 September 2017

technologist must be pursued in collaboration with a dental practitioner, since that requirement applies, by that legislation, to clinical dental technologists who obtained their professional qualifications in another Member State and who wish to pursue their profession in the first Member State.

The fourth preliminary reference, Case C-896/19 *Repubblika v Prim Ministru* was lodged on 5 December 2019, and the hearing and final judgement are still pending at the time of writing. The case was filed in the Maltese Constitutional Court at a time when the local NGO Republika was claiming the procedure of appointment of members of the Maltese judiciary may not be in line with the fundamental provisions of the Treaty and some members of the Maltese judiciary may have their appointment *ultra vires*. The questions asked by the national court to the CJEU are the following:

1. Should the second [subparagraph] of Article 19(1) TEU and Article 47 of the Charter of Fundamental Rights of the European Union, read separately or together, be considered to be applicable with respect to the legal validity of Articles 96, 96A and 100 of the Constitution of Malta?
2. If the first question elicits an affirmative answer, should the power of the Prime Minister in the process of the appointment of members of the judiciary in Malta be considered to be in conformity with Article 19(1) TEU and with Article 47 of the Charter of Fundamental Rights, considered as well in the light of Article 96A of the Constitution, which entered into effect in 2016?
3. If the power of the Prime Minister is found to be incompatible, should this fact be taken into consideration with regard to future appointments or should it affect previous appointments as well?

This is one of the most interesting and important cases involving European Union law from Malta. However, it is still pending at the time of writing with the oral hearing set for 27 October 2020. Hence one cannot elaborate further.

3.2   Enforcement Actions Against Malta

In exercising its function as guardian of the Treaties, the European Commission ensures and monitors the uniform application of EU law by the Member States. After a relatively short honeymoon, in 2005 the European Commission started its first infringement proceedings against

Malta. Only in 2005, Malta received 55 formal notices, and the number increased to 77 in 2006.[57] The 2006 statistics do not provide a good impression of Malta in terms of the implementation of EU law. During those two years, Malta was the worst of the ten new Member States in terms of reception of formal notices and out of the EU 25, Italy only surpasses Malta, the Member State with the highest number of formal notices, 126 in all, followed by Greece, Portugal and France respectively. Malta received 19 reasoned opinions in 2005 followed by 18 reasoned opinions in 2006.[58] 2006 saw Malta's first infringements referrals to the CJEU (one of them was later removed from the register).[59] There were three in all making Malta the new Member State with the second-highest number of referrals, exceeded by one by the Czech Republic and at par with Poland.[60] Out of the 77 formal notices received in 2006, 58 related to the non-communication of the transposition measures for directives.

Further, nine resulted in the non-conformity with a directive while three resulted from a bad implementation of a directive. The final nine notices were received as a result to direct infringement of the TFEU.[61] In 2007 Maltese Government received 69 formal notices as well as 25 reasoned opinions.[62] In case of formal notices, 44 dealt with non-communication of transposition measures, 7 with non-conformity of domestic law with directives and 10 with the bad application of directives. Reasoned opinions covered 13 instances of non-notification, 2 of

[57] Commission Staff Working Document: Annex to the 24th Annual Report from the Commission on Monitoring the application of Community Law (2006), SEC (2007) 975; Commission Staff Working Document accompanying the 25th Annual Report from the Commission on Monitoring application of Community Law (2007), SEC (2008) 2855.

[58] Commission Staff Working Document: Annex to the 24th Annual Report from the Commission on Monitoring the application of Community Law (2006). *loc. Cit.* n. 75 at p.10.

[59] See Action brought on 10 March 2006—*Commission of the European Communities v. Republic of Malta (Case C-136/06)*, OJ 2006 C 131/30; Action brought on 14 December 2006—*Commission of the European Communities v. Republic of Malta (Case C-508/06)*, OJ 2007 C 56/15.

[60] Commission Staff Working Document: Annex to the 24th Annual Report from the Commission on Monitoring the application of Community Law (2006). *loc. Cit.* n. 75 at p.10.

[61] Commission Staff Working Document: Annex to the 24th Annual Report from the Commission on Monitoring the application of Community Law (2006). *loc. Cit.* n. 75 at pp.11–12.

[62] Commission Staff Working Document accompanying the 25th Annual Report from the Commission on Monitoring application of Community Law (2007), *loc. Cit.* n. 75, p. 11.

non-conformity and 5 cases of bad application. Eight letters of formal notice and five reasoned opinions covered breaches of the Founding Treaties, regulations and decisions. Other 3 cases were referred to the CJEU.[63]

By 2020 there have been 587 infringement proceedings communicated and closed against Malta.[64] Most of the cases are settled at the administrative stage of the infraction procedure. However, some do reach the judicial stage. Still, one has to remember that an action can be withdrawn by the European Commission when a case is pending at the CJEU. Action in case C-269/08 *Commission v. Republic of Malta* may serve as an excellent example. The action was submitted to the Court on 20 June 2008,[65] however following the transposition of Directive 2004/83/EC[66] into Maltese law,[67] the European Commission withdrew its application thus the President of the Chamber—to which the case had been assigned—removed the case from the register.[68] It merits attention that from 2007 to 2008 the European Commission withdrew all three actions submitted in 2007 and consequentially they were removed from the register of the Court of Justice of the EU.[69]

---

[63] Action brought on 15 February 2007—*Commission of the European Communities v. Republic of Malta (Case C-87/07), OJ* 2007 C 82/46; *Action brought on 13 February 2007—Commission of the European Communities v. Republic of Malta* (Case C-79/07), *OJ* 2007 C 82/43; *Action brought on 20 December 2007—Commission of the European Communities v Republic of Malta* (Case C-563/07), *OJ* 2008 C 51/61.

[64] https://ec.europa.eu/atwork/applying-eu-law/infringements-proceedings/infringe-ment_decisions/index.cfm?lang_code=EN&typeOfSearch=true&active_only=2&noncom=0&r_dossier=&decision_date_from=&decision_date_to=&EM=MT&title=&submit=Search last accessed on 1 October 2020

[65] Action brought on 20 June 2008—*Commission of the European Communities v. Republic of Malta* (Case C-269/08), *OJ* 2008 C 197/16.

[66] Council Directive 2004/83/EC of 29 April 2004 on minimum standards for the qualification and status of third country nationals or stateless persons as refugees or as persons who otherwise need international protection and the content of the protection granted, *OJ* 2004 L 304/12.

[67] An amendment to Refugees Act 2000 was adopted in 2008. See Refugees Act, Act XX of 2000, Chapter 420 of the Laws of Malta (as amended by Act VIII of 2004; Legal Notices 40 of 2005 and 426 of 2007; and Act VII of 2008). Text available at http://docs.justice.gov.mt/lom/legislation/english/leg/vol_13/chapt420.pdf

[68] CJEU, Case C-269/08 Order of the President of the Seventh Chamber of the Court of 5 February 2009, *OJ* 2009 C 141/65.

[69] Order of the President of the Seventh Chamber of the Court of 10 August 2007—*Commission of the European Communities v. Republic of Malta* (Case C-87/07), *OJ* 2007 C 297/65; Order of the President of the Court of 8 August 2007—*Commission of the*

The first-ever judgment in an infraction case against Malta was rendered in case C-508/06 *Commission v. Republic of Malta*.[70] The CJEU held that by failing to communicate plans and outlines required by a directive on the disposal of chemicals Malta has failed to fulfil its obligations under EU law.[71] It is fitting to mention that a good number of infringements against Malta concerns environmental protection. Most of these deal with the impact of major development projects on the environment. The earliest controversial infraction so far was case C-76/08 *Commission v. Republic of Malta*. The factual and legal background is as follows. The European Commission has submitted that Malta failed to comply with Article 9 of a directive on the conservation of wild birds.[72] Malta insisted that it had negotiated a special derogation on spring hunting, while the EU Commission argued that any derogation had to be in line with Article 9 of the Directive with which Malta has allegedly failed to comply.

This was a standard infringement proceeding, yet one of the few where the President of the CJEU entertained a Commission's request for interim measures. According to an order of 24 April 2008 Malta had to refrain from adopting any measures applying the derogation laid down in Article 9 of the Directive for the 2008 spring migration of two species of birds.[73] The CJEU finally decided that by authorising the opening of a hunting season for quails (*Coturnix coturnix*) and turtle doves (*Streptopelia turtur*) during the spring migration period in the years 2004 to 2007, without complying with the conditions laid down in Article 9(1) of Council Directive 79/409/EEC of 2 April 1979 on the conservation of wild birds, as amended, in respect of 2004 to 2006, by Council Regulation (EC) No 807/2003 of 14 April 2003, and, in respect of 2007, by Council Directive 2006/105/EC of 20 November 2006, the Republic of Malta has failed to fulfil its obligations under that directive. This was followed by a second

European Communities v. Republic of Malta (Case C-79/07), *OJ* 2007 C 297/65; Order of the President of the Fifth Chamber of the Court of 18 August 2008—*Commission of the European Communities v. Republic of Malta* (Case C-563/07). *OJ* 2008 C 313/37.

[70] ECJ, Case C-508/06 *Commission of the European Communities v. Republic of Malta* [2007] *ECR* I-172.

[71] Council Directive 96/59/EC of 16 September 1996 on the disposal of polychlorinated biphenyls and polychlorinated terphenyls (PCB/PCT), *OJ* 1996 L 243/31.

[72] Council Directive 79/409/EEC of 2 April 1979 on the conservation of wild birds, OJ 1979 L 103/1.

[73] ECJ, Order of the President of the Court in case C-76/08R *Commission of the European Communities v. Republic of Malta*, n.y.r.

case dealing with trapping of birds. Case C-557/15 *Commission v Malta* decided on 21 June 2018 dealt with the failure of Malta to fulfil its obligations under Directive 2009/147/EC, dealing with the conservation of wild birds, trapping of birds and the Member States' power of derogation. The CJEU decided that by adopting a derogation regime allowing the live-capturing of seven species of wild finches (Chaffinch *Fringilla coelebs*, Linnet *Carduelis cannabina*, Goldfinch *Carduelis carduelis*, Greenfinch *Carduelis chloris*, Hawfinch *Coccothraustes coccothraustes*, Serin *Serinus serinus* and Siskin *Carduelis spinus*), the Republic of Malta has failed to fulfil its obligations under Article 5(a) and (e) and Article 8(1) of Directive 2009/147/EC of the European Parliament and of the Council of 30 November 2009 on the conservation of wild birds, read in conjunction with Article 9(1) of that Directive.

Other well-known infringements against Malta include Case C-12/14 *Commission v Malta* dealing with the failure of Malta to fulfil its social security obligations. The European Commission asked the Court to declare that, by deducting the value of civil-service old-age pensions from the other Member States from Maltese old-age pensions, the Republic of Malta has failed to fulfil its obligations under Article 46b of Council Regulation (EEC) No 1408/71 of 14 June 1971 on the application of social security schemes to employed persons, to self-employed persons and to members of their families moving within the Community. The CJEU disagreed with the European Commission, and Malta carried the day.[74]

Another case is C-178/11—*Commission v Malta*. The Commission claimed that Malta failed to establish strategic noise maps in respect of major roles and agglomeration identified in its report under the second subparagraph of Article 7(1) of Directive 2002/49EC, and to make them available and disseminate them to the public, and to send the information from the strategic noise maps to the Commission. Malta claimed that the report is submitted in 2006 in line with the directive mentioned above concerning 43 major roles on the island for the scope of the said directive. Malta settled, and the Commission finds a note for the case to be removed, Malta bearing the costs of the case.

Another important Case is Case C-351/09, *Commission v Malta* decided on 22 December 2010, dealing with environmental issues with regards to Articles 8 and 15 of Directive 2000/60/EC dealing with the status of inland surface water, and the establishment and operation of

---

[74] Decided on 3 March 2016

monitoring programmes. The CJEU declared that in failing, firstly, to establish monitoring programmes on the status of inland surface water and make them operational per Article 8(1) and (2) of Directive 2000/60/EC of the European Parliament and of the Council of 23 October 2000 establishing a framework for Community action in the field of water policy, and, secondly, to submit summary reports on the monitoring programmes on the status of inland surface water in accordance with Article 15(2) of that directive, the Republic of Malta has failed to fulfil its obligations under Articles 8 and 15 of that Directive.

This case was followed by Case C-376/09 *Commission v Malta* dealing with failure to fulfil obligations on the Regulation (EC) 2037/2000 decided on 19 May 2011. This was about the requirement to decommission fire protection systems and fire extinguishers containing halons for non-critical uses onboard ships. The CJEU ruled in favour of Malta.

Other important infringement proceedings deal with file no.2005/4534 about car registration tax on second-hand cars infringing Article 110 TFEU. Malta had a very high registration tax on second-hand cars which makes it very difficult to import second-hand cars from the other EU Member States. The European Commission insisted that this was discriminatory and in fact the car registration tax regime was amended and a new law based on emissions was enacted in 2009. Perhaps one of the clearest infringement proceedings against Malta is file no. 2005/4778 concerning departure tax on all air passengers starting their itinerary in Malta. The discrimination is evident as the same departure tax was not levied on Maltese domestic flights when they existed. These cases never made it to the CJEU as the Commission chose to drop proceedings once the local law was amended.

Another very important infringement proceedings against Malta were initiated on 20 October 2020 with the regards to the sale of EU citizenship. The Commission considers that the granting by Malta and Cyprus of their nationality—and thereby EU citizenship—in exchange for a predetermined payment or investment and without a genuine link with the Member States concerned, is not compatible with the principle of sincere cooperation enshrined in Article 4(3) of the TEU. This also undermines the integrity of the status of EU citizenship provided for in Article 20 TFEU. Due to the nature of EU citizenship, such schemes have implications for the Union as a whole. When a Member State awards nationality, the person concerned automatically becomes an EU citizen and enjoys all rights linked to this status, such as the right to move, reside and work freely within the EU, or the right to vote in municipal elections as well as elections to the European Parliament. As a consequence, the effects of investor citizenship schemes are neither limited to the Member States operating them, nor are they neutral concerning the other Member States and the EU as a whole. The Commission considers that the granting of EU citizenship for pre-determined payments or investments without any genuine link with the Member States concerned undermines the essence of EU citizenship.[75]

This appears to be a very serious infringement by Malta, a complete disregard to European values. The conditions for obtaining and forfeiting national citizenship are regulated by the national law of each Member State, subject to due respect for EU law. As nationality of a Member State is the only precondition for EU citizenship and access to rights conferred by the Treaties, the Commission has been closely monitoring investor schemes granting the nationality of Member States. The Commission has frequently raised its serious concerns about investor citizenship schemes and certain risks that are inherent in such schemes. As mentioned in the Commission's report of January 2019, those risks relate in particular to security, money laundering, tax evasion and corruption and the Commission has been monitoring wider issues of compliance with EU law raised by investor citizenship and residence schemes. In April 2020, the Commission wrote to the Member States concerned setting out its concerns and asking for further information about the schemes. In a resolution adopted on 10 July 2020, the European Parliament reiterated its earlier calls on the Member States to phase out all existing citizenship by investment (CBI) or residency by investment (RBI) schemes as soon as possible. As stated by President von der Leyen in the State of the Union Address of 16 September 2020, European values are not for sale. As infringement proceedings have just started at the time of writing, it is not possible to discuss further this matter.

---

[75] European Commission Press Release IP/20/1925

4   THE INFLUENCE OF EU LAW ON SUBSTANTIVE
MALTESE PRIVATE LAW

Mixed legal systems, like the Maltese one, owe their *mixité* mostly to legal transplants, that is, the borrowing of legal institutions and rules by one country from another, often initiated by the national courts. Reid and Zimmermann, in their introduction to an important book on Scots law, state:[76]

> If, therefore, the establishment of an intellectual connection between civil law and common law is regarded as an important prerequisite for the emergence of a genuinely European legal scholarship, it should be of the greatest interest to see that such connection has already been established (...) in a number of 'mixed' legal systems. Such systems provide a wealth of experience of how civil law and common law may be accommodated within one legal system.

This statement is closely related to the idea that Scots law and the other mixed jurisdictions are an optimal mix of the best that both civil law and the common law can offer. Mixed legal systems present a mix of national mentality and European uniformity. Thus Malta, with a mixed legal system, is in an excellent position to adopt and integrate the workings of the EU legal order with that of the Maltese one. This reduces the possibility of legal irritants and therefore increases the success of the application of EU law.

Taking advantage of this mixed legal heritage, over the past years since independence Malta has, in certain instances, successfully adopted a comparative approach in its formulation of new legislation. Comparative law could give an insight into how more and to what extent legal integration of private law could take place. Indeed, legal families have their similarities which may facilitate the adoption of legal principles from the other family. Watson controversially argues that a society's laws do not usually develop from within, but are borrowed from other societies.[77] One could agree that comparative law would ease the borrowing from other societies. However, it could also be argued that the Europeanization of private law

---

[76] K. Reid & R. Zimmermann, 'The Development of Legal Doctrine in a Mixed System', in Reid and Zimmermann (eds), *A History of Private Law in Scotland*, Vol 1 (OUP 2000) 3.
[77] See A. Watson, *Legal Transplants: An approach to Comparative Law* (Scottish Academic Press 1974).

is also an opportunity for European law to develop within. Strictly speaking, Watson is referring to the adoption of legal principles from one national legal system to another. Referring to the subject under evaluation, European private law building goes a step beyond that. While a unifying private law at European level would encourage the borrowing from the national legal systems, because such a project may be supported by the needs of achieving the proper needs of as internal market, one should not rule out the creation of new rules at a European level from within the existing fragmented European private law.

The above places Maltese law in an excellent position to continue to adopt the ongoing developments in substantive European private law. The Maltese Trusts Act has been successfully integrated into Maltese law.[78] Trust law by its nature is a common law concept of private law which does not tally with the civil law concept of Maltese private law in general. The possibility of legal irritants in the Maltese legal system is infrequent, and thus, it is easier for it to adopt reforms or new concepts. Following the Communication on European Contract Law,[79] the European Commission adopted a further Communication in February 2003 entitled 'A More Coherent European Contract Law—An Action Plan'.[80] This is considered to be a further step in the ongoing discussion on developments in European Contract Law. One of the key measures proposed in the Action Plan is the elaboration of a CFR. To increase coherence in the contract law *acquis*, the CFR should provide a common terminology (e.g., contract, damages) and rules (e.g., non-performance of contracts). The CFR serves two different aims: (a) It should serve as a tool for the improvement of the *acquis*. The addressee of this tool is in the first place the European Union institutions, above all the Commission, to increase the quality of drafting provisions; (b) It could be the basis for the so-called optional instrument on European Contract Law. In both scenarios, Maltese law would be able to adapt to European developments. From a substantive point of view, no serious problems can be envisaged in the relationship between Maltese and European law.

In 2010 the European Commission published the Green Paper on policy options towards a European contract law for consumers and

---

[78] Chapter 331 of the Laws of Malta.
[79] COM (2001) 398 final.
[80] COM (2003) 68 final.

businesses.[81] The Green Paper proposes several options for the development of European Contract Law including an Optional Contract Code through a Regulation, a Directive on European contract law and a Regulation for a new European contract law or a European Civil Code among other options. From the wording of the Green Paper, one can come to the conclusions that the European Commission will likely continue pursuing the option of an Optional European Contract Law. While not entering the merits of this discussion, it is clear that the Maltese legal order will be able to adopt any of the proposals and if the Optional Code is eventually pursued it is likely that this will have a positive influence on Maltese contract law itself.

EU regulations and directives are the most important legal instruments which would have to be examined to see the effect of EU law on Maltese law. Regulations are binding upon all Member States and are directly applicable within all such States. On accession, all EU regulations became binding in Malta unless a transitory provision or derogation covers them in the Accession Treaty. This means that EU regulations are to be considered as primary law, and they should not be transposed. They are the law. Member States may need to modify their law to comply with a regulation. This may be the case where Regulation has implications for different parts of national law. However, this does not alter the fact that the Regulation itself has legal effect in the Member States independently of any national law, and that the Member States should not pass measures that conceal the nature of an EU regulation. In case national law is not amended, the Regulation would prevail. In the *Variola* case,[82] the CJEU was asked by a national court whether the provisions of a regulation could be introduced into the legal order of a Member State in such a way that the subject-matter is brought under national law. The CJEU explained that under the obligations arising from the Treaty and assumed on ratification, Member States are under a duty not to obstruct the direct applicability inherent in regulations and other rules of Community law.[83] The CJEU explains:

> … Member States are under an obligation not to introduce any measure which might affect the jurisdiction of the court to pronounce on any question involving the interpretation of Community law or the validity of an act

---

[81] COM (2010) 348 final.
[82] See Case 34/73 *Variola v Amministrazione delle Finanze* [1973] ECR 981.
[83] Ibid para 10.

of the institutions of the Community, which means that no procedure is permissible whereby the Community nature of a legal rule is concealed from those subject to it.[84]

As regulations need no transposition, there is no need to elaborate further. Analysis of the implementation of directives proves to be a more effective way to gauge the effectiveness of the transposition of EU law into Maltese law. Directives have been generally transposed either by an Act of Parliament into primary legislation such as the Company Directives[85] or the VAT Directives,[86] or through a Legal Notice such as most of the Labour Directives,[87] or by a combination of both primary and secondary legislation. The best method of implementation would depend on the objectives of the particular directive. An Act of Parliament is usually reserved for the implementation of a directive which is either a framework law on which subsidiary legislation can be enacted, or it is a matter of high national importance. Being transposed through an Act of Parliament would often mean that a national debate is held on the subject matter, and the law would be better publicised.

On the other hand, transposition through a legal notice is faster though less publicised. However, it may be a better way of transposing European law, mainly if the directive is technical and needs to be transposed in a very short time. In practice, it would be impossible to use Acts of Parliament every time, given the number of directives that need to be transposed and the time needed to pass through Parliament. By a combination of primary and secondary legislation as a way of implementing EU directives, an economy of scale in parliamentary time is possible.

5   CONCLUSION

From the above one can come to the conclusion that the integration between Maltese law and EU law has to some extent been a success while more can be done to improve the relationship between these two legal orders which now co-exist side by side. Improvement can come if the state invests more in legal resources for the civil service including the judiciary

---

[84] Ibid para 11.
[85] Chapter 386 of the Laws of Malta.
[86] Chapter 406 of the Laws of Malta.
[87] Regulations 78 to 100 under Chapter 452 of the Laws of Malta.

and the office of the Attorney General/State Advocate as well as the University. Maltese lawyers cannot keep up to date unless they have access to the various legal resources that are mushrooming in Europe, which are making the use of comparative law more accessible and more widespread. Also, the utility of studying the development of Maltese law as a laboratory for European law mentioned earlier on in this chapter is being lost as the lack of adequate legal material on Maltese law makes the Maltese legal order inaccessible to foreign jurists. As a result, it remains unknown and without any influence in the European sphere.

Finally, one of the major challenges still to be tackled seriously facing the 'marriage' between these two legal orders comes not from the legal sphere but the public sphere. Educating the Maltese public about the relationship between the two legal orders is essential as the public at large is its ultimate consumer. The vast majority of Maltese look towards the European Union as a being a rebirth of the now-defunct 'Privy Council' which will have the supreme authority to put right whatever happens to be wrong in the Republic of Malta. Unfortunately, certain politicians and journalists do not help this cause by giving the wrong impressions such as that the European Court of Justice is a Court of Appeal which it is not, and that one can go to it whenever local redress is not obtained which is not the case. Putting matters into context and a proper information campaign could help save a future tragedy for the confidence that the Maltese public has in the EU institutions could hit rock bottom if it would be based on false pretences. Perhaps it is time to realise that EU law is not a superior foreign law but part of domestic law which the Maltese state has enacted in partnership with the other Member States through the EU institutions. Both legal orders exist side by side for the benefit of the individual who must not be afraid to fight for his or her rights should it be the case. Considering the hybrid nature of the Maltese legal order, legal irritants are also highly unlikely.

CHAPTER 3

EU Law in the Republic of Malta: The Judicial Protection Point of View

Jelena Agranovska

1 INTRODUCTION

Upon joining the European Union in May 2004, Malta agreed to respect the rule of EU law in good faith and comply with obligations stemming from the '*acquis communautaire*' in a correct and timely manner. The core essence of the Union would be undermined if the Member States that form it would be allowed to disregard the binding force of policies agreed at the EU level by infringing EU law or by maintaining national laws which are contrary to the Treaties. Any form of non-compliance with the *acquis*, be it through action or inaction on behalf of the signatories to the Treaties, could render the efficacy and uniformity of Union law non-existent. In order to guarantee effective application of Union law, two procedural avenues to the Union judicature were created through which enforcement could be achieved at both the public and private levels.

J. Agranovska (✉)
University of Malta, Msida, Malta
e-mail: jelena.agranovska@um.edu.mt

I. Sammut, J. Agranovska (eds.), *The Implementation and Enforcement of European Union Law in Small Member States*,
https://doi.org/10.1007/978-3-030-66115-1_3

47

Firstly, there is a centralised avenue for public enforcement through direct actions in the Court of Justice of the European Union (CJEU). In cases of non-compliance the EU Commission, acting as a 'guardian of the Treaties', could employ enforcement system provided for in Article 258 of the Treaty on the Functioning of the European Union (TFEU), which foresees the matter being brought before the CJEU under a so-called infringement action. Designed to be a system based on dialogue, the core prerequisite of Article 258 TFEU is to find an amicable solution during the pre-litigation stage of the procedure in order to remedy the infringement and avoid referral to the CJEU altogether. The infringement action system is successful in persuading the erring Member States to rectify their conduct since in around 95% of all infringement cases the parties were able to find an amicable solution to the dispute. Therefore, throughout the years, it has become evident that Member States choose to duly comply with their obligations before the case reaches the judicial stage of the Article 258 TFEU procedure. However, in those few cases where the Member States resist complying and are prepared to go all the way to the Court, a ruling confirming an infringement of EU law would consequently impose an additional compliance obligation on the Member State in question. This post-judgement obligation is re-enforced with the financial sanction procedure envisaged in Article 260(2) TFEU which could potentially impose heavy fines on the Member State which resorts to persistent non-compliance in spite of the condemning judgement under Article 258 TFEU.

Although a success story, the enforcement action procedure has its obvious flaws. One of the most evident shortcomings is the fact that this system is likely being engaged only as a weapon of last resort and only for those few select cases where the Commission is highly confident that it has all the trumps to thwart any defences put forward by the Member States. This "strategic" use of the Commission's powers and EU's own resources (both financial resources and its political bargaining powers) rests on the premise that other infringement cases of less blatant non-compliance or borderline cases would reach the same result via the second decentralised avenue of the Union's judicature, designed for enforcement at the private level. This decentralised or indirect route starts at the national level whereby a national court refers a question to the CJEU on validity or interpretation of EU law through the preliminary ruling procedure envisaged in Article 267 TFEU. Therefore, although private parties can never make use of the enforcement system provided for under Article 258

TFEU, they may successfully attack the very same national provision through this indirect action of the preliminary ruling procedure.

Although both the centralised and decentralised procedural routes to the Union judicature are two very different enforcement channels with incomparable 'philosophies' underpinning them, the ultimate goal is to ensure that the Member State in question complies with the *acquis* by whichever means necessary in order to rectify the confirmed breach. However, as this chapter will argue, this status quo on the division of direct and indirect enforcement channels will sometimes not amount to an optimal solution in the local context, since the preliminary reference procedure is highly unlikely to be sought after or used in order to attack any incompatible national measures and specifically those relating to the environment. In addition, compared to the other Member States' record, infringement cases involving Malta are relatively few, which, on the one hand, could be indicative of Malta's overall good record of compliance with EU law. This statement could further be supported if one considers a number of infringement actions which have been terminated following Malta's compliance. Yet, on the other hand, a very low number of infringement proceedings against Malta coupled with just a handful of preliminary reference requests over the span of sixteen years could also indicate that the combination of direct/indirect enforcement systems is not as effective as generally perceived. Therefore, this chapter will seek to assess the perceived effectiveness of the combined EU enforcement system in Malta, by first analysing whether there are areas where non-compliance remains a significant problem which could persist even following the condemning judgement under Article 258 TFEU, and secondly, whether the decentralised avenue via Article 267 TFEU could be seen as an effective tool to remedy national non-compliance.

The chapter starts with defining the scope and role of the enforcement system envisaged in Article 258 TFEU and its 'sister' provision Article 260 TFEU in Sect. 2, also briefly touching upon another type of enforcement actions which allows Member States to take another Member State before the CJEU according to Article 259 TFEU. The aim of this section is to emphasise the true nature of the enforcement system, this being its ability to persuade the erring Member State to comply in good faith with their obligations without the need of a condemning judgement by the Court. Section 3 then briefly reflects upon compliance theories, subsequently applying those to the Maltese situation in Sect. 4, which will assess Malta's compliance with case-law of the CJEU in the area of the environment.

This chapter will analyse the practical application and effects of enforcement actions on national turf. It is in this context that the effectiveness of the infringement and sanction procedures will be analysed, specifically by looking at instances where sanction mechanism has been employed against Malta. The findings of Sect. 4 will also be compared with similar situations vis-à-vis sanction procedures prevalent in another three small EU Member States (Latvia, Estonia and Lithuania). This comparative analysis allows one to draw relevant conclusions on the effectiveness of the enforcement actions. Section 5 of this chapter will also examine the role played by the preliminary reference procedure in Malta over the past sixteen years of EU membership and contrast it with the extent and scope of the local jurisdiction's recourse to this mechanism and the experience in small EU Member States (Latvia, Estonia and Lithuania) and attempt to draw relevant assessments from this comparison.

2   ENFORCEMENT MECHANISMS

2.1   Infringement Procedure: Article 258 TFEU

Upon joining the club, Malta conformed to its rules: it had agreed to be loyal to the EU, to sincerely cooperate with it and to generally act in good faith towards all the obligations stemming from the Treaties. This, the so-called principle of 'sincere co-operation' or 'loyalty to the EU' principle, is enshrined in Article 4(3) TEU[1], which states:

> Pursuant to the principle of sincere cooperation, the Union and the Member States shall, in full mutual respect, assist each other in carrying out tasks which flow from the Treaties.

> The Member States shall take any appropriate measure, general or particular, to ensure fulfilment of the obligations arising out of the Treaties or resulting from the acts of the institutions of the Union.

> The Member States shall facilitate the achievement of the Union's tasks and refrain from any measure which could jeopardise the attainment of the Union's objectives.

[1] Treaty on European Union 2012/C 326/01. Previously Article 10 EC and Article 5 EEC Treaty.

In brief, the 'sincere co-operation' principle obliges Member States to comply with the EU *acquis* by duly implementing all binding measures and by ensuring that there is no national law which is contrary to the Treaties. Hence, broadly speaking, there could be two instances when Member States could fail to adhere to the principle enshrined in Article 4(3) TEU—either by act or by omission. The latter could be a result, for example, of a failure to transpose a Directive into national legal order or a failure to comply with a condemning judgement of the CJEU. The former breach could come as a consequence of incorrect transposition of a Directive or persistent maintenance of national law which is contrary to EU law. The matter is relatively clear-cut as regards the so-called 'non-communication' cases where the Member State fails to transpose a Directive on time and communicate the result of national transposition to the Commission. Likewise, any somehow defective transposition of a Directive would also be a rather straight forward infringement. In both these cases, the infringement action would likely be straightforward, as the Member State in question would barely have any defences that the CJEU would be willing to accept justifying this type of breach. Non-communication cases alongside the poor transposition cases and cases which were ruled in favour of Malta are outside the scope of this study and will not be considered at further depth. Other breaches, where the Member State implements or maintains national law which is contrary to the Treaty are much more difficult to detect, and there could be valid justifications which the Member States could present in Court in order to defend their national practice. As a result, non-compliance in these cases could be of much greater concern—this being the target of this study.

The EU Commission acts as a 'watchdog' by ensuring that all the Member States remain loyal to the Union—the general institutional duty imposed on the Commission by Article 17 TFEU. Obviously, the 'watchdog' does not have the eyes and ears in every backyard of every province of every Member State or a capacity to detect all possible ongoing infringements. Many incompatible national laws which came under the Commission's radar were attributed to the provinces and were rather archaic.[2] Hence, the Commission heavily relies upon complaints received

---

[2] As in the infamous 'Volkswagen' Case C-112/05 *Commission v Germany* [2007] ECR I-8995 where the law which was complained about was dating back to 1960s' (Law governing the transfer of share rights of Volkswagenwerk GmbH to private parties of 21/07/1960 (BGBI. I 1960 and BGBI. III).

from aggrieved natural and legal persons, who would rely on the Commission's ability to act in lieu of themselves having the standing to challenge the national measure directly. Since 2008 the Commission employs a new way of handling the complaints by means of the administrative system of the EU Pilot, which Malta has joined in 2012. Most of the infringement actions go through the EU Pilot system before the infringement action procedure is engaged. The 'watchdog', however, is not obliged to take action and bite at every incoming infringement by engaging the enforcement mechanism envisaged in Article 258 TFEU.

The Commission's discretion as regards initiation of the infringement action rests on two pillars on which Article 258 TFEU is based: firstly, on an explicitly wide discretion evident throughout all the lengthy stages of the enforcement procedure, as will be discussed below, and secondly, on the structure of the procedure itself which is designed not to be a punitive measure, but rather one of co-operation and dissuasion. Article 258 TFEU provides that:

> If the Commission considers that a Member State has failed to fulfil an obligation under the Treaties, it shall deliver a reasoned opinion on the matter after giving the State concerned the opportunity to submit its observations.

> If the State concerned does not comply with the opinion within the period laid down by the Commission, the latter *may* bring the matter before the Court of Justice of the European Union.

The official part, therefore, consists of pre-judicial and judicial proceedings. The aim of the entire enforcement procedure is to give the erring Member State sufficient time to reach a friendly, out-of-court settlement with the Commission and to ultimately comply. Given that only around 5% of all infringement cases are referred to the CJEU, it could be maintained that generally the Member States strive to comply in order to avoid facing the Court. The said procedure is a lengthy multi-stage negotiation process, based on compliance bargaining, which initially begins with negotiations behind the scenes through an exchange of informal correspondence (first stage). When infringement is detected, the Commission would first resort to informal bargaining by employing political pressure through dialogue with national authorities. Ideally, either throughout bilateral meetings or through an exchange of informal letters, the Member

State officials who adhere to the principle of sincere co-operation would aim to assist the Commission in good faith. Historically, during these so-called 'package meetings' many infringements have been rectified, making this friendly out of the Court solution a very effective alternative dispute resolution mechanism. However, in some instances, especially where sensitive interests of Member States were at stake, national authorities have turned a deaf ear and a blind eye on any informal attempts to make them change their national position on the matter. Informal dialogue could easily become a monologue since Article 258 TFEU does not impose any compliance obligations on the Member State concerned. It is in tough non-compliance cases like these that the formal enforcement procedure of Article 258 TFEU could be employed. However, it does not mean that it unequivocally will or indeed should be. The Commission enjoys full discretion on the matter[3], and it could choose not to pursue the matter any further, and there may[4] or may not be certain valid reasons for this.

The first informal stage is followed by the pre-judicial stage (second stage) which consists of official correspondence to which the text of Article 258 TFEU refers. During this stage, the Commission issues two types of formal written warnings to the Member State concerned: a formal letter which is then followed by a reasoned opinion. Although the former (the so-called 'letter of formal notice') is a key procedural requirement under Article 258 TFEU without which the action may not commence,[5] it is not binding. The letter is the first step in the formal pre-judicial stage of the procedure, which serves a dual purpose. First, it allows the Commission to kickstart the infringement action mechanism by informing the Member State of all[6] the charges which may be raised in action before the CJEU. Secondly, the letter of formal notice gives the Member State concerned the opportunity to submit its observations in relation to all the grounds of complaint put forward by the Commission and to prepare its defence.

---

[3] As confirmed through numerous case-law of the CJEU such as e.g., Case 48/65 *Alfons Lütticke v Commission*.

[4] as suggested by the Advocate General Roemer in the infringement case against France Case 7/71 *Commission v France* [1971] ECR 1003.

[5] as confirmed by the Court in Case 51/83 *Commission v Italy* [1984] ECR 2793.

[6] as confirmed by the Court in Case 31/69 *Commission v Italy* [1970] ECR I-00025. Importantly, the letter of formal notice must relate to proceedings relating to Article 258 as stated in *Commission v France* case C-230/99 [2001] ECR I-01169.

The letter must give the Member State concerned sufficient time to respond, and it used to be the case prior to around 2007 that the letter would not set a deadline by which a reply would be expected. Only in the extraordinary circumstances and so when urgency was required, would the Commission set such a deadline.[7] Nowadays it is common practice that the letter of formal notice contains a deadline by which the Member State is to submit its observations, however, this is a rather recent invention aimed at streamlining the procedure.[8] Although the setting of the deadline is at the Commission's discretion and its length could vary from case to case, the Member State would normally have two months within which to submit their reply.

Two points should be mentioned here. First, sometimes additional letters of formal notice could be sent to the Member State concerned.[9] Such additional letters would allow the Commission to reply to the Member State's observations in order to clarify some points mentioned in the first formal letter or then to add some new charges which may be eventually raised at the judicial stage of the procedure. In a similar vein, the Member States are not precluded from sending additional letters to the Commission after they have already replied to the letter of formal notice. This further set of correspondence once again elucidates on the role played by the infringement procedure—the one of a dialogue which aims to settle the case amicably without the need to take ones' own member of the club to court. The second point is that since the letter of formal notice does not impose a positive obligation to reply on the national authorities, they may as well ignore the letter and fail to reply to it[10] (or indeed any subsequent

---

[7] As was the case in C-174/04 *Commission v Italy* [2005] ECR I-4933 and C-112/05 *Commission v Germany* [2007] ECR I-8995 where the Commission requested Italy and Germany to submit their observations within two-month period.

[8] Following the re-organization of the way the Commission handles the potential infringements in its 2007 Communication 'A Europe or Results—Applying Community Law' COM (2007) 502 final, the Commission is now committed to decide on whether the case.

[9] As is the case in active infringement case against Malta in relation to VAT on yachts, see European Commission (INF/20/202), 12 February 2020, February infringements package: key decisions, Taxation: Commission sends an additional letter of formal notice to Malta for not levying the correct amount of Value Added Tax on yachts, available at: https://ec.europa.eu/commission/presscorner/detail/EN/INF_20_202, last accessed on 10 September 2020, also see the now closed Case C-178/11 *Commission v Malta*, Order of the Court, ECLI:EU:C:2012:227.

[10] As was the case for example, in Case C-274/06 *Commission v Spain* [2008] ECR I-00026.

letters) altogether, or reply to it after the specified deadline (if any) established by the Commission.[11] There would be no repercussion for the Member State if any of the above omissions occur.

What happens after the initial exchange of the official correspondence is the following. Either the Commission takes some time to try once again and persuade the Member State concerned to comply by employing political pressure, or it may move on to the second step in the formal pre-judicial stage by issuing the second written warning to the Member State—the reasoned opinion. Another outcome would be that the Commission decides not to pursue the matter any further and the enforcement action ends here with the closure of the case. How much time may pass between the issuing of the letter of formal notice and the reasoned opinion depends entirely on the Commission as many different variables could affect this period being either very long (when there are possible national compliance measures in the pipeline) or making it very short (when there is the need to take the matter to court as soon as the procedure of Article 258 TFEU permits).

The reasoned opinion is the expression of the Commission's official position. It requires the Member State to comply by a specified deadline, which is usually set for two months, but in cases of urgency could be much shorter.[12] Similarly, as with the letter of formal notice, the Member State's authorities could fail to reply on time[13] or fail to reply altogether.[14] However, in contrast to the formal letter, there could be repercussions for such an omission, specifically, if this omission is coupled with non-compliance. Likewise, additional reasoned opinions could be issued.[15] Suppose there is no compliance by the time specified in the reasoned

---

[11] For example, as in Case C-174/04 *Commission v Italy* [2005] ECR I-4933.

[12] As in Case C-178/11 *Commission v Malta*, Order of the Court, ECLI:EU:C:2012:227 where the Commission has set a one-month compliance period for Malta to establish strategic noise maps required under Article 7(1) of Directive 2002/49/EC, to make them available and disseminate them to the public, and to send the information from these strategic noise maps to the Commission. See Commission Report of 24 June 2010 (IP/10/832), available at https://ec.europa.eu/commission/presscorner/detail/en/IP_10_832, last accessed on 10 September 2020.

[13] As in Case C-367/98 *Commission v Portugal* [2002] ECR I-4731.

[14] For example, as in Case C-174/04 *Commission v Italy* [2005] ECR I-4933, where the two-month period lapsed with no response from Berlusconi's government, so the matter got referred to the Court; similarly, in C-274/06 *Commission v Spain* [2008] ECR I-00026 Spain has not replied to the reasoned opinion and the matter got referred to the CJEU.

[15] As in Case C-178/11 *Commission v Malta*, above.

opinion. In that case, the Commission may refer the matter to the CJEU bringing the infringement action procedure to its culminating step—the third stage in the form of a judicial procedure. When assessing the infringement at stake, the Court refers to the situation as it stood at the end of the period laid down in the reasoned opinion, so it will not take account of any subsequent amendments to the contested measures.[16] Consequently, compliance on the Member State's own initiative can be effectively achieved only before the period specified in the reasoned opinion has lapsed. Having said this, it is important to note, that the Commission may still withdraw its application to the Court while the case is still pending, which may occur in the event of due compliance by the Member State.

During the judicial stage, the CJEU examines the merits of the case and determines whether the breach has occurred, subsequently issuing a declaratory judgement on whether or not the Member State has failed to fulfil its obligations under the Treaty, specifically by acting contrary to EU law or by infringing the principle of sincere co-operation and loyalty to the EU enshrined in Article 4(3) TEU. Currently, on average, it takes around 32 weeks to handle infringement cases.[17] Although Article 258 TFEU remains the predominant enforcement action used against the Member States, and indeed the only enforcement action relevant in the Maltese context, the second type of direct enforcement action provided in the Treaty needs also be mentioned here.

2.2   Infringement Procedure: Article 259 TFEU

Article 259 TFEU allows Member States to take other Member States before the CJEU. However, Article 259 TFEU actions are extremely rare[18] due to the possible political implications. Firstly, it is one of the core

---

[16] Case C-58/99 *Commission v Italy* [2000] ECR I-03811, para. 17; Case C-463/00 *Commission v Spain* [2003] ECR I-4581, paras. 25–28; Case C-196/07 *Commission v Spain* [2008] ECR I-00041, paras. 26–28.

[17] Commission Staff Working Document, part I: General Statistical Overview, Accompanying the Document Monitoring the Application of European Union Law, 2019 Annual report, p. 14.

[18] There are total of five cases to date C-141/78 *France v United Kingdom* (Fisheries dispute over Re Fishing Net Mesh sizes), C-388/95 *Belgium v Spain* (Designation of origin of 'Rioja' wine), C-145/04 *Spain v UK* (Eligibility to vote in EP elections in Gibraltar, C-364/10 *Hungary v Slovakia* (Refusal to allow entry to President of Hungary), C-591/17 *Austria v Germany* (Passenger car vignette) and C-457/18 *Slovenia v Croatia*, concerning a maritime border dispute.

tasks of a supranational institution—the Commission—to act as an independent and neutral arbiter and take the defaulting Member States to court. Therefore, in some cases, the Commission has intervened to take over the action as it did in two cases against France[19] which commenced by the UK under Article 259 TFEU concerning French measures which continued after the Commission's UK beef export ban had been lifted. Secondly, the administrative procedure provided for in Article 259 TFEU aims at avoiding the judicial stage because there is a real threat of retaliation by the defendant party. Above all, the liberal recourse to Article 259 TFEU enforcement action would conflict with the core aims of the Union, which was based on the premise of peace and sincere co-operation between its members. Subsequently, in only one case the CJEU has ruled in favour of a Member State, dismissing the actions in full or in part or denying jurisdiction in another five.

The judgement issued pursuant to enforcement action under Article 259 TFEU is also of a declamatory character, however, it also imposes an independent compliance obligation on the Member State, pursuant to provision of Article 260(2) TFEU which is discussed in the subsequent section. Ideally, in line with the sincere cooperation obligation, the Member State has to cooperate with the Commission post-judgement and sincerely try to resolve the matter and comply with the ruling of the Union Court.

2.3   Sanction Procedure: Article 260 TFEU

The CJEU has no jurisdiction to oblige Member States to comply with the Court's judgement issued pursuant to either Articles 258 and 259 TFEU in any particular way or within a specified period of time. Yet, the national authorities are obliged to initiate a compliance process immediately and to fully comply without delay. It is therefore logical that the appropriate action of the respective government in such a case should be relatively simple: comply as soon as possible—this would not only see the Member State acting in good faith as per Article 4(3) TEU principle but likewise, it would conform to additional compliance burden which stems from Article 260 TFEU. Pursuant to sanction procedure envisaged in Article 260(1) TFEU, the Member States are explicitly obliged to take all

---

[19] Case 232/78 *Commission v France* ECR [1979] I-02729 and 1/00 *Commission v France* [2001] I-09989.

the necessary measures and comply with judgments of the Court. If despite the compliance obligations and sincere cooperation principle, the breach is not promptly remedied following the infringement action judgment, the Commission's last resort to ensure compliance is to initiate a sanction procedure under Article 260(2) TFEU, which foresees the imposition of financial penalties for non-compliance with a judgment:

> If the Commission considers that the MS concerned has not taken the necessary measures to comply with judgment of the Court, it may bring the case before the Court after giving that State the opportunity to submit its observations. It shall specify the amount of the lump sum or penalty payment to be paid by the MS concerned which it considers appropriate in the circumstances. If the Court finds that the MS concerned has not complied with its judgment it may impose a lump sum or penalty payment on it.

As evident from the text, the sanction procedure is simplified in the way that there is only one procedural step during the pre-litigation stage—the Commission has to notify the Member State of the perceived breach. Although Article 260(2) TFEU provides for a single notification, it does not preclude the Commission from issuing an additional letter of formal notice[20] mirroring the practice employed under sister provision of Article 258 TFEU.

Even more so than under Article 258 TFEU procedure, Member States are eager to avoid the embarrassment of being sued for obstinate non-compliance with the condemning judgement (and face hefty financial fines that come with it) so for as little as 10% of all the cases delivered by the CJEU the sanction procedure under Article 260 TFEU was ever used. In those few cases where the Member State persisted in non-compliance even under threat of Article 260(2) TFEU the likelihood that the Member State will be the winning party is extremely slim. To the best of the present author's knowledge, there is to date only one instance in which the Court found that action by the Commission under Article 260(2) TFEU has been unfounded.[21] From the year the sanction procedure has been intro-

---

[20] For example, in C-326/07 *Commission v Italy* [2009] ECR I-02291 the Commission issued additional letter of formal notice in the course of infringement procedure pursuant to Article 258 TFEU and then additional letter of formal notice course of sanction procedure pursuant to Article 260 TFEU.

[21] See Case C-95/12 *Commission v Germany* [2013] ECR I-0000, For relevant discussion see Agranovska, J. 'Free movement of capital and Golden Shares in Volkswagen: unexpected twist or foreseeable outcome?', available at: https://blogs.kcl.ac.uk/kslreuropeanlawblog/?p=678#.X5Hh5IgzaUk.

duced by the Treaty of Maastricht until 2020, there was a total of thirty-eight judgements imposing sanctions on the Member States. Similarly, as with infringement action procedure under Article 258 TFEU, the bulk of cases which go through the sanction procedure derive from the area of the environment, and the analysis of the Maltese situation will confirm this trend.

The good record of compliance with the original infringement action judgements comes in contrast with the analysis presented in Sect. 4 of this contribution since it will be demonstrated that the ratio of infringement *vs* sanction procedure is much higher when we consider judgements against Malta in comparison to the three Baltic states.

3   Why Comply?

As mentioned above, the compliance obligation derives from the legally binding duty enshrined in Article 4(3) TEU, the so-called 'loyalty to the EU' or 'sincere cooperation' principle, obliging Member States to duly comply with the EU *acquis*. Therefore, Article 4(3) TEU is of fundamental importance, which signifies that the very essence of the Union rests on the Member States' sincere willingness to cooperate and comply in good faith with Union law. This positive obligation is then re-enforced by another compliance obligation stemming from Article 260 TFEU. There is an overall consensus[22] that the enforcement system created by Articles 258 and 260 TFEU is successful in facilitating compliance. However, both the Commission and academic literature also agree that non-compliance remains a serious concern.[23] How serious is this a concern within the Maltese context will be analysed below.

Simply looking at the number of all the infringement proceedings commenced against Malta cannot be taken as a yardstick for measuring the actual level of compliance since such proceedings would culminate in an

---

[22] *See* e.g., Beach, D. (2005) 'Why governments comply: an integrative compliance model that bridges the gap between instrumental and normative models of compliance', *Journal of European Public Policy*, 1466–4429, Volume 12, Issue 1, 2005, pp. 113–142; Panke, D. (2010) 'The Effectiveness of the European Court of Justice: Why Reluctant States Comply', November 2010, MUP, p. 256.

[23] *See* Tallberg, J. (2000) 'Supranational influence in EU enforcement: the ECJ and the principle of state liability', *Journal of European Public Policy*, 7:1, 2000, pp. 104–21; Börzel, T.A. (2001) 'Non-compliance in the European Union: pathology or statistical artefact?', *Journal of European Public Policy* 8(5), pp. 803–24.

actual judgement only in particularly hard cases of non-compliance. Therefore, this assessment will only consider cases which concern issues other than non-communication and poor transposition of EU law, as significant resistance to comply could be expected in such instances.

Member States have to comply with the entire EU *acquis*, and this includes complying with agenda-setting jurisprudence of the Court. One would expect, that if there are condemning judgements on similar measures in one Member State, this will prompt all other Member States to 'see the light' and comprehensively comply in good faith by embarking on wide-ranging policy changes. It could be assumed that in cases where there exists an agenda-setting body of case-law on violation of a particular EU provision (or any ongoing infringement actions)—this would send a clear message to all: amend your national provisions as soon as possible – otherwise, it will soon be your turn to face the Court. However, other Member States may believe that their national provisions are justified by some overriding reasons and relentlessly try to defend their position, specifically when provisions at stake are seen as important to the general populace as will be the case in Case-studies 1 and 2 on hunting and trapping derogations in Malta.

Since the Member States are giving 'flesh and blood' to the smooth operation of Union law, non-compliance with agenda-setting judgments of the CJEU could be seen as one of the most serious forms of non-compliance. Failure to comply with such judgments would signify that the defending Member State may be acting in bad faith towards its obligations enshrined in the Treaty, revealing a wider resistance to the policy setting of the EU's institutions on the issue at stake. This scenario can be seen as the most severe form of non-compliance, which qualifies as obstructionist non-compliance in bad faith. Any such obstructionist non-compliance conduct questions the authority of the Court, the effectiveness of the EU enforcement system and the policy-making abilities of the Commission.

Regarding compliance with the rulings, the Court has consistently held that 'the incompatibility of national legislation with [...] [the EU's] provisions, even provisions which are directly applicable, can be finally remedied only by means of national provisions of a binding nature which have the same legal force as those which must be amended.'[24] This implies that overruled provisions could only be validated by adequate national law that would amend or repeal them within the shortest time possible. However,

---

[24] Case C-367/98 *Commission v Portugal* [2002] I-04731 at p. 41.

as this study claims, some Member States would repeatedly fail to comply in good faith, specifically when important national interests are at stake. Unwillingness to completely overhaul national provisions following the infringement action demonstrates that for Maltese authorities EU law is important, yet national interests may sometimes prevail. Therefore, persistent non-compliance with obligations stemming from the Treaties by retaining national provisions that are subject to infringement action raises an important question of distribution of power between the States and the EU.

To understand and predict obstructionist behaviour in relation to the infringement actions in the Republic of Malta, it is necessary to explore some of the factors which could prompt or preclude compliance in good faith. The following paragraphs will explore the prerequisites and tendencies which could predict Malta's pull towards comprehensive *vs* minimalist compliance or non-compliance in bad faith, which in turn would reveal the actual state of the effectiveness of the infringement and sanction procedures on national grounds.

Firstly, it is necessary to comment on the overall compliance problems which could affect the effectiveness of the enforcement system and to analyse whether these are applicable to compliance within the national context. Much of the current academic research is concentrated on the effectiveness of a combined compliance approach (management and enforcement) used by the European enforcement system.[25] Here, enforcement assumes that the Member States violate law voluntarily because they are not willing to bear the costs of compliance. At the same time, the management approach accepts that Member States are generally willing to comply with the law of the EU but lack the capacity.[26] The combined approach was claimed to be made very effective in its battle against Treaty violations, reducing non-compliance to a temporal phenomenon as sooner

[25] See ex, Börzel, T.A.; Hofmann, T.; Panke, D.; Sprung, C. (2010), 'Obstinate and inefficient: why Member States do not comply with European Law', Comparative Political Studies and Tallberg, J. (2002) 'Paths to compliance: enforcement, management, and the European Union', *International Organization* 56(3), pp. 609–43.
[26] Börzel, T.A. (2003) 'Guarding the Treaty: The Compliance Strategies of the European Commission' in Cichowski R., Börzel T. (eds), 'The State of the European Union, 6', September 2003, pp. 197–221(25), p. 199; however earlier Börzel suggested that the lack of the Member States' compliance with the EU law was not attributed to the lack of willingness or capacity to comply in Börzel, T.A. (2001) 'Non-compliance in the European Union: pathology or statistical artifact?', *Journal of European Public Policy* 8(5): 803–24, p. 804.

or later all Member States comply. However, this study challenges this theory by assessing the effectiveness of the judicial instruments applied repeatedly against Malta, against the same governments and within the same policy area of environment protection.[27]

Conversely, the present study challenges the view that non-compliance is a temporal phenomenon, by opposing it to the obligation to comply with a judgement without delay and the fact that Malta should not only amend its laws as soon as possible and effectively address the Court's ruling by shifting to comprehensive compliance in good faith, but also to withhold from implementing and maintaining any similar measures. The compliance obligation is again re-enforced with the existence of the agenda-setting case-law of the Court, which addressed similar national measures in the other Member States. The following question arises: 'to what extent is non-compliance with the environment-related judgements a temporal phenomenon in Malta?'

To understand and predict Malta's behaviour in relation to enforcement actions on environmental breaches, it is necessary to explore some of the factors that could influence and/or predict compliance in good faith. For this purpose, it is necessary to outline different factors which will be taken into account for contextual compliance analysis. The following analysis of issue-related factors and variables, though by no means exhaustive, can be helpful in setting the scene for predicting and explaining Malta's compliance with environmental judgments. The aggregate effect of the reasons below could potentially be the reason for obstructionist non-compliance.

(a) *Overall compliance record.* The Commission reports on compliance with EU law demonstrate that some Member States are more likely to violate the Treaty freedoms than others. When comparing the overall number of infringement actions started against Malta and the three Baltic states it will be clear that overall Malta could be seen as a less compliant Member State;

(b) Malta's *administrative capacity,* (such as the training, motivation and availability of the administrative staff) and legitimacy (a moral obligation entailing that the rule of law ought to be obeyed);

---

[27] National measures infringing Directive 2009/147/EC of the European Parliament and of the Council of 30 November 2009 on the conservation of wild birds.

(c) *Historic* pre-requisites, such as a country's traditions in exercising a particular environmentally harmful practice;

(d) The existence of *alternative legitimate policies/practices* which could substitute for the outlawed ones.

(e) Even though the CJEU has long established a principle[28] that national political difficulties could never qualify as an acceptable reason for non-compliance with EU law, this study nonetheless reflects on the political situation in Malta at the time of the judgment if it could potentially influence compliance. If there is a political crisis (such as pending elections), the chances are high that compliance will be postponed or minimalist measures implemented.

Another issue worth mentioning is *time*. When it comes to compliance with judgements on environmental matters, time is a decisive factor as the longer the Member State persists in maintaining unlawful national laws/practices in place the greater the damage caused to the environment and the firmer the requirements for compliance become. Since the infringement procedure of Article 258 TFEU is a multi-stage bargaining tool, it would grant Malta with more than sufficient time to settle the infringement. When the case is before the Court, compliance could still be achieved, yet generally, Malta tends to wait until the binding judgment and beyond. Following the judgment, even though the national authorities in question have been aware of the perceived breach since the issue of an informal letter, the government is not required to comply immediately. Still, it can use 'reasonable time' to facilitate compliance without unnecessary delay and initiate comprehensive steps towards compliance immediately. This study aims to demonstrate whether or not the Republic of Malta initiates comprehensive compliance measures immediately following the judgment on environmental issues. Even when the national law is outlawed, it may remain in force if there is no comprehensive compliance, resulting in obstructionist non-compliance that is in direct violation of sincere cooperation obligation. It is true to say that dissatisfied public may challenge national practice in national and European courts and claim damages sustained, however with regards to hunting and trapping pastime practices it is impossible to casually link some dead or injured birds to personal damages sustained.

---

[28] See e.g., *Commission v Belgium (Belgian Wood)* case 77/69 [1970] 34.

The Republic of Malta's government's behaviour, such as press statements, compliance initiatives or non-action at the pre-judicial stage, at the hearing and post-judgment stage, will be assessed. In this regard, it could be hypothesised that in cases where Malta replies with delay or altogether fails to reply to the Commission's correspondence, it could be assumed that it moves towards non-compliance. In a similar vein, if the Republic of Malta challenged the Commission's application merely on its incompleteness or pleads its inadmissibility on vague or unsubstantiated grounds, it would point towards a desire to resist compliance and protect national position by any means possible. Such conduct may imply that Malta resisted cooperation in good faith, acting contrary to the obligations imposed by the Treaty. Additionally, suppose during the judicial stage of the infringement procedure, the Republic of Malta continuously argued at cross purposes with the Commission, never reaching an agreement on the legality of the national provisions. In that case, this could imply that the relevant government was heading towards non-compliance.

The management approach, which is occupied with improving the capacity of the Member States to comply, may be ineffective when dealing with environmental breaches analysed in subsequent Sect. 4 because non-compliance in this instance may be deemed voluntary, and there may be no genuine willingness to comply. To demonstrate this initial absence of an inclination to comply, it is pertinent to distinguish obstructionist non-compliance involving Maltese hunting/trapping cases from non-communication cases referred to the CJEU under Article 260(3) TFEU.

Late or incorrect implementation of the EU's secondary law could be harder to remedy since it requires the Member State to correctly implement the directives, which at times could be achieved only through comprehensive legislative reforms of the existing national measures. In such cases, the Member State is obliged to legislate in order to comply extensively and comprehensively. Hence, the breach here is harder to remedy. Also, given that the wording of some of the directives could be obscure and imprecise, prompt and comprehensive compliance would be harder to achieve. In contrast, in the hunting/trapping cases, Malta has not been obliged to implement any particular EU provision correctly, and all that was required is to repeal defeated rules once and for all. In the case of judgments discussed in this study in Sect 4.2 of this study, the legislative adjustments which have to be initiated in Malta in order to achieve compliance are purely documentary—there is no need to clear up an illegal dump or restore polluted marshlands to their original state (as some environmental judgements mandate). Therefore, in the case of Maltese hunting/trapping judgments, compliance could be achieved swiftly.

There is neither particular uncertainty about the precise nature of the obligations imposed by the judgments nor uncertainty about their exact meaning so that the compliance obligations stemming from the hunting/ trapping judgments are equally clear. It is important to emphasise that in comparison to other cases which can result in non-compliance post-judgement, hunting/trapping cases stand out as being politically sensitive although not legally complex. However, the outcome of the judicial procedure is not excessively obscure—incompatible measures must be abolished. Therefore, since the Commission normally sets the ultimate compliance deadline for all judgments at twelve months, this study envisages that full compliance with hunting/trapping judgments must be anticipated much sooner.

Current theories on compliance with EU law generally assume that the Member States comply with the Court's judgments when the net benefits of compliance exceed the net benefits of non-compliance. From this point of view, non-compliance could be prevented by increasing the costs of non-compliance, and these costs could be increased by mobilising social and *political pressure*, as well as by increasing the publicity of the case and shaming the offending Member State.[29] The level of *publicity* and the *visibility* of a case could be seen as two of the factors that directly influence the possibility of compliance. The general public can encourage their governments into compliance from below via shaming. Similarly, the price for non-compliance could be considered for the Member States in much-publicised cases that reach the headlines, as governments generally do not like bad publicity. The joint effect of these factors could increase the reputational costs for the government and Member State concerned.

Given that hunting/trapping cases receive rather unique publicity, it could be assumed that there would be increased social and political pressure, as well as considerable reputational losses. However, this study demonstrates that in the local context the large proportion of the public and the government could strongly oppose (or are indifferent) to the Union's position on the matter so that the Courts' judgment could be seen as an attack on national sovereignty and old-engrained traditional practices. This, in turn, would see the Republic of Malta likely to resort to procrastination post-judgement, thus leading to sanction threats. In hunting/

---

[29] *See* Panke, D. (2010) *above*.

trapping cases, the self-interest compliance would seem not to be an option, as compliance with such politically unfavourable judgments may lead to high electoral losses and political resistance.

Consequently, it could be predicted that national shaming campaigns are less likely to occur in environment-related cases in Malta since the broad public generally sides with the government. Therefore, it could be claimed that the enforcement of compliance via shaming would not apply to environmental cases; on the contrary, the Maltese government could be strongly opposed to repealing national rules to avoid electoral losses. This study reveals that 'visibility' prerequisite is of little relevance in ensuring Malta's compliance with environmental judgements. In contrast, in cases where the proceedings and the judgment under Article 258 TFEU resonate well with the on-going national politics, one would expect prompt and effective post-judgment compliance.

4   ASSESSMENT OF MALTA'S COMPLIANCE RECORD

As noted before, both the Commission and the Member States seek to avoid going all the way to the Court: from the one hand, a condemning judgement should always be bad publicity for the Member State's government concerned since not only it confirms that the Member State acted in bad faith towards its Union obligations, it also means that the taxpayers would have to pick up the lawyers' bill. The Commission selects its targets carefully, normally taking the Member State to judicial stage only when it is confident that it is in the right. Given the success rate of the Commission in winning the case, it is obvious that once the watchdog took the Republic of Malta to court, the latter was likely to lose with all the subsequent repercussions.[30]

To date, there have been a total of 160 infringement actions started against Malta, with 57 cases relating to the area of the environment which confirms the EU-wide trend. In 27 cases the action got to the reasoned opinion stage, while on two occasions there were additional reasoned opinions.[31] On 18 occasions the case got referred to the CJEU—10 of the

---

[30] For exception within the Maltese context see Case C-508/08 *Commission v Malta* [2010], 2010 I-10589 ('Gozo Channel contract') where the Court issued a judgement in favour of Malta; and for the more recent example see Case C-12/14 *Commission v Malta* [2016] ECLI:EU:C:2016:135 on old-age pensions which culminated in a judgement in Malta's favour.

[31] Case C-178/11 *Commission v Malta*, Order of the Court, ECLI:EU:C:2012:227.

cases related to environment with the total of 5 judgements confirming infringements on the part of Maltese state, which are *all cases dealing with the environment*:

Case C-508/06 on non-communication of measures required by EU Directive on disposal of chemicals;[32]
Case C-252/08 on an incorrect application of air quality Directive to exhausts from Delimara and Marsa power stations;[33]
Case C-76/08 on infringement of directive on the conservation of wild birds;[34]
Case C-351/09 on failure to provide information on the status of inland surface water;[35]
Case C-557/15 on trapping of wild birds.[36]

Overall, there have been three sanction proceedings initiated against Malta—all relating to environmental cases mentioned above: C-351/09 (surface water), C-252/08 (exhausts from power plants) and C-557/15 (bird trapping).

To put these numbers into perspective, it is now appropriate to look at cases from the other three small Member States which joined the EU at the same date as Malta—Lithuania, Latvia and Estonia.

Lithuania: 110 infringement cases, 5 referrals (no environmental cases), 3 condemning judgements;[37]
Latvia: 139 infringement cases, 4 referrals (no environmental cases), 1 condemning judgement;[38]

---

[32] C-508/06 *Commission v Malta* [2007] I-00172.
[33] Case C-252/08 *Commission v Malta* [2009] I-00159 on Failure to correctly apply Directive 2001/80/EC on the limitation of emissions of certain pollutants into the air from large combustion plants.
[34] Case C-76/08 *Commission v Malta* [2009] ECR I-08213.
[35] Case C-351/09 *Commission v Malta* [2010] I-00180.
[36] Case C-557/15 *Commission v Malta* [2015] ECLI:EU:C:2018:477.
[37] Case C-61/12 *Commission v Lithuania* [2014] ECLI:EU:C:2014:172 on rules relating to registration of motor vehicles—Articles 34 TFEU and 36 TFEU; Case C-350/08 *Commission v Lithuania* [2014] 2010 I-10525 on Medicinal products for human use; Case C-274/07 *Commission v Lithuania* [2008] I-07117 on single European emergency call number '112' established under Directive 2002/22/EC ('Universal Service Directive').
[38] Case C-151/14 *Commission v Latvia* [2014] ECLI:EU:C:2015:577 on infringement of Article 49 TFEU ('Notaries').

Estonia: 104 infringement cases, 13 referrals (incl. 6 environmental cases), 1 condemning judgement.[39]

Only on one occasion, the Commission had to resort to sanction procedure against Lithuania for failure to comply with the judgement in Case C-274/07 on Single European emergency call number. In the case of Lithuania, the sanction mechanism proved to be a successful deterrent since it took Lithuania just 5 months to comply after which the case was closed.

What is apparent from the above findings is that Malta marginally excels on all fronts: the overall number of infringement cases, the total number of referrals to the Court, the total number of judgements confirming an infringement and the number the sanction procedure had been engaged. What is even more telling is the prominence of environmental cases emanating from the Republic of Malta—all five judgements which confirmed infringement are environmental cases. At the same time, all three sanction proceedings have been used in this area.

Before turning to examine Malta's conduct during the infringement actions, it is first necessary to make a couple of preliminary remarks regarding factors which could have influenced such a level of non-compliance, specifically concerning environmental issues. As previously noted, some of the country-specific factors and variables may explain or predict the level of compliance with the EU *acquis*. The three Baltic states were chosen due to their relative size and population, which could qualify them as 'small' EU Member States. However, no other EU Member State is as small and as densely populated as is Malta. With 1633 people per square kilometre, it may not be compared to sparsely populated Latvia ($29,6/km^2$), Estonia ($28/km^2$) or Lithuania ($43/km^2$). Besides being the 4th most densely populated country in the world, it is the smallest of all EU Member States, and geography-wise it is little more than a rock in the sea: there are no forests, no rivers, no available land, no space. It could be argued that due to its unique geography, environmental issues are pre-programmed.

National wealth could be another country variable to be assessed as it could also potentially explain poor compliance with environmental cases. The Gross Domestic Product per capita in Malta was recorded at around 28,950 US dollars in 2019—the highest when compared to the three

---

[39] Case C-39/10 *Commission v Estonia* [2012] ECLI:EU:C:2012:282 on infringement of Article 45 TFEU.

Baltic states. This could signify that the Republic of Malta is more likely to 'afford' non-compliance when compared with the less wealthy Baltic states. Yet this could be too simplistic of a view, since Greece while being one of the worst non-compliers on environmental matters in the EU, stands at 24,024 US dollars per capita in 2019. What these numbers could be telling, is that in reality, Malta stands in line with some of the less wealthy EU countries, so no wonder that its society has different priorities than compliance with the environmental *acquis*. Once the wealth of the general Maltese population increases to the level like the ones found in Germany or the Netherlands, then environmental issues would become more prioritised. And above all, the need to address environmental issues is a novel idea in Malta which largely came as a result of the necessity to comply with the *acquis communautaire* before the EU accession.

There is another important difference between the Baltic states and Malta, which could potentially explain higher levels of non-compliance in Malta—its historical background. All the Baltic states, sharing a socialist past as they do, were eagerly anticipating to join the EU and be associated with the West—a desire that was somehow alien to Malta. Having evolved into the western capitalist nation it is nowadays, it was not eagerly anticipating to 'join the club', and it took a referendum to confirm that general Maltese populace agree to the idea. This could be another telling factor which distinguishes Malta from the three Baltic states as regards its compliance record: the latter are still striving to please the EU, while the former had always experienced a degree of Euroscepticism.

Malta's administrative capacity could also be one of the core factors influencing poor compliance since human resources (which are required to cope with correct transposition and application of the EU *acquis*) are very limited. As seen from the hunting/trapping cases—one of the stumbling stones for confirming Malta's inability to comply with EU law, was Malta's inability to ensure proper enforcement and monitoring of the concerned activities. Enforcement and compliance are two of the weakest spots in a tiny country like Malta. This means that legitimacy in the form of respect for the rule of law is also an issue, as the latest request for a preliminary ruling in Case C-896/19 *Repubblika v Prim Ministru*[40] vividly demonstrates.

---

[40] Case C-896/19: Request for a preliminary ruling from the Qorti Ċivili Prim'Awla — Ġurisdizzjoni Kostituzzjonali (Malta) lodged on 5 December 2019 — Repubblika v Il-Prim Ministru.

4.1   Case-Study 1: Spring Hunting—Between a Rock and a Hard Place

The first case to be analysed is Case C-76/08 on infringement of Wild Birds Directive on the conservation of wild birds.[41] The issue of Malta's non-compliance has received much academic and public attention, which is rather unique since non-compliance rarely triggers any public debate. This high level of attention is due to the national importance of bird hunting and trapping practices in Malta for one part of the population on the one hand, and relatively strong opposition to such practices by national NGOs and conservationists on the other, specifically due to persistent infringements of hunting regulations and EU laws on environmental protection. There are high numbers of active hunters and trappers in Malta, and they have an extensive and powerful lobby,[42] which could not act as a catalyst for 'shaming from below' as current theories on compliance with EU law generally assume. The cost of non-compliance with EU law may not be increased because of the importance of hunting and trapping in Malta. The importance of such practices could be seen as historic prerequisite, which is rather unique. Currently, there are around 12,500 licences for hunters and trappers in Malta—one of the highest per capita in the EU—with hunting licence fees being some of the lowest. The pastime of shooting and trapping birds has been Malta's tradition for hundreds of years before it became necessary to protect wild birds in Europe. So, the case at hand hits at the very essence of the Maltese heritage, and it could be anticipated that the Republic of Malta would defend its stand eagerly on all stages of the infringement action and even beyond.

The Union issued the Wild Birds Directive which seeks to protect all species of wild birds in the EU, as there was a growing concern that the traditional hunting of migratory birds, which sees hundreds of millions of migratory birds and songbirds killed and captured during their migration between Europe and Africa, could result in an environmental disaster with

---

[41] Council Directive 79/409/EEC of 2 April 1979 on the conservation of wild birds, OJ 1979 L 103/1 repealed and consolidated by Directive 2009/147/EC of the European Parliament and of the Council of 30 November 2009 on the conservation of wild birds OJ L 20, 26.1.2010, pp. 7–25.

[42] through the Federazzjoni Kaccaturi Nassaba Konservazzjonisti—FKNK (Federation for Hunting & Conservation—Malta).

many species brought to the brink of extinction.[43] The Directive provides that the killing, trapping or injuring of wild birds is not permitted. However, Article 7(4) provides that some species which are abundant across the Union can be hunted and otherwise exploited as long as it does not take place during the breeding or spring migration season. However, the spring-hunting ban was not absolute as derogations were provided in Article 9, which allowed the Member States to allow the capture or killing of birds in small numbers under strictly supervised conditions outside of the normal hunting season for a limited number of reasons, although such derogations are only applied when there is no alternative solution to be found. Any derogations had to be strictly regulated and supervised as per Article 9(2) of the Directive, and annual report on management and execution of derogations has to be sent to the Commission pursuant to Article 9(3) of the Directive. Before joining the EU Malta has discussed the issue of a derogation with the Union and the Commission confirmed that a derogation would be possible where the strict conditions set out in the Wild Birds Directive were met.[44]

Other Member States such as France, Finland and Austria have used the derogation of Article 9 to justify the opening of spring hunting season. All three cases ended up in the CJEU, with the Court narrowly interpreting the derogation. The three cases dealing with the same derogation found in Article 9 of the Directive were quoted in the Court's judgement against Malta were: Case C-344/03 *Commission v Finland*,[45] Case C-182/02 *Ligue Pour la Protection des Oiseaux and Others*,[46] Case C-507/04 *Commission v Austria*.[47] These cases all confirmed that it is extremely difficult for a Member State to derogate from the overall prohibition of hunting during springtime. For example, in Austrian case, the national authorities tried defending opening of the hunting season in spring due to the severe weather conditions which, as they have claimed, precluded hunting in autumn. In the French case which was referred to the Court

---

[43] Martin Hedemann-Robinson, 'Enforcement of European Union environmental law: Legal issues and challenges', 2nd Edition, 2006, Routledge, pp. xv–721.

[44] European Commission (IP/08/647), 'Court orders ban on spring hunting in Malta', Brussels, 25 April 2008, available at: https://ec.europa.eu/commission/presscorner/detail/en/IP_08_647.

[45] Case C-344/03 *Commission v Finland* [2005] ECR I-11033.

[46] Case C-182/02 *Ligue pour la Protection des Oiseaux and others v Premier Ministre and Ministre de l'Aménagement du Territoire et du l'Environnement* [2003] ECR I-12105.

[47] Case C-507/04 *Commission v Austria* [2007] ECR I-5939.

under the preliminary ruling procedure, the CJEU emphasised that any opening of the spring season must be carried out under strictly supervised conditions and on a selective basis, apply only to certain birds in small numbers. There must be an efficient system of control and monitoring in place which had to be duly communicated to the Commission annually. These three judgements could be seen as agenda-setting jurisprudence of the Court which other Member States must respect in good faith. However, when there is a law which allows for derogations, it may be ripe for testing by other contending Member States, and this is exactly what happened in case of Malta, where hunting is the way of pastime for so many.

Malta relied on derogations found in Article 9 of the Wild Birds Directive to open spring-hunting season on quails and turtle doves during their spring migration in 2004. Having been aware of the issue from bilateral pre-accession discussions, the Commission monitored the situation closely, urging Malta to conform to the Wild Birds Directive. At the time the issue of derogations has by now prominently featured on the Commission's and the CJEU's agenda. In 2003 the CJEU had already issued a preliminary ruling on the French case interpreting the criteria which make it possible to establish the limits of Article 9 derogations. In its ruling the CJEU confirmed that Article 9 may be relied upon only in exceptional situations:

> when there is no other satisfactory solution. That condition would not be met, inter alia, if the sole purpose of the derogation authorising hunting were to extend the hunting periods for certain species of birds in territories which they already frequent during the hunting periods fixed in accordance with Article 7 of Directive 79/409.[48]

Likewise, the Finnish and Austrian cases were already before the CJEU, with the infringement proceedings commencing as early as in 1998 for the former.

Following the informal stage of bilateral negotiations, the Commission started an infringement action by sending a letter of formal notice on 4th July 2006. The Commission believed that the facts of the Finnish case were similar to the Maltese situation since alternative solutions to spring hunting existed because there was the possibility to hunt quails and turtle

[48] Case C-182/02, *above*, para. 19.

doves in autumn. However, Malta resisted complying and has been relying on the derogation to open spring hunting seasons in 2005 and 2006. At the time, a number of grave hunting illegalities took place in May 2006. A purported massacre of honey buzzards forced the government to close its 2006 spring hunting season 10 days early. Malta's resistance to comply prompted the Commission to issue an additional letter of formal notice on 23 March 2007, which widened the scope of the dispute to include subsequent years.

The Maltese authorities were extremely quick to react and issued their reply on the same day, with an additional reply sent a month later on 23 April 2007. It seems that the legal advisors to the government at the time have not consulted the case-law on the issue which was already available on similar measures introduced in Finland. Or rather, they may have been well aware of indefensibility of their position, however prohibiting spring hunting would mean political suicide for the ruling party. Hence, the Maltese authorities replied that since very few quails and turtle doves were available to hunt in autumn, there was no 'other satisfactory solution' but to open hunting season in spring. In addition, national authorities argued that the Commission could not challenge the opening of spring hunting season for 2005 to 2007 as it had not yet received annual reports which the government itself was under the obligation to provide in accordance with Article 9 of the Wild Birds Directive. This literally means that the government justified non-compliance with EU law by its own non-compliance with EU law! This is a rather telling point on the desire of a Member State to conform to EU law in good faith, which was further aggrieved by its decisions to open three consecutive spring hunting seasons after the infringement proceedings were already commenced. This could also be a telling point as regards Malta's administrative capacity to conform with the *acquis* as it has repeatedly failed to issue the reports necessitated under Article 9 of the Wild Birds Directive and only providing the Commission with some general information on bird migration on 28 June 2007. The next step of the Commission was to issue Malta with its reasoned opinion on 23 October 2007 and setting the two-month deadline for compliance. There was no compliance by the date, and instead, the Maltese authorities replied by a letter of 31 December 2007 reiterating their position on the legality of national derogations.

A new spring approaching soon, the Commission considered that opening another hunting season would cause irrevocable and significant damage to the environment and hence on 21 February 2008 it successfully applied for interim measures for the third time in the Union's history.[49] The interim measures applied to 2008 spring season and the Republic of Malta refrained from authorising spring hunting during that year but not for any subsequent years.

Before the Court the Maltese authorities pleaded the Commission's action as inadmissible on the same grounds they have challenged it in their reply to the official correspondence: the Commission could not challenge the decision to open spring hunting unless it had based its decision on the annual report on the implementation of Article 9 of the Directive, which Malta had to send to it. In response to these claims, the Commission reminded that it is the guardian of the Treaties and it is alone empowered to decide whether or not to initiate infringement proceedings. The Court dismissed all the pleas of inadmissibility, re-emphasising the Commission's wide discretion on the starting of infringement proceedings and that such discretion was not subject to any conditions.

During the Court submissions the Commission emphasised that similarly as with other two cases on Article 9 derogations, namely against Finland and Austria, spring hunting could only be allowed only 'if there is no other satisfactory solution'. Since, according to national reports for 2004 and 2005 both quails and turtle doves were present in Malta during the autumn season, it constituted a 'satisfactory solution', so there was no justification to open spring hunting seasons.[50] The Commission also submitted that Malta failed to comply with other conditions for the application of Article 9(1) of the Directive, set out in subparagraphs (a) to (c) in particular.

In reply, the Maltese authorities claimed that the Commission infringed on the principle of legitimate expectations since during the pre-accession negotiations it promised to allow Malta to continue spring hunting of quails and turtle doves under Article 9 of the Directive. Malta also submitted that due to very specific circumstances, hunting of these two bird species during the autumn season in Malta does not constitute 'another satisfactory solution' as there are very few birds passing over Malta at that time of the year and the very conditions of their overflight of the islands permit killing of only an inconsiderable number of them. Therefore, Malta

---

[49] The previous cases concerned spring hunting in Liguria, Italy and a road-building project in the Rospuda valley in Poland.

[50] Case C-76/08, para. 28.

took the view that the first condition laid down in Article 9(1) of the Directive is satisfied when national specifics are considered.

When addressing the claim put forward by the national authorities that the Commission infringed on the principle of legitimate expectations, the CJEU replied that first, any such pre-accession agreement was not apparent from the documents before the Court. Second, this is irrelevant to the assessment of compliance with the conditions provided for in the Directive.[51] In its verdict, the Court confirmed that the derogation under Article 9 of the Directive may be used only so far as necessary, where hunting opportunities during the autumn season are so limited as to upset the balance sought by the Directive between the protection of species and certain leisure activities. Hence, the Court agreed that the Maltese situation was different from Finnish and Austrian cases, ruling that Article 9 derogation could, in principle, be used in Malta.[52] However, after considering whether the other conditions on which the Republic of Malta authorised spring hunting of the two species fulfil the requirement for proportionality principle and other requirements provided for in the directive, the Court concluded that such derogation was not used under strictly supervised conditions in the Maltese case.

In its declaratory ruling of 10 September 2009, the CJEU ruled that by opening spring hunting seasons in the years 2004 to 2007, without complying with the conditions laid down in Article 9(1) of the Wild Birds Directive, Malta has failed to fulfil its obligations under that directive. Following the condemning judgement, Malta had to comply as soon as possible. Naturally, compliance measures would be not to authorise any subsequent spring hunting seasons without first ensuring that the conditions laid down in Article 9(1) of the Directive are satisfied. However, the spring hunting was again authorised in 2009. In April 2010, Malta informed the Commission about the adoption of framework legislation[53] which would permit the spring hunting in future years of a maximum of 25,000 birds, with a three-week hunting period. It is evident that the Maltese authorities sought to find some sort of a solution, however, it seemed to be a sub-optimal one. It could be concluded that when assessed

---

[51] Case C-76/08, para. 67.
[52] Case C-76/08, para. 56.
[53] S.L.549.57 Framework for Allowing a Derogation Opening a Spring Hunting Season for Turtle Dove and Quail Regulations, available at: https://legislation.mt/eli/sl/549.57/eng/pdf.

together both the implementation non-comprehensive amendments to the national provisions and the decision to open spring hunting in 2009 could be seen as a shift towards minimalist compliance. The fact that these 'compliance initiatives' have been implemented eight months following the original judgement could once again demonstrate that this was in fact a minimalist compliance measure which could result in obstructionist non-compliance.

Unsurprisingly, given the flaws in the proposed national measures, the Commission concluded that this measure was not proportionate with the overall conservation objectives of the Wild Birds Directive due to the following three reasons: (a) there was no obligation to consider the conservation status of quails and doves when setting bag limits; (b) there was no provision to consider the possibilities for autumn hunting in that year before opening a spring season, and (c) the maximum limits established in the legislation were too generous.[54] Therefore, on 28 October 2010, the Commission initiated sanctioning action for non-compliance with the original judgement. In the meantime, the Maltese authorities opened 2010 spring hunting season.

The Maltese authorities implemented further amendments to the law in 2011, 2013 and 2014 to address the Commission's concerns. Since the Court confirmed that Malta has a unique situation which could justify the application of derogations, the government sought to do everything in its powers to draft the law in the way which would satisfy the Commission. More so, they were obliged to find a workable solution and comply, as following the national referendum on spring hunting held in April 2015 the government had a mandate to maintain the practice. On 28 May 2015, shortly following the referendum which confirmed the public support for spring hunting, it was proclaimed that the sanction procedure was terminated. Given the termination of the procedure, it could be argued that the additional amendments to the law comprised a comprehensive compliance measure which was in itself sufficient to terminate the breach. As of today, Malta is the only EU Member State which has a derogation for opening of spring hunting seasons.[55] However, it needs to be emphasised, that from the initiation of sanction proceedings to withdrawal of the case four-

---

[54] European Commission (IP/10/1409), 'Environment: Commission requests Malta to comply with Court ruling on bird hunting, Brussels, 28 October 2010.

[55] Framework for Allowing a Derogation Opening a Spring Hunting Season for Turtle Dove and Quail Regulations has been further amended in 2016, 2017 and 2020.

and-a half years have passed, which is a considerable amount of time specifically given the combined burden of obligations stemming from Article 4(3) TEU and Article 260(1) TFEU. In fact, at the time it must have seemed that the Republic of Malta had comprehensively complied by rectifying the breach, however it took a number of years, a sanction threat and multiple minimalist amendments to the national law.

In a small Member State where hunting-license holders constitute nearly 10% of the voting population (as those hunters have voting family members), the government had to please both the EU and its population. At the time, it was thought that Malta has eventually succeeded in drafting a law which is a workable solution, however, it took the national authorities more than five years following the condemning judgement to finally address all the Commission's concerns. The law was once again amended in 2016, 2017 and 2020. However, it takes more than black letter law to protect the EU interests at stake, as effective application and enforcement are also of vital importance. To which extent the law is enforced, is an entirely different case. For example, although in 2020 spring hunting was supposedly permitted only for quail, the chosen dates for the season overlapped with the peak migration of the turtle-dove (a protected species). Thus, given that in 2018 and 2020 there were record numbers of illegal killings of birds (including the protected species), both during closed and open seasons, the legality of national status quo could have been once again undermined, which eventually has happened in 2020. As the 2020 rolled to an end, the Commission announced that it has started another infringement procedure against Malta for its spring hunting derogations. On 3 December 2020 the Commission sent a letter of formal notice pursuant to Article 258 TFEU, urging Malta to comply within two months, otherwise the reasoned opinion will be issued. The Commission is of the opinion that Malta has failed to fulfil the basic conditions for granting derogations under the Wild Birds Directive, since the derogations fall short systematically of the requirements set out in the legislation, specifically in relation to poor supervision of the conditions set out in the derogations. In its letter of formal notice, the Commission has also expressed its conceres over the high numbers of wild birds illegally shot in Malta which in itself constitutes a major and systemic failure to establish a general system of protection as required by Article 5 of the Wild Birds Directive.

As one could see, Malta's situation is special. Although there were other agenda-setting cases on spring hunting derogations in other Member

States available, Malta's uniqueness allowed the hundreds of years old practice to persevere despite the condemning infringement action which is not yet fully resolved more than a decade following the condemning judgement. Had the Court found that Malta's situation disallows derogating from the Directive in principle, as was the case in Finland, it would conflict with the view of the nation so vividly expressed at the 2015 referendum. In such a case, the government would have the mandate not to comply with the judgement. Any solution to find a balance between the sincere co-operation principle and obligations towards its constituents would result in sub-optimal solutions. It would have become an impossible balancing act, and the government would find itself between a rock and a hard place.

Although losing the case, Malta relentlessly defended its position and was able to demonstrate that national provisions may be justified by overriding reasons and specifically when provisions at stake are seen as important to the general populace. The original infringement action under Article 258 TFEU proved to be successful in persuading the Member State to legitimise its conduct. Nevertheless, since the new infringement action seems to be inevitable due to the Maltese Government's stance on the issue, it could be concluded that the Republic of Malta has failed to comply in good faith and resorted to obstinate non-compliance.

4.2   Case-Study 2: Trapping of Birds—A Foreseeable Outcome

This case concerned the infringement by Malta of the same EU laws as in the previous case—the Wild Birds Directive. Same as with hunters, Maltese bird trappers are not an odd relic, as in many other Member States, but rather an active minority that practices sport which is millennia old. There are over 4000 active license holders with thousands of registered trapping stations (although there are also hundreds of illegal trapping stations, found for example even in EU-funded Natura 2000 nature reserves) and very little enforcement. Following the pre-accession negotiations, Malta was allowed to phase out finch trapping until 2008 and to establish a captive breeding programme for finch rearing.[56] Malta found itself in a virtually identical battle (to that of spring hunting) when it comes to wild bird

---

[56] European Commission (IP/14/1154), Environment: Commission urges Malta to refrain from finch trapping, Brussels, 16 October 2014, available at: https://ec.europa.eu/commission/presscorner/detail/en/IP_14_1154.

trapping practices, as in 2017 the CJEU found that by using a derogation regime of Article 9 of the Wild Birds Directive and allowing the live-capturing of seven species of wild finches, the Republic of Malta has failed to fulfil its obligations.

This time the infringement action concerned a derogation[57] of the opening of an autumn live-capturing season for finches in 2014.[58] Pursuant to the Directive, wild birds, such as finches, are strictly protected. Although under Article 9, there could be a derogation from the general prohibition of capture and keeping of birds when 'other satisfactory solution' could not be found and if the derogation is used judiciously, with small numbers and strict supervision. On 17 October 2014, the Commission sent the Republic of Malta a letter of formal notice stating that the derogation regime did not meet the conditions laid down in Article 9 of Directive 2009/147. Essentially, as with the case on hunters, it was claimed that Malta failed to show that no 'other satisfactory solution' to trapping existed and had not complied with the conditions relating to judicious use, small numbers and strict supervision laid down in Article 9(1)(c) of that Directive. The Maltese authorities duly replied to the letter stating that the derogation was legitimate. Despite the formal notice, the Maltese authorities went on with opening the season for trapping of finches. The Commission issued a reasoned opinion in May 2015 to which Malta answered in time, reiterating its position. The Commission brought the issue before the CJEU. While the case was still pending before the Court, the Government of Malta opened an autumn live-capturing season for finches in 2015 and 2016.[59]

At the hearing which took place on 15 February 2017, the Commission argued that the Maltese derogation regime fails to provide a clear and sufficient statement of reasons why no 'other satisfactory solution' is possible for finch trapping since captive breeding would be a satisfactory alternative

---

[57] S.L.549.91 Subsidiary Legislation on Conservation of wild birds (declaration on a derogation for a 2014 autumn live-capturing season for finches) regulations, of 15th July, 2014 which was based on S.L.549.93 Framework for allowing a derogation opening an autumn live-capturing season for finches regulations, 15th July, 2014, as amended by Legal Notices 288 and 447 of 2014, and 319 of 2016, revoked by Legal Notice 383 of 2018.

[58] Case C-557/15 *Commission v Malta* [2015].

[59] S.L.549.98 Conservation of wild birds (declaration on a derogation for a 2015 autumn live-capturing season for finches) regulations,16th October, 2015 and S.L.549.98 Conservation of wild birds (declaration on a derogation for an autumn 2016 live-capturing season for finches) regulations, 7th October, 2016.

solution. In response, Malta very reasonably argued that since trapping has been practised for generations and makes an important part of a Maltese tradition, the whole idea behind acquiring a bird was the thrill of catching it, which breeding would not deliver. Several months after the hearing, on 17th October 2017, Malta went on to open another autumn live-capturing for 2017.[60]

In its judgement of 21 June 2018, the Court ruled that contrary to the Commission's observations Malta's Framework Law on the conservation of wild birds sets out the criteria for derogation clearly and precisely and requires the authorities responsible for their application to take them into account. However, after considering whether the authorities responsible for the opening of the trapping season indeed have done so, the Court found that the conditions on which Malta authorised the trapping did not fulfil these requirements. The CJEU ruled that when opening an autumn finch trapping season, the reasons as to why there is no other satisfactory solution within the meaning of Article 9(1) of Wild Birds Directive must be stated, which was not the case for the 2014 trapping season. Likewise, it ruled that the Republic of Malta has not demonstrated that its trapping derogation allows for trapping of birds 'in small numbers' which would ensure the maintenance of the birds' populations at a satisfactory level. In conclusion, the Court ruled that the trapping of birds may be permitted only under strictly controlled conditions, which the national authorities failed to ensure.

Contrary to the Court's conclusions in the case of hunters, the practice of trapping of birds in Malta could not be potentially justified, since there was no assessment on the part of the Maltese authorities before authoris-ing the trapping of finches whether another satisfactory alternative solu-tion (such as captive breeding) exists. In the case of hunters, there was no alternative solution to hunting in spring, which saw the Maltese deroga-tion on spring hunting satisfying the first limb of the justification pursuant to Article 9 of the Directive, that is—whether the derogation *may be applied*. Therefore, in order to rely on the derogation in good faith, the Maltese authorities had to comply with *how* it is applied (proper supervi-sion, capture in small numbers, etc.). On the contrary, in the case of trap-pers, the national authorities have failed to satisfy both limbs on the derogation justification—whether the derogation *may be applied* and *how*

---

[60] S.L. 549.117 Conservation of wild birds (declaration on a derogation for a 2017 autumn live-capturing season for finches) regulations,19th October 2017.

it is applied. What the national authorities have successfully satisfied is a national passion for bird trapping by opening subsequent trapping seasons, since the practice could continue until the condemning judgement of the Court was delivered. However soon following the judgement, the Framework Law for allowing a derogation for the opening of the autumn trapping season has been revoked, which presumably could be seen as due compliance with the Court's judgement. The case was closed on 7 February 2019, that is eight months following the judgement. However, does the termination of the infringement proceedings mean that Malta has duly complied with EU law? Unsurprisingly, the answer to this question is in the negative. First, trappers continued to operate illegally as there were free-for-all violations and enforcement remained next to non-existent. Secondly, the Maltese authorities came up with a new derogation scheme adopted in October 2020 which authorised the trapping of finches for 'research purposes'. Such disguised compliance in fact circumvents the condemning judgment of the CJEU. The Commission was quick to react and initiated a new set of infringement proceedings under Article 258 TFEU, setting up a two-month compliance deadline in its letter of formal notice.

On one hand it could be argued that in both hunting and trapping cases, Malta could be seen as acting in a relatively good faith towards the sincere co-operation obligation since it has duly responded to all the official correspondence issued pursuant to infringement procedure. This praise both goes to the previous government, and the current one since the change in government accompanied the hunting saga. Likewise, in case of hunting, the current government went to great lengths to come up with a legislative solution which would satisfy both camps—the hunters and the Commission. The fact that there were seven amendments to the national law on spring hunting supports the previous finding. On the other hand, however, it is nonetheless true that the Maltese authorities resorted to obstinate non-compliance post judgement with final compliance with the original judgement achieved nearly five years later. Along the same lines it could be argued, that maintaining and authorising spring hunting seasons throughout the infringement and sanctions procedures does not show Malta in the best light. Above all, it could be concluded that since the Maltese authorities failed to fulfil the basic conditions for granting derogations for spring hunting and since enforcement on the ground remained next to non-existent, the legislative compromise which sought to pacify the Commission is nothing but a smokescreen, in reality being only a new step in this never-ending saga. A new set of infringement proceedings targeting both hunting and trapping practices vividly demonstrates that in certain Member States and in certain areas the mechanisms envisaged in Articles 258 and 260 TFEU would fall short of yielding a workable solution. Given that in both hunting and trapping cases it took on average four years to issue a condemning judgement and given that compliance post-judgement is unlikely to be swift or effective, it may be predicted that the outlawed national practice on spring hunting and trapping is likely to remain for years to come.

4.3   Pending Infringement Actions

When the Commission initiated new infringement proceedings against Malta on 20 October 2020 by issuing a letter of formal notice, it sent shockwaves throughout the national and Union press, since this time a genuinely 'trademark' national law on Investor Citizenship Scheme was under attack. Although the law in question has been the source of significant revenue for the Maltese State since its launch in 2014, it has been long criticised by the EU officials. The Commission's main point of contention is that the Maltese scheme goes contrary to the general understanding that one's nationality is the expression of a special relationship of allegiance, solidarity and a genuine link between the state and its people. How nationality of a given Member State is granted, is solely a matter of national law, however, alongside the national passport a person also gets to become an EU citizen. The Commission argues that selling national passports is not compatible with the principle of sincere co-operation enshrined in the EU treaty and undermines the essence of EU citizenship. The government announced that it would defend its law eagerly.[61]

The hunting-trapping cases aside, there are currently 29 active infringement cases against Malta which are currently at the pre-litigation stage, including, for example, a case on levying the incorrect amount of Value Added Tax on yachts.[62] Environmental cases feature prominently among

---

[61] EU officially launches infringement action against Malta's passport scheme, available at https://timesofmalta.com/articles/view/eu-action-on-maltas-golden-passport-scheme-officially-launched.825982, last accessed on 10 September 2020.

[62] see European Commission (INF/20/202), 12 February 2020, February infringements package: key decisions, Taxation: Commission sends an additional letter of formal notice to MALTA for not levying the correct amount of Value Added Tax on yachts, available at:

active infringement cases (7 in total plus the hunting-trapping cases), however, as this study has demonstrated, those cases which are on the list are the most likely candidates to proceed to the judicial stage. Another, very recent infringement action on the environment is on restrictions of access to justice under the Environmental Liability Directive.[63] In the latter case, the Commission called on Malta to make sure its legislation allows for natural and legal persons to request the competent authorities to take remedial action for environmental damage.

5   A QUEST FOR PRELIMINARY REFERENCES IN MALTA

This study will now briefly turn to examine Malta's experience with preliminary rulings procedure envisaged under Article 267 TFEU—which serves as a decentralised avenue to the Union judicature for private enforcement. It will be shown to which extent this procedure may be successfully embarked on by individuals to challenge incompatible national measures and arrive at the result, which is similar to the judgement issued pursuant to infringement procedure.

The preliminary ruling procedure is rightfully regarded as the 'Jewel in the Crown' of the EU judicial system, as it played a vital role in the development of the Union as we know it today.

Under the Article 267 TFEU procedure, the CJEU may give preliminary rulings concerning the interpretation of the Treaties and the validity and interpretation of acts of the institutions, bodies, offices or agencies of the Union. Through this procedure, private parties may indirectly challenge the validity of national law. Once the national court refers the question to the CJEU, the latter interprets EU legislation, so that it becomes clear whether national provisions at issue are compatible with the Treaty or not. Following the preliminary ruling, it is up to the national court to decide on the facts of the case at hand. Therefore, this indirect way of challenging both the Union and national provisions proves to be indispensable for individual citizens in defending their rights and interests.

https://ec.europa.eu/commission/presscorner/detail/EN/INF_20_202, last accessed on 10 September 2020.
[63] Directive 2004/35/CE of the European Parliament and of the Council of 21 April 2004 on environmental liability with regard to the prevention and remedying of environmental damage, Official Journal L 143, 30/04/2004, pp. 0056–0075.

Throughout the EU in the majority of cases, it is the ordinary courts of the Member States which tend to be rather active users of the preliminary reference procedure. For example, according to the statistics of the CJEU, between 2004 and 2020 Maltese courts referred to the CJEU in total on four[64] occasions (1 case[65] currently pending), while Latvian courts referred on 70 occasions (18 cases pending), Estonia—27 times (5 cases pending) and Lithuania—65 times (8 cases pending). Malta, with only four references in sixteen years, is the EU's Member State with the least number of references. However, what could explain this low level of references from Maltese courts and which country-specific factors and variables are responsible for this?

It could be argued, that being the bigger states, the Baltic states have more ordinary courts and tribunals than Malta, so the likelihood of referrals is greater. Civil and criminal proceedings in Latvia can be heard in 40 courts, in Lithuania, there are 56 courts of general jurisdiction, in Estonia, there is a total of 16 courts. Malta has 7 courts, which are divided into Superior and Inferior courts. The Superior Courts are: The Constitutional Court, the Court of Appeal, the Court of Criminal Appeal, the Criminal Court and the Civil Court. The Inferior Courts are the Court of Magistrates (Malta) and the Court of Magistrates (Gozo). Therefore, in the assessment of court *vs* population ratio, Malta outperforms Estonia, where there is one court per every 83,000 people, while for Malta, this ratio is 1 to 73,000. However, the relatively low number of national courts does not explain why a Maltese case is *14 times less* likely to end up in Luxembourg, where the CJEU is based, than a case originating from Baltic states. In this regard, the relationship between the number of national courts vis-à-vis population could not be seen as a factor explaining low referral rates in Malta. The number of judges that make up a court could also be one of the factors to consider. In Malta, there are only 22 judges and 21 magistrates.[66]

---

[64] C-221/09 *AJD Tuna Limited v Direttur tal-Agrikoltura u s-Sajd u Avukat Ġenerali* [2009] OJ 2009/C 205/41; Case C-71/12 *Vodafone Malta ltd. and Mobile Communications ltd.v Avukat Ġenerali and Others* [2013]; Case C-125/16 *Malta Dental Technologists Association and John Salomone Reynaud v Superintendent tas-Sahha Pubblika and Kunsill tal-Professjonijiet Kumplimentari għall-Mediċina* [2017].

[65] Case C-896/19 *Repubblika v Prim Ministru* lodged on 5 December 2019.

[66] From the website on The Judiciary of Malta, available here: https://judiciary.mt/en/Pages/default.aspx.

This discussion needs to look at some other factors which could be the reason behind this low referral rate. Academic literature divides these factors into two broad categories being structural and behavioural factors.[67] Firstly, structural factors comprise the country's population size, the likelihood of engaging in litigation and the level of compliance by the Member States with the EU *acquis*. The relationship between the number of national courts vis-à-vis population could fall into this category. Secondly, behavioural factors concern the behaviour of national judges when they must decide on whether to make a reference or not.

In relation to the first structural factor, it has also been argued that size matters and 'big states simply refer more questions than small states' because there is much more litigation going on.[68] Naturally, it could be argued that if the size matters, it being the smallest Member State, Malta should be the one with fewer references made. However, the correlation between population size and the number of references for Malta is still much lower. In relation to the second structural factor—that is the level of compliance of a Member State with EU law—it has been suggested that the national courts of Member States which have a high level of compliance have less possibility of making a reference than national courts of Member States which do not fulfil their legal obligations.[69] This factor may not be usefully applied in the national context, since in comparison to the three Baltic states, Malta has a larger number of infringement proceedings, which could indicate that it is less compliant. Yet, there are still very few preliminary references made. Another country-specific variable which was found to influence the number of references is the length of Union membership.[70] However, as the above analysis of reference rates for the three Baltic states clearly demonstrates, there is a significant gap between Malta and the Baltic states although all four joined the EU at the same

---

[67] See e.g. Broberg, M. Fenger, N., 'Variations in Member States' Preliminary References to the Court.

of Justice— Are Structural Factors (Part of) the Explanation?' (2013) 19 *EurLJ* 488–501, p. 488.

[68] Maarten V. et al., 'Explaining the Use of Preliminary References by Domestic Courts in EU Member.

States: A Mixed-Method Comparative Analysis' (2009) Paper presented at the 11th Biennial Conference.

of the European Union Studies Association 21.

[69] Broberg, M. Fenger, N. *above*, p. 42.

[70] Broberg, M. Fenger, N. *above*.

time. Hence, there must be some other factors influencing low reference rates in Malta's case, apart from the length of EU membership and the overall level of compliance with EU law.

One of the factors to be mentioned is the effectiveness of the national judicial system, which is one of the national pet peeves. There goes a saying that *you may not exhaust all the local remedies before going to the Court of Human Rights in Strasbourg simply because local remedies are going to exhaust you instead.* There is a tendency in Malta for cases to remain in courts for decades on end without any resolution. Effectiveness of the national judiciary is also undermined by the way the judges are appointed, which brings about the question on the level of professionalism. Disputed levels of professionalism of judges, which result in poor overall familiarity with EU law, could be seen as one of the main factors which significantly undermines the ability of the national judiciary to duly apply EU law[71] and refer questions for preliminary rulings to the CJEU. In cases where judiciary is unfamiliar with the EU *acquis* the judges would be required to apply unfamiliar substantive and procedural rules, which inherently precludes any such application. This factor could be specifically relevant in the national context since, in Malta, judges are appointed not according to their professional achievements and abilities, but due to their alliance to a ruling party. The case on the legality of the national system of appointment of judges is currently under the CJEU's scrutiny as it became the subject of the latest judicial reference in Case C-896/19 *Repubblika v Prim Ministru.* This preliminary reference could be the beginning of the much-needed reform of the national system of appointments to judicial office, which in turn could increase the overall effectiveness of national courts and their ability and willingness to rely on Article 267 TFEU in their daily work. Hopefully, in the very near future, preliminary references from Malta will not be akin to endangered spices of birds, but rather a common trend in the national application of EU law.

A very low rate of preliminary references from Malta undermines the coherence of enforcement system, since its 'indirect' limb specifically designed for private enforcement is not particularly effective. The weakness of preliminary reference mechanism for challenging national environmental laws and practices is specifically revealing, since none of the references to date deal with the EU environmental *acquis.* As a result, it

---

[71] This situation on has already occurred in case *Izola Bank Ltd v Commissioner of VAT,* Application 18/2006 Court of Appeal decided on 9/5/2007.

could be concluded that the decentralised avenue via Article 267 TFEU could not be seen as an effective tool to challenge national non-compliance in the area of environmental protection.

6   Conclusion

As this study on Malta has demonstrated, some national laws are aiming at protecting of long-ingrained national practices, so that the Member State could be expected to behave very differently when it comes to compliance with infringement actions on those matters (compared to the broader compliance trends). This study clearly demonstrated Malta's attitude towards the Union institution's agenda-setting when it comes to hunting/trapping of wild birds. Although the Maltese authorities duly replied to the Commission's correspondence during the infringement action proceedings, the very same authorities failed to settle the case amicably as there was little to no impetus for self-interest compliance. More so, the concerned authorities maintained the national provisions which were under the Court's scrutiny and implemented new ones by opening subsequent hunting/trapping seasons.

As a result, this chapter demonstrated that direct and indirect enforcement channels do not always amount to an optimal solution in the local context, since preliminary reference procedure is highly unlikely to be used to attack any incompatible national measures relating to environment (specifically hunting and trapping activities) while the infringement actions may see the national authorities resorting to obstinate non-compliance. As a result, this chapter clearly demonstrated that in certain cases, the Member States could repeatedly fail to 'see the light'. However, these conclusions cannot be taken in a factual vacuum, and the particularities which distinguish a small island state with a long history and traditions must also be taken into consideration.

CHAPTER 4

The Transposition and Implementation of European Union Directives: A Case-Study of the Maltese Legal Order

Ivan Sammut

1 INTRODUCTION

Directives as legal instruments are the backbone on which the European Union's Internal Market is built. Unlike regulations, on the one hand, directives are not the law itself, but they are instructions to all of the Member States or to some of them to ensure that the domestic legislation satisfies the criteria and the parameters of the directive. Article 288 TFEU provides that directives are only binding upon each addressed Member State, as to a result to be achieved. The advantage of this instrument is that it combines the creation of Union-wide 'master rules' on a Union level with the competence and responsibility of the Member States to enact the concrete and directly applicable rules that are deemed to be adequate

I. Sammut (✉)
University of Malta, Msida, Malta
e-mail: ivan.sammut@um.edu.mt

I. Sammut, J. Agranovska (eds.), *The Implementation and Enforcement of European Union Law in Small Member States*, https://doi.org/10.1007/978-3-030-66115-1_4

according to the specific national legal order.[1] Directives could be seen as less intrusive to national sovereignty than regulations. Also, they show several advantages when compared with private law harmonisation through treaties and through so-called 'Restatements', in the tradition of the idea of pre-existing common private law rules in Europe.[2] On the other hand, a regulation is a straight-way means of implementation, having a direct effect. Basedow argues that:[3]

> The primary purpose is to reproduce the common rules and the principles of law that is to state the law and not to shape it.

The Regulation requires no transposition but is capable of having immediate direct effect and supremacy over any existing conflicting law as it stands. As an instrument, a regulation is the natural choice of an instrument if codification is to be the desired effect.

Directives are useful to achieve harmonisation of EU law. Harmonisation or approximation or coordination[4] is the process whereby legal rules from different jurisdictions are brought closer to each other in scope.[5] Harmonisation is a common method used by the European Union to bring the laws of the Member States closer to each other by means of directives to achieve the Internal Market. An essential characteristic of directives that is affecting the new European legal culture is that a directive leads to 'Impressionistic harmonisation.'[6] Directives deal with specific subjects that in most legal systems form part of a broader subject which may, in turn, be systematically connected with other subjects. This patchwork, characteristic of harmonisation of directives is a direct result of the instrumental approach to law.

The Commission from which directives originate is concerned with certain specific changes in the law which it may regard as necessary to fulfil

---

[1] Hartkamp A., et al. (eds.), *Towards a European Civil Code*, (2nd ed.), Kluwer Law International, Amsterdam, 1998, p. 77.

[2] Hartkamp A., et al., Ibid. note 21 p. 78.

[3] Basedow J., 'Codification of Private Law in the European Union: the making of a Hybrid', (2001), 9.*ERPL*. p. 35–49 at p. 39.

[4] These are different terms that are sometimes used interchangeably in the EC Treaty, for example, Article 6, 27, 40 41, 43, 54(3) (g), 56, 57, 63, 70, 75, 99, 100, 101, 102, 105, 111, 112, 113, 145, 220 and 235 (numbering as stood before the Amsterdam amendments).

[5] Zapiriou G., 'Harmonisation of Private Rules between Civil and Common Law Jurisdictions', *The American Journal of Comparative Law*, 1990, Vol. 38, p. 71.

[6] Hesselink M. W., *The New European Private Law*, Kluwer, 2002, p. 36.

the function of the Internal Market and which are politically desirable. The directive is not concerned with the result it may have on the national legal system, and even the same effect could vary from one system to another. This functional and impressionistic approach to private law could lead to friction within the national legal systems. While the directives aim at unity at the European level, they may cause disunity at the national level.[7] The disruptive effect is a direct result of the impressionistic approach. As Muller-Graff argues, to make matters even worse, directives are frequently incoherent among themselves.[8] This has led to the impressionistic approach to be lamented by private scholars and is one of the main reasons for pleas for a systematic unification in the form of a European Civil Code.[9]

The objective of this chapter is to show how directives are implemented in the Member States using Malta, the smallest member state of the EU as a case-study to determine the effectiveness of a directive as the legal instrument. The first part of the chapter tackles the process of harmonisation in the European Union to achieve the interests of the Internal Market further. It then briefly analyses the characteristic of a directive resolving the doctrine of direct effect. It then moves the focus precisely on how the Maltese legal order absorbs directives. The entire process is from the very first stage when the European Commission issues its draft legislative proposal up until the actual adoption of the EU directives is discussed. Here the reference is made to Malta's established EU and national structures available for its involvement in the EU's legislative process. A discussion is made about Malta transposition procedures and its performance over the past 15 years from its accession to the European Union in 2004.

2   DIRECTIVES AS BINDING INSTRUMENTS OF LEGISLATIVE ACTION TO ACHIEVE HARMONISATION

Harmonisation designates the legal mechanism by which national legislations are aligned to reduce or eliminate the inconvenience arising from their disparities. Having established the EEC in 1957, the Member States intended to achieve a common market which has now developed into an Internal Market. As the then EEC, now EU was being established, it was

---

[7] Joerges C., op cit p. 385.
[8] Muller-Graff P.C., 'EC Directives as a Means of Private Law Unification', op cit p. 77.
[9] Lando O. & Beale H. (eds.), Principles of European Contract Law, Parts I and II, Prepared by the Commission on European Contract Law, The Hague 2000, p. xxii.

realised that it would be of limited use if technical standards legally imposed in one Member State differed from those of the other Member States. Until standards were 'harmonised' they would constitute obstacles to the four freedoms.

Of the three terms, coordination, approximation or harmonisation, the latter was established in legal parlance towards the middle of the twentieth century. The other two terms were new. The word 'harmonisation' was introduced in the legal sphere by René David, who was a French legal comparatist of international reputation. If one were to examine the etymological meaning of 'harmonisation' one can refer to Dembour's analysis from the French dictionary *Littré* of 1958.[10] The dictionary defines the word *'harmonie'* in six parts. Reference to the first and second definition found in the dictionary is enough to make it clear that 'harmony' etymologically refers to an arrangement between different parts of a whole, in such a way as making these parts serve a single purpose. This can be easily transposed in the European legal context. National legislations need to be adapted to further the aim of a common purpose, the establishment of a common market.

Lawyers can now distinguish between various methods of harmonisation. They are not necessarily provided for in the Treaties or secondary legislation but can be identified in an academic exercise as an introduction one can mention them at this stage. For example, one can speak of 'total harmonisation' or uniformisation. This allows no derogation in the pre-empted area except for safeguard measures or to the extent permitted in the directive. In the seventies, the term 'optional harmonisation' was coined to remedy the perceived excesses of the former. This tool allows producers to apply national norms or Union norms. Some directives also allow the Member States to exercise the right of opting-out. Partial harmonisation regulates some aspects of the subject matter, for example, only rules for certain cross-border transactions. Minimum harmonisation allows the Member States to provide for more stringent rules. Alternative harmonisation allows the Member States to choose between alternative methods of harmonisation. This is particularly relevant for mutual recognition of control whereby the Member States are required to recognise each other's control. Often harmonisation leads to a piecemeal legislative

[10] Dembour M., Ibid. p. 6–8.

method. Finally, one can also speak of 'bottom-up' or 'top-down' harmonisation depending on the reasons why it would be taking place.[11]

Harmonisation is necessarily partial. Each specific harmonisation measure requires a sufficient legal base. In light of the principle of subsidiarity, harmonisation measures cannot go further than is necessary and are not desirable with a view of the proper functioning of the Internal Market.[12] They must genuinely have as their objective the improvement of the conditions for the establishment and functioning of the Internal Market. A mere finding of disparities between national rules and of the abstract risk of obstacles to the exercise of fundamental freedoms or of distortion of competition liable to result there, from is insufficient to justify Article 114 TFEU as a legal basis.[13] Even if there is a sufficient legal basis, the Union is allowed to take legislative action only insofar as the objectives of the proposed action cannot be sufficiently achieved by the Member States. The principle of subsidiarity and proportionality prevents any action taken from going beyond what is necessary to achieve the objectives of the Treaty—the creation and functioning of the Internal Market.

Harmonisation is also unsystematic. Internal consistency between directives is challenging to achieve as they are often prepared in different DGs of the Commission. For example, directives concerning contract law can be developed in DG Sanco, which is in charge of the CFR-Net and DG Markt. Drafting may also be incoherent, and often directives are drafted by civil servants in a language that may not be their native language. Directives do not focus on or contain a comprehensive regulation of the entire substantive law of the matter in question. Often they only regulate specific issues such as information to be provided before the conclusion of the contract, and they may also apply to one type of contract, for example, time-share contracts. Different 'sector-specific' directives often use different concepts. Directives are also entirely flat in the sense that in a directive, all rules are located on the same level of abstraction.[14]

---

[11] Van Gerven W., 'Harmonisation Within and Beyond' in Empel M. v. (ed.), *"From Paris to Nice" Fifty Years of Legal Integration in Europe,* The Hague, Kluwer, 2002, p. 2.

[12] Articles 114 & 115 TFEU.

[13] See Case C-376/98 *Germany v European Parliament and Council* [2000] ECR I-8419, at [83].

[14] See Hesselink M. W., 'Codification and Europeanisation in the Netherlands', in Vogenauer S. and Weatherill S., *'The Harmonisation of European Contract Law'*, Hart Publishing, Oxford, 2006, p. 48 ff.

Harmonisation takes place on two different levels of governance, the European and the national level. The European and national legislators share legislative responsibilities, and neither one nor the other has the final responsibility for the whole. There is no superior body or authority such as a Supreme Court who can make use of a Constitution to claim the final say on who is responsible for what competence. National courts apply the national law as it has been transposed, but they have to do so in conformity with the directive.[15] The national court is free to refer a question of interpretation of the Directives according to the parameters of Article 267 TFEU, and the parties do not have the right of appeal as such. If a reference is made, the CJEU does not go into the merits of the case, nor does it have the power to invalidate conflicting national law. It merely has jurisdiction to interpret and clarify the directive in question and provide guidelines for application. This methodology is also dynamic. Directives are instrumental as they aim at change. In particular, they aim at improving the conditions of the establishment and functioning of the Internal Market.[16]

Having established how harmonisation works, one can also consider why one should use this tool towards achieving the Europeanisation of private law. Here one can borrow Professor Stephen Weatherill's thesis, which explains that two rationales have historically driven harmonisation.[17] The first is the assumption that harmonised rules promote market integration while the second is that in so far as the TFEU is deficient in allocating competence to act in particular areas of non-market regulation, then the legal base authorising harmonisation may be borrowed to fulfil that role.

As regards the first rationale, Weatherill has two objections on connecting harmonisation with effective market-building. These are the cultural and economic objections.[18] With regards to cultural objections, it could be argued that harmonisation, as a technical process devoted to market-building, tends to disregard the rich and deep historical roots of national laws that are subjected to its influence. Cultural tradition could be

---

[15] See Case C-106/89 Marleasing v La Comercial Internacional de Alimentación [1990] ECR I-4135.
[16] Hesselink M. W., op cit p. 51.
[17] Weatherill S., 'Why Harmonise?' in Tridimas T. & Nebbia P. (eds.) *European Union Law for the Twenty-First Century,* Oxford, Hart Publishing, 2004, p. 11 ff.
[18] Ibid. p. 13.

sacrificed for economic gain.[19] For private law, this could be more important since private law is rich in legal doctrines that could easily be ignored in a simple harmonisation process. It could lead to incoherence in legal principles within the same legal system. However, while the above could be true, it does not necessarily justify the non-use of this methodology. It justifies a more proper and careful use to reduce cultural objections as much as possible. The economic objection to harmonisation is primarily driven by proponents of inter-jurisdictional regulatory competition as a model for the EU. This perspective would portray harmonisation itself as anti-competitive as it would distort competition. Some literature is beginning to examine what 'distort' can and should imply in the context of legal diversity within the EU and to explore the case for and against the regulatory competition in particular sectors such as contract law.[20] For harmonisation to be successful, economic losses have to offset gains.

It can be observed that harmonisation is conventionally understood as a process of generating standard rules for a common market. It increasingly co-exists with other 'softer' forms of governance and a general willingness to tolerate a high degree of flexibility and diversity in coverage under the EU umbrella. The TFEU itself in Articles 114 and 115 recognises that harmonisation is a sensitive matter and it includes provisions that reveal a concern to feed in a degree of respect for variation and adequate regulatory protection within the Internal Market.[21]

As regards the second rationale for legislative harmonisation mentioned earlier on, as far as the TFEU is deficient in allocating competence to act in a particular area of 'non-market' regulation, then the legal base authorising harmonisation may be borrowed to fulfil that role.[22] Harmonisation of laws for defined ends associated with the market building has always been an EU competence recognised by Article 115 TFEU and follows the SEA Article 100a, then, Article 95 EC and now Article 114 TFEU. Many harmonisation measures adopted according to these provisions are based on the perception that legislative diversity damaged integration. The principle

---

[19] See Harlow C., 'Voices of Difference in a Plural Community' 50 *American Journal of Comparative Law* (2002), 339.

[20] See Wagner G., 'The Economic of Harmonisation: the Case of Contract Law' (2002) 39 *CML Rev* 995.

[21] Sammut I., 'Tying the Knot in European Private Law', (2009) 17.*European Review of Private Law*, p. 813–840.

[22] Weatherill S., 'Why Harmonise?' in T. Tridimas & P. Nebbia (eds.), *European Union Law for the Twenty-First Century*, Hart Publishing, 2004, p. 19.

of attributed competence gave way in community practice to the capacity of the Council, acting unanimously to fix the scope of EU action. In the field of harmonisation, it appeared to assume that it enjoyed a *carte blanche*.[23] This is what Pollack describes as a competence creep.

The above shows that harmonisation is limited by competence and competence has expanded as the European Union deepens and widens. The limitations on what could be harmonised means that often harmonisation leads to legal disintegration and fragmentation. However, besides the official legislative harmonisation, which is steered by the European Commission, at European level, one can also mention various non-legislative harmonisation attempts and this bottom-up approach is also worth mentioning at this stage.[24] This involves non-legislative preparatory work undertaken by legal scholars and practitioners to bring European legal systems closer together. Here one can mention the "Principles of European Contract Law". This compilation was first presented in 1995 and has been re-issued in 1998 by the Lando Commission named after its initiator and Chairman, Professor Ole Lando from Copenhagen.[25] This work is confined to the more technical issues of contract law. This restatement is elaborated on a comparative law basis and consists, just as its American predecessors, of rules, illustrations and comments. These Principles attempt to show what a future European Civil Code might look like and provide a platform for debate.

Besides the above strategy, there have been other initiatives that rely on the harmonisation potential of the Europeanisation of legal science and education through synoptic compilations of what might become a new Common Law of Europe.[26] This is based upon the conviction that lawyers too are encouraged to think in European terms. Three books can be mentioned as an example, *European Contract Law* by Hein Kötz,[27] The

---

[23] See Pollack M., 'Creeping Competence: The Expanding Agenda of the European Community', (1994), 14 *Journal of European Public Policy* 95.

[24] This expression seems to have been coined by Hayek F., *Law, Legislation and Liberty*, 2 vol. (1973 and 1976).

[25] Lando O. & Beale H. (eds.), *Principles of European Contract Law*, 1995 [part I].

[26] Scmid C. U., 'Bottom-up Harmonisation of European Private Law: *IUS COMMUNE* and Restatement' in Heiskanen V. & Kulovesi K., *Function and Future of European Law* Helsinki 1999 p. 75 ff.

[27] Vol. 1 : Formation, Validity and Content of Contracts, Contracts and Third Parties, English translation by Tony Weir, Oxford, Clarendon Press, 197.

Common European Law of Torts, by Christian von Bar[28] and *Cases, Material and Text on National, Supranational and International Tort Law: Scope of Protection* by Walter van Gerven, Jeremy Lever, Pierre Larouche, Christian von Bar and Geneviève Viney.[29] These books, adopting a comparative functional perspective informed by the historical genesis and the social and economic tasks of private law, represent attempts in the classical fields of contract and tort law, the foundations of a new European common law. Another project which is worth mentioning is the Trento Project entitled "The Common Core of European Private Law".[30]

An effective and sensitive way of harmonising the standards of protection of certain basic interests of European citizens could be convergence in the case-law of the Member States.[31] This could be more effective because the intensity of protection of a certain right depends primarily on the law in action and not on the law in books.[32] Harmonisation of this type could be more sensitive because case-law convergence operates even in the context of the great diversity of legal cultures. All that matters is that the courts of different European states achieve similar results in the same cases, regardless of the norms, doctrines or procedures they apply to reach this end.[33] The mechanism for ensuring top-down harmonisation in the EU is available. The judgments of the CJEU and those of the European Court of Human Rights form legally binding guidelines to be compiled by the Member States. This method of harmonisation can be applied to every private law matter touching upon European fundamental rights.[34] Since every citizen of the EU should enjoy the common European fundamental rights without any discrimination on the ground of nationality,[35] one may argue that the standards of private law protecting these rights in their

---

[28] English translation (Beck Munich 1998).

[29] Hart Publishing, Oxford, 1998.

[30] http://www.jus.unitn.it/dsg/common-core.

[31] Colombi Ciacchi A., 'Non-Legislative Harmonisation: Protection from Unfair Suretyships' in Vogenauer S. & Weatherill S., *'The Harmonisation of European Contract Law'*, Hart Publishing, 2006, p. 198.

[32] Pound R., 'Law in Books and Law in Action' 44 *American Law Review* (1910), 12.

[33] Collins, H., 'European Private Law and the Cultural Identity of States' (1995) 3 *European Review of Private Law* 353.

[34] Colombi Ciacchi A., 'Non-Legislative Harmonisation: Protection from Unfair Suretyships' op cit p. 205.

[35] This follows from the non-discrimination principle enshrined in both Article 12 EC Treaty and Article 14 ECHR.

horizontal dimension should become equal. This could be easily achieved through case-law convergence.

It could be argued that the seductive appeal of harmonisation is today tarnished. Its role is increasingly contested. The tension between centralisation and respect for local autonomy is becoming more problematic in a geographically and functionally expanded EU. The debate about the function of harmonisation has essentially become a debate about the function of the EU itself.[36] If the EU were to widen and deepen, the Europeanisation of private law could become more feasible. Certainly, with all its pros and cons, harmonisation and uniformisation remain a very good methodology in achieving greater harmony in private law. Harmonisation is the most common tool because it represents the least common denominator for Europeanisation. For many instances, it would satisfy the principles of subsidiarity and proportionality when one comes to deal with the national legal orders and the European legal order. However, although harmonisation is more commonly used than unification and codification, the latter would certainly represent a more advanced level of Europeanisation than the former. Nevertheless, these two tools complement each other in the eventual Internal Market building.

3   THE IMPLEMENTATION OF DIRECTIVES IN MALTA

When it comes to the implementation and enforcement of directives, size does not matter. The smallest Member State has the same obligations as the largest one, albeit with significantly fewer resources in its civil service. The same objectives of the respective directive still need to be achieved in domestic law.

Like every other EU Member State, Malta had to considerably change and adapt its government structures and procedures for it to meet with the changes brought about by EU accession. This process started immediately after the application for accession was filed in July 1990 but intensified after Malta reactivated its application in September 1998. The changes and introduction of new civil service structures and procedures were the only way Malta could ever cope with all its commitments as a member. It was only once such structures and procedures were in place that Malta could be in a position to give its utmost input and leave its desired impact

---

[36] See Weatherill S., 'Why Harmonise?' in Tridimas T. & Nebbia P. (eds.), *European Union Law for the Twenty-First Century*, Hart Publishing, 2004, p. 31–32.

at EU level and also gain and make the best use of the advantages while mitigating as much as possible the downsides of membership.

Such structures introduced slowly over a period of fifteen years before membership were and are still constantly being updated particularly during the first years of membership. Initially, Malta's system was heavily centralised. Following the first change of Government since membership in 2013, the system was adjusted to the new administration's needs. The challenges brought about by EU membership are countless, irrelevant if we are speaking of big countries or small countries. The smaller the country, the more challenging it is due to obvious reasons, particularly due to restricted resource, including but not limited to financial limitations. Malta's fundamental response to triumph the challenges posed was by vigilantly selecting and establishing an effective national coordination system for EU affairs which suits our necessities. Every Member State has its national coordination system or something equivalent to, with their respective structures and organisation making up the system. Some have opted for a system which is highly centralised such as those found in Britain, Finland and Malta, with the latter possibly having *"the most highly centralised system to be found anywhere in the EU"*.[37] In contrast, others have opted for a more decentralised system such as those found in Italy and Belgium'.[38]

Malta's coordination system is broadly split into two branches; on one part having Malta's Permanent Representation which is based in Belgium (Brussels), which despite being the Representation of the smallest Member State, it is quite large when compared to that of other small Member States, while on the other, having the EU Secretariat which is based in Malta in Valletta. Both are linked to one another and together with other national players make up Malta's coordination system for EU Affairs. It is beneficial to note that both the Permanent Representation and the EU Secretariat fall under the auspices of the executive, i.e. the Government of Malta.

The Permanent Representation, headed by Malta's Representative to the EU, is based at Malta House in Brussels. It has a twofold task; it deals directly with EU institutions on behalf of the Government and acts as a channel to pass on information coming from Brussels to Malta and vice-versa. The Permanent Representation can be deemed to be the extension of the Government in the Brussels, particularly by participating within COREPER I and II. Its main role is to convey Malta's voice at EU level and also act as a conduit between the two. The Permanent Representation's direct contact in Malta is the EU Secretariat. Until 2013 this fell directly under the Office of the Prime Minister. After the change of government, it fell within a specific ministry. The administration set up is not set up in law and can change from one administration to another.

The EU Secretariat plays a vital role in the coordination system for two particular reasons, the first because it is responsible for the general coordination and the smooth running of the system, and secondly because it acts as a reference point between all the key players based in Malta and the Permanent Representation in Brussels. Moreover, the EU Secretariat is tasked with the coordination of the national process on EU affairs both at the proposal stage and post-legislative stage.

At the proposal stage, when the Commission issues a draft legislative act, the EU Secretariat is burdened with the monitoring and coordination of the national process which establishes Malta's official position on a particular proposal. A similar task is performed post-legislative stage once the EU legislator crystallises a proposal into law, this time by coordinating and overseeing transposition in the Maltese legal order. Besides these two core key players, individual ministries also feature in this coordination system. Every ministry has an EU Affairs Directorate that coordinates all EU affairs related matters within that particular ministry, including with the departments and authorities that fall under its responsibility. The size and staff complement of these Directorates vary according to the size and responsibilities of that ministry which very often follows the EU's *acquis* covered by that particular ministry.

3.1   The Political Process

All proposals, including legislative proposals emanating from the European Commission, have to be conveyed to among other recipients such as other applicable institutions, to all the governments of Member States. This is done through an online system where both the Permanent Representatives and local coordination offices (such as the EU Secretariat in Malta) are linked and have access. Thanks to this electronic system, all Member States are instantly informed of all EU proposals together with any related documentation which might exist then. The practice is that the Permanent Representation transmits a given proposal and all accompanying documentation via electronic mail to the Head EU Secretariat and the responsible coordinator within the EU Secretariat. The responsible coordinator here would be that person which proposal falls under his direct responsibility to coordinate locally.

The EU Secretariat is structured into several offices, mirroring the Council configurations. Illustrating this through an example, if the Commission issues a draft directive regulating an area dealing with land transport, the Permanent Representation transmits that draft directive to both the Head EU Secretariat and the Coordinator responsible for Transport, Telecommunications and Energy affairs within the same Secretariat. From there on, the EU Secretariat is responsible for coordinating the whole process locally, which at the very end of the process should bring about Malta's official position on that particular proposed directive (Fig. 4.1).

The initial step which the EU Secretariat takes is that of filtering and forwarding that particular proposal to the Ministry concerned, which is referred to as the implementing Ministry. It is at this stage that the implementing Ministry embarks on a consultation process with the civil society and all stakeholders involved. This consultation process takes place through MEUSAC (Malta-EU Steering and Action Committee) which is

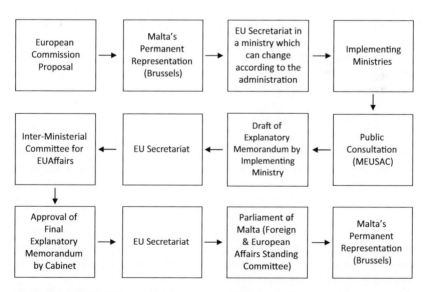

Fig. 4.1 Malta's EU coordination system. (Diagram taken from Harwood Mark *Malta in the European Union*, Ashgate, 2014, p. 102)

the Government's arm responsible for consultation with the civil society and the general public on EU affairs. MEUSAC nevertheless is included in the EU's decision-making process. One of its main duties is to precisely discuss and inform those concerned with the impact (either positive or negative) of such a proposed legislative measure could leave on sectors, industries, institutions, the citizens and Malta in general.

The next step is that both the EU Secretariat and the implementing Ministry work together to formulate a document referred to as the 'explanatory memorandum'. This explanatory memorandum can be defined as that document which provides a preliminary snapshot of what such a proposed directive is all about; its legal basis emanating from the EU Treaties, the consultation processes which took place both within Government and with external stakeholders, Malta's formulated position, official positions of other Member States (if already known) and what initiatives and changes need to be affected in domestic law for its transposition if and when the EU legislator adopts such a proposal. As one can attest from the contents of this document, the explanatory memorandum is of paramount importance, primarily because it consists of Malta's official position, which position once approved and conveyed to Brussels, is to be strictly followed by all representatives representing Malta in the Council.

Once this draft explanatory memorandum materialises, the document appears on the list of what is referred to as the Inter-Ministerial Committee for EU Affairs. The Head EU Secretariat chairs this Committee. It is convened once every month or two according to exigencies, very much depending on the number of items featuring on the list. The other members that make up this Committee are the Directors for EU Affairs within every Ministry, the Head of MEUSAC and also a representative from the Secretariat of the Ministry responsible for EU affairs. It is the principal task of this Committee to thoroughly vet and go through these draft explanatory memoranda for endorsement. Once an agreement has been reached, the EU Secretariat passes on such memoranda to the Ministry responsible for EU affairs, which in turn transmits them to the attention of Cabinet within the Office of Prime Minister. Cabinet discusses, and the usual practice is that the explanatory memoranda presented are adopted without any delay. Cabinet's final approval solidifying Malta's official position is conveyed to the implementing Ministry (the same Ministry which drafted it) for the Minister's signature (rubber stamp).

As soon as the Minister officially adopts that memorandum, it is then tabled in front of the House of Representatives, more specifically in front of the Standing Committee on Foreign and European Affairs'. 'The Committee has a total of four working groups, with Working Group 1 being tasked to filter the explanatory memoranda and also examine whether there are any issues which are to be referred to other working groups or Standing Committees within Parliament'.[39] 'The main reason why the Ministry (and therefore Government) lays such a document in Parliament is precisely to inform members of Parliament of Malta's position on that particular proposal. Parliament's function here is rather contained, having a mere scrutiny role without any particular say or power to change the Government's adopted position. Having said so, however, Parliament not only has this right to be informed but also may give its feedback or even ask the implementing ministry questions or for clarifications concerning that tabled explanatory memorandum. It is beneficial to note that Parliament here is merely informed and not even consulted, so much that virtually at the same time the implementing ministry tables the explanatory memorandum in front of the House, it is also communicated to the Permanent Representation in Brussels for it to follow when representing Malta at EU level.

The process mentioned above under Malta's EU Coordination system ensures that Malta has a single strong voice which is clear and consistent in the EU institutions. It is precisely thanks to this national process which formulates Malta's position on any given legislative proposal. Besides the process which is held on a national level in all Member States once a draft legislative proposal has been issued by the Commission, work will also kick off in the two main EU institutions which are directly involved in the process of EU law-making; the Council and the European Parliament, jointly making up the EU legislator. Both institutions can be deemed to serve as means for the Member States to voice their respective positions when it comes to decision making, each from a completely different perspective. While the Council represent the official positions of Member States directly through the involvement of national Ministers, the EP can also be said to represent the Member States through MEPs directly representing the citizens of that particular Member State from which they were elected.

---

[39] Mark Harwood (2014). 'Ten Years of EU Membership – The Maltese Parliament.' *Reflections of a Decade of EU Membership: Expectations, Achievements, Disappointments and the Future Occasional Papers*, No. 1, Institute for European Studies, Malta, https://www.um.edu.mt/__data/assets/pdf_file/0005/228074/The_Maltese_Parliament_final.pdf last accessed on 1 February 2020.

A working party is composed of delegations sent by every Member State, which delegations are usually made up of individuals referred to as attachés, being specialised officials based at the Permanent Representations in Brussels and national experts on travel coming directly from the Member States. These so-called national experts can be sent to represent Malta by the implementing Ministry which such a proposed legislative act being discussed falls under the responsibility of and which experts may also be selected from a Government department or Authority which falls under that Ministry's political responsibility'. 'At the final stages of the work assumed by the working party, a conclusion is drawn up which may take one of the following two different directions. If the working party reaches an agreement, the proposed act appears on Part I of the COREPER (Committee of Permanent Representatives in the EU) Agenda. If on the other hand an agreement has not been attained, the proposal appears on Part II of the COREPER Agenda'.[40]

Once all meetings of the working party come to an end, its work and outcomes are transmitted to COREPER where Member States are represented by the Deputy Permanent Representative at COREPER I and the Permanent Representatives at COREPER II respectively.[41] 'COREPER's task is twofold; it either meets to discuss further and hopefully reach an agreement on those areas which were left without agreement at working party level or if an agreement has been reached at the working party level, to give its formal approval before transmitting the work to the Council. COREPER's most crucial and significant role is when it actively intervenes and through its political impetus irons out the remaining disputed points.

Once discussions at COREPER level come to an end, the conclusion would be either one of an agreement or one where a final agreement could not be fully reached. In case of an agreement, the proposed legislative act with all its amendments (if any) made at the working party, and COREPER levels appear as an A item on the Council's agenda. In this scenario agreement is invariably reached by the national Ministers in the Council without debate, simply giving a rubber stamp. Suppose there is no final

[40] The official website of the Council of the EU—The decision-making process in the Council; http://www.consilium.europa.eu/en/council-eu/decision-making/ last accessed on 1 February 2020.

[41] COREPER I deals and prepares the work for all Council configurations, expect the General Affairs and External Relations, Economic and Financial Affairs (ECOFIN) and Justice & Home Affairs configurations which are dealt with by COREPER II since they are deemed to be more political sensitive areas.

agreement at COREPER level. In that case, the proposed act appears as a B item on the Council's agenda, which entails that debate is held between the national Ministers to strike a consensus'.[42]

Nevertheless, in the vast majority of the instances, the Council moves to adopt its position on that particular legislative proposal without the need for any further discussion between Ministers themselves. Of course, exceptions do exist, and where even COREPER has failed to reach an agreement, it is then up to the political will of national Ministers to try and find a plausible solution and come to a common position. A description of the EU's legislative procedure is beyond the scope of this chapter.

One might argue that Malta's voice in the European Parliament is limited because Malta has only six MEPs. Malta has successfully managed to overcome this quantity handicap by having generally qualitative hardworking MEPs, with a number of them also being appointed as rapporteurs to the EP on several proposed legislative acts. When it comes to voting in the European Parliament a paramount principle is that every MEP is free to vote as he/she desires, hopefully keeping in mind the views of the citizens who have directly elected them. This, therefore, prescribes that MEPs can either vote according to his/her country's official position or otherwise. The EU Secretariat takes the initiative to inform Maltese MEPs of the Maltese Government's official position on a particular proposal once Cabinet has approved the explanatory memorandum. It is up to every MEP to decide whether to follow such a position or otherwise, keeping in mind that in no way an MEP is obliged to do so. This heavily contrasts with the situation of attaches, national experts and the Permanent Representative who are all required to abide with the Government's position when representing Malta at the Council.

3.2   The Legislative Process

Once a directive is approved and adopted by the EU legislator according to the type of legislative procedure being followed, it no longer a 'draft' but rather becomes a fully-fledged EU law which needs to be first and foremost transposed into the national legal orders of the Member States. Transposition has to take place within the set timeframes laid down in the

---

[42]The official website of the Council of the EU—The decision-making process in the Council; http://www.consilium.europa.eu/en/council-eu/decision-making/ last accessed on 1 February 2020.

directive itself, usually somewhere between six months and two years. While transposition entails an act performed by every Member State for a directive to be ultimately included in their national legal orders, implementation goes further than that. For effective implementation, there has to be a system and a watchdog in place that oversees and ensures the correct implementation of any given directive.

Before membership, each Member State had to cater for a set of legal provisions which permit EU legal acts including directives, to be binding on them and therefore allowing transposition into their national legal order. The European Union Act,[43] through Article 3(1) provides that the Treaty and existing and future adopted EU acts *"shall be binding on Malta and shall be part of the domestic law"*, with Article 3(2) going a step further declaring the supremacy of EU law on domestic law so much that whenever *"any provision of any law…is incompatible with Malta's obligations under the Treaty"* shall *"be without effect and unenforceable"*.

The very first stage before the commencement of national measures by a Member State to transpose a directive is that of notification. This stage is deemed to be a formality since the Member States to whom that act is addressed are very well aware of it, having been involved in the entire process and from the very beginning. Nevertheless, the Commission publishes the adopted directive in the Official Journal of the EU to formally notify all addressees in a manifested manner.

The Maltese transposition system is very much ministerial centred, where the implementing ministry drives the transposition procedure. Every ministry has its *modus operandi* on how to transpose directives which fall under its ministerial portfolio. One is to note that when speaking of the implementing ministry which is ultimately responsible for carrying out the respective transposition, one is also including that entity which falls under its political responsibility and which has been entrusted with all the work being necessary for transposition. The intrinsic details of transposition are naturally performed by both internal and/or external legal experts tasked by the implementing ministry or the responsible entity'. This wide discretion of the implementing ministry does not mean that the ministry works in isolation. During transposition stage, the implementing ministry has to closely liaise with both the EU Secretariat and the Justice Unit. The fact that ministries are by and large in control of the

---

[43] European Union Act (Chapter 460 of the Laws of Malta), https://legislation.mt/ Legislation.

process and manner for transposition with no sign of uniformity across ministries may lead to some confusion or worst ending with transposition instruments of varied quality. The EU Secretariat maintains its coordination role or more appropriate, its supervisory role on a national level even at the transposition stage. It informs ministries about every adopted directive which falls under their respective responsibility and what is referred to as a working plan is formulated jointly with the implementing ministries.

If the transposition requires the enactment or amendment of primary legislation, the House of Representatives needs to be involved in the process. This process inevitably entails that transposition takes longer to materialise than if a Subsidiary Legislation (through a Legal Notice) is used as a legislative tool to transpose directives. One is to bear in mind that a Subsidiary Legislation does not pass through the entire formal process requiring the active involvement of the House of Representatives. Legal Notices are signed (and eventually published in the Government Gazette) by the implementing minister and are merely tabled in front of the members of the House for their notification. Parliament then has a period of four weeks within which it can voice its objection to any tabled Subsidiary Legislation.[44]

If a public consultation is required, civil society needs to be involved through MEUSAC. Here consultation revolves on how the implementing ministry should go around transposition and the fundamental ways and means to be used. A practical example where and when consultation is necessary is when a directive negatively affects a particular industry or sector. Stakeholders contribute and give their views and suggestions on how the government can mitigate or neutralise as much as possible any negative effects, while at the same time fully transpose and implement that directive. Again, in such a scenario, the work plan has to take into consideration that if and when public consultation needs to take place, the period for transposition will probably take longer.

If transposition requires national legislation to go beyond the requirements laid down in the directive, such transposition measures require notification under the TRIS (Technical Regulation Information System) Directive 98/34/EC.[45] The scope of the TRIS directive is one which

---

[44] See Article 11 of the Interpretation Act (Chapter 249 of the Laws of Malta), https://legislation.mt/Legislation last accessed on 1 February 2020.

[45] Directive 98/48/EC of the European parliament and of the Council of 20 July 1998 amending Directive 98/34/EC laying down a procedure for the provision of information in

establishes a notification procedure to anticipate and ultimately prevent the Member States from creating any possible barriers hindering the smooth function of the Internal Market through their enactment of domestic laws. This prescribes that whenever a national measure goes beyond the requirements as laid down in a given directive and which measure has the possibility of impacting on the smooth running of the Internal Market, this must be flagged and stated in the work plan. The reason behind this is that a particular procedure must be followed before actually adopting that national measure.

The notification procedure under this TRIS directive is of particular importance since if not correctly followed might bring about the nullity of the national measure. Any Member State who is in the process of enacting national law (whether to transpose a directive into national law or otherwise) and where such national law consists of technical matters that could potentially hinder, obstruct or distort the smooth functioning of the Internal Market, is bound and therefore obliged, before publishing that proposed law in the Government Gazette to notify the Commission and the other Member States with the said law through what is referred to as the TRIS database. The TRIS database is therefore used as a means to convey information or receive information. Each Member State has an office that is responsible for the administration of this database, where the MCCAA (Malta Competition and Consumer Affairs Authority) is the responsible office which handles and administers the database on behalf of Malta.

Whenever a notification is sent via TRIS database by a Member State, this directly reaches the Commission and the remaining Member States. They, in turn, may either choose to comment or submit a detail opinion on such a law being proposed by that particular Member State. By way of example, let us say that a particular Maltese ministry drafts a Subsidiary Legislation which might potentially impinge on the Internal Market as per TRIS Directive. The ministry is obliged to communicate that proposed law to the MCCAA for it to be notified to the Commission and the other Member States via this database. Once notification has taken place, the ministry has to wait for three months for any comments or six months in the case of reasoned opinions by the Commission or the Member States before proceeding with the publishing and eventual entry into force of

the field of technical standards and regulations: http://eur-lex.europa.eu/legal-content/EN/TXT/PDF/?uri=CELEX:31998L0048&from=EN last accessed on 1 February 2020.

that law. Suppose the Commission and/or a Member State comments/ submit a reasoned opinion. In that case, the proposing Member State is obliged to reply by either changing its draft national measure or rebut to such comments/reasoned opinions received. This envisages that both the Commission and the Member States cannot be ignored once they have decided to intervene. It is likewise important, that in the case where a Member State had to notify its national measure as per TRIS Directive, yet failed to do so, that national law is deemed to be null and void.

Malta often makes use of the this TRIS database, particularly to comment or make explicit opinions according to the case and necessity on proposed national laws by the other Member States. An area of particular interest to Malta is precisely that of the gaming industry, where through the TRIS database Malta monitors and vets the proposed measures by the other Member States in a rigorous manner. Whenever a Member State notifies through this database a new or amending national measure dealing with the gaming industry attempting to introduce taxes based on the place of origin and which has the potential of distorting the internal market, Malta promptly utilises the TRIS database to voice its concern in safeguarding its local gaming industry.

The Justice Unit features at the final stages of the transposition process, with its primary roles being those of reviewing the drafted transposition measure compiled by the implementing ministry, crystallising the measure into a proper legal instrument and ultimately coordinating the publishing of the law on the Government Gazette. Once the implementing ministry finalises its draft transposition text in both the Maltese and the English languages, these are sent to the Justice Unit for its review. The review and process differ slightly according to the type of legal measure being used, that is whether transposition will take place through secondary law— Subsidiary Legislation or through primary law—an Act of Parliament.

Whenever transposition takes place through subsidiary legislation, the Justice Unit, upon receiving the draft text reviews the legal basis of the measure. The verification as to whether the minister is empowered by primary law (main Act) to make such Regulations is established. A review extends to verify as to whether the proposed measure has the potential to conflict with other national laws. Even if this is an infrequent occurrence, whenever established, this has to be flagged to the implementing ministry and also given solutions. The next stage of review consists of that of scrutinising the actual legal text of the measure with the text of the directive. The wording used in the national measure is to mirror the wording used in the Maltese version of the directive. Finally, the review exercise has to ensure that the directive is properly and fully transposed meaning that whatever needs to be transposed is included in the transposition measure. Once all the review work has been concluded by the Justice Unit, the draft is sent back to the implementing ministry in the form of a proper legal instrument, in this case being a subsidiary Legislation. The minister after vetting it and is satisfied with the result of the proposed law brings it to the attention of Cabinet, where it is customary that together with the signature of the minister concerned, the Prime Minister also signs the law signifying Cabinet's endorsement. The signed legal instrument is once again conveyed to the Justice Unit for its publication on the Government Gazette. Once published, the Subsidiary Legislation is deemed to gain the status of a fully-fledged law and is consequently incorporated into the Maltese Legal Order.

Transposition through Acts of Parliament more or less involves the same review process which is conducted by the Justice Unit when dealing with subsidiary legislation. Since the legislative instrument under review is a primary law, there is no need to verify whether the minister is empowered to make regulations, naturally because here no regulations will be enacted and because the process involves the legislator—Parliament. Once the review exercise is concluded, the draft legal instrument is sent to the implementing minister for his approval, which once approved, the Justice Unit will move on with the publication of the bill. The presentation of the bill to the House of Representatives is the first reading. The second reading requires the minister piloting the bill to briefly explain the rationale of each article to the members of the House. The piloting minister may before the bill being thoroughly examined during Parliament's Committee stage, ask the Justice Unit to modify the bill, very often taking into account any proposals or submissions made by the general public or the civil society after its publication. During the Committee stage, the bill may be further amended until a vote approving it for its third reading takes place.

The Justice Unit converts the bill as approved by the Parliamentary Committee concerned into a proper legal instrument, here is an Act of Parliament. This is sent back to the piloting minister and Parliament, where the President of the Republic is notified of this quasi-Act which is in front of the House for its third and final reading. Once Parliament (in plenary session) adopts the Act during its third reading, and the President of the Republic assents to it, the Justice Unit is informed accordingly for the Act to be published on the Government Gazette. Once this is executed, the Act is formally declared to be part and parcel of the Laws of Malta.

Malta generally transposes directives into its legal order by subsidiary legislation (through Legal Notices), with as much as roughly 80–90% of its transposition obligations taking place in this manner. One can get at these figures by looking at the various sectoral directives and see how they are implemented in Malta. These figures suggest that the time for transposition in Malta is significantly reduced since the formal procedure used for enacting/amending primary legislation in the House of Representatives is so to speak circumvented. The reason for this is that the primary act empowers the government (ministers) to pass secondary legislation without the need of going through Parliament. This has both positive and negative attributes. Positive because transposition takes place swiftly and rapidly, which undoubtedly contributed to Malta's satisfactory transposition results during the last decade. The downside of this is that the highest institution of the country, Parliament is not fully and effectively involved in the process, but rather is merely informed of the Legal Notice being tabled to the attention of the members of the House by the implementing minister. Legal Notices are as enforceable as primary legislation.

Article 4 of the European Union Act gives enormous powers to the Government of Malta when it comes to transposition, *"which as long as they are not abused are positive"*.[46] Under this Act, Parliament gave the right to the Government to amend an Act of Parliament (principle law) in cases of extreme urgency provided that the aim is to adopt EU legislation. This entails that the Prime Minister, through the issuing of an order and a Legal Notice can amend primary law with the usual national legislative process in Parliament being bypassed. In other words, this Act provides for an exception to the rule that the Government can only issue Legal Notices concerning Subsidiary Legislation. This Act extends this right to also include Primary legislation in cases of extreme urgency and where the need is one to adopt EU legislation'.

The final stage of the transposition process is that of communication. Member States are obliged to notify the European Commission with the national measures transposing and implementing EU directives. This is done through yet another system which Member States are logged to directly with the Commission—the NEM (National Execution Measures) system. The Commission's secretariat is logged to the NEM system in

---

[46] Chapter 460 of the Laws of Malta.

Malta, where once the implementing ministry finalises the transposition and the national legal measure has been published in the Government Gazette, this is to be notified to the Commission. The publishing of the national measure in the Government Gazette and the date of entry coming into force are essential before notification since the NEM system requires that both a copy of the Government Gazette where the national legal measure has been published, and the actual legislative instrument (text) transposing the directive are to be uploaded on the system. Member States are also obliged to inform the Commission as to whether such a national measure being notified has fully or partially transposed the directive in question. This is because a single national measure such as single subsidiary legislation might not fully transpose a directive. Therefore subsequent national measures have to be adopted for it to be fully transposed into national law.

4   CONCLUSION

From the above, one can appreciate that Malta has adopted a very centralised structure to transpose and implement European Union directives. The individual ministries which tend to change from one administration to another retain an important role in the implementation of directives that fall within their sectoral responsibility. One can argue that there may be no standard process of how the individual ministry goes about implementing the directives that fall within the competence of more than one ministry. However, the Justice Unit, offers some standardisation as it is the body responsible for the review and finalisation of the legal instrument, this in turn ensures the highest quality of legislative instrument possible. As one can appreciate from above, the transposition and implementation procedure adopted by Malta seems to have catered for the country's needs since its accession to the EU. Nevertheless, there will always be room for improvement in the system if Malta wants to retain its records on the top of the scoreboard for the Member States when it comes to the implementation and transposition of directives. Fine-tuning the functions and work of implementing ministry could be a primary area which would need to be seriously revisited targeting both the qualitative aspect of the legal instruments fabricated by the ministries as well as improving the efficiency of implementation. This would help to consolidate and strengthen Malta's achievements in the area of transposition and implementation of EU directives.

CHAPTER 5

Legal Translations: The Translation of EU Law into the Maltese Language—*Quo Vadis?*

Ivan Sammut

1   INTRODUCTION

Sometimes it may be argued that multilingualism in the European Union or legal translation could be an obstacle to the proper functioning of the EU's Internal Market due to discrepancies that may result from translating one language version to another. In practice, the EU cannot function as an Internal Market without multilingualism. Subsequently, this chapter seeks to argue that after all, legal translation is an inherent element of legal harmonisation, intrinsically connected to the very foundations of the EU and therefore, it cannot be an obstacle.

'Legal Translation is not Transcoding, i.e. substituting words and phrases of the source legal system by the corresponding expressions of the target legal system'[1] The basic unit of translation is not the word but the concept. This is particularly true in the case of the European Union (EU)

---

[1] Šarčević, S. (1997), *New Approaches to Legal Translation*, Kluwer: The Hague p. 229.

I. Sammut (✉)
University of Malta, Msida, Malta
e-mail: ivan.sammut@um.edu.mt

I. Sammut, J. Agranovska (eds.), *The Implementation and Enforcement of European Union Law in Small Member States,*
https://doi.org/10.1007/978-3-030-66115-1_5

which currently has twenty-four language versions. Council Regulation 1/58/EEC stipulates that once a language is recognised as official, according to Article 2 and 4 of the said Regulation, the EU Institutions are required to communicate with citizens and enact legislation in all the recognised official languages. This includes the legislative instruments adopted for legal harmonisation. Legal harmonisation is the process by which national laws are brought closer to each other for the better functioning of the Internal Market.[2] This is mainly done through EU directives. Hence the multilingual nature of EU law is inherently linked with the need for uniform interpretation and application of EU law. When Malta joined the EU, in 2004 as Maltese is an official and the national language one of two languages the other being English in which law in Malta is enforced and implemented, through Regulation 1/58/EEC, Maltese had to become an official language of the EU.

This chapter examines the importance of EU legal translation to the harmonisation of the EU's Internal Market, and it then seeks to study how the Maltese language, the least spoken language in the EU, spoken by less than half a million people, fits into the EU's multilingualism. It also studies the effect that the European Union and EU law has on the evolution of the Maltese language as the national language of Malta.

2   THE IMPORTANCE OF EU LEGAL TRANSLATION

EU legal translation contributes to the achievement of harmonisation of EU law and the evolution of the European legal culture. The Court of Justice of the European Union (CJEU) has regularly clarified that a uniform interpretation and application of EU law entails uniformity of all the language versions in which EU law exists. In fact, in numerous judgments, the CJEU has emphasised that the need for the uniform interpretation and application of EU law entails that EU legislation must be interpreted and applied 'in the light of the versions in all … Languages' (Case 29/69 *Stauder* [1969][3] and more recently, Case C-375/07 *Heuschen & Schroff* [2008].[4] In fact, in the *Regina v. Bouchereau* case in 1977, the CJEU

---

[2] Baaij, C.J.W. (2012), *The Role of Legal Translation in Legal Harmonisation*, Wolters Kluwer: The Hague p. 2.
[3] ECR 419, para 3.
[4] ECR I-8691, para 46.

added that 'the different language versions ... must be given a uniform interpretation' (Case 30/77 *Regina v. Bouchereau* [1977].[5]

Thus the Court makes it clear that while the EU Institutions operate in various legal cultures and languages, institutional multilingualism must still result in the uniform interpretation of the law.[6] Legal harmonisation is the process by means by use of directives, the EU instructs the Member States to bring their national laws within the parameters set by the Directive. The national laws are written in the official language/s of the Member States, and EU law also requires directives to be available as the authentic version in the official language of the Member State. EU legal translation is not just a 'standard' legal translation from one Source Language (SL) to another but requires the establishment of new legal and linguistic concepts to be introduced. 'New' in the sense that this legal culture is created specifically for the EU legal order. As Šarčević's work mentioned earlier on points out, a proper legal translation is not just being faithful to the text but also recreating the spirit of the text.[7] In the translation of EU legal texts, one can argue that Šarčević's observation can be taken even further, as the legal translator needs to recreate not necessarily the spirit of the Target Language (TL) but must contribute to the creation of a 'new' European legal translation.

Multilingualism is the EU law's greatest challenge, and the paradoxical role of legal translation is very evident.[8] On the one hand, translation is essential for the functioning of EU law as it enables the production of equally authentic texts of EU legislation. On the other hand, legal translation may be seen as inherently imperfect and a potential obstacle to the very goal of legal harmonisation. In the quest for a better translation, which makes up 23 of the 24 authentic linguistic versions, the EU tries to improve the quality of the basic texts of EU legislation.[9] In fact, in 2009, DGT has launched a *Programme for Quality Management in Translation*

---

[5] ECR 1999, para. 14.

[6] Šarčević, S. (ed.) (2015), *Language and Culture in EU law – Multidisciplinary Perspectives*, Ashgate: Surrey p. 3.

[7] Šarčević, S. (1997), *New Approaches to Legal Translation*, Kluwer: The Hague p. 229.

[8] Kjaer, A., 'Theortical Aspects of Legal Translation in the EU: The Paradoxical Relationship between Language, Translation and the Autonomy of EU Law' in Šarčević, S. (ed.) (2015), *Language and Culture in EU law – Multidisciplinary Perspectives*, Ashgate: Surrey, p. 91.

[9] Šarčević S, 'Coping with the Challenges of Legal Translation in Harmonisation' in in Baaij, C.J.W. (ed.) (2012), *The Role of Legal Translation in Legal Harmonisation*, Wolters Kluwer: The Hague p. 84.

(European Commission 2009).[10] At this stage, it makes sense to outline what makes EU translation unique from the perspective of legal translation studies.

Nowadays, there is a growing awareness of the inherent link between law, language and culture. This has resulted in greater interaction between lawyers and linguists. Legal translation studies is a truly disciplinary field that borrows from translation theory, the theory of law, comparative law and comparative legal drafting.[11] Like in other areas of translation, the legal translator's basic tasks are to translate texts anchored in a specific legal context and intended for a specific purpose or *skopos*, as it is often called in Translation Studies. Normally this is a duel operation involving an SL and a source legal system with a TL and a target legal system. EU legal translation is more complex, but one must keep in mind that EU law is regarded as an independent supranational legal system with its autonomous conceptual system.

In this sense, Professor De Groot[12] remarked that the translation of EU texts might be 'relatively easy' because equivalents for EU legal concepts exist in all the official languages. However, one can disagree and argue that this is a narrow approach given that most EU concepts are borrowed from several national systems, from international law, and legal transplants and their linguistic terminology acquires an autonomous EU meaning. One can refer to Anna Lise Kjaer,[13] who said that legal translation in the EU is neither translation within one legal system nor translation across legal systems. She argues that EU translation is so complex that it requires 'theoretical categories of its own', which take into account the special characteristics of multilingual law-making in the EU to which traditional concepts of translation theory may no longer apply.

---

[10] ec.europa.eu/dgs/translation/publications/studies/quality-management_translation_en.pdf last accessed on 10 September 2020.

[11] Šarčević S, 'Coping with the Challenges of Legal Translation in Harmonisation' in in Baaij, C.J.W. (ed.) (2012), *The Role of Legal Translation in Legal Harmonisation*, Wolters Kluwer: The Hague, p. 84.

[12] De Groot, G., 'The Influence of Problems of Legal Translation on Comparative Law Research', in Baaij C.J.W. (ed.) (2012), *The Role of Legal Translation in Legal Harmonisation*, Wolters Kluwer: The Hague, p. 20.

[13] Kjaer, A., 'Theortical Aspects of Legal Translation in the EU: The Paradoxical Relationship between Language, Translation and the Autonomy of EU Law in Šarčević, S. (ed.) (2015), *Language and Culture in EU law – Multidisciplinary Perspectives*, Ashgate: Surrey, p. 91.

As regards translation in EU legal harmonisation, it is necessary to identify the text producers and above all the receivers in the unique multi-level process of harmonisation. EU legal instruments (Regulations and Directives) are produced and adopted by the EU institutions. The former are directly applicable and enforceable in all the Member States while the later would need to be transposed into the laws of the Member States. This two-level of governance (the EU level and the Member State level) brings about a corresponding two-step translation process which is inter-lingual at EU level but intra-lingual at the national level.[14] The two steps are inseparably linked and mutually dependent on each other. It follows that EU translators need to take account of both phases when selecting an appropriate translation strategy. At EU level these legal instruments are normally drafted in English or French and after being approved by the Legal Service, they are translated into the other 23 languages. The second phase of harmonisation in the case of Directives takes place at Member State level. It is at this point that the normally translated version of the language of the particular Member State is taken to draft the transposing local legislation. At this point, the EU linguistic concepts meet with the national, linguistic concepts. If there are variations or neologism, the challenge of integration into national law would be even more demanding.

From the above one can argue that one of the greatest challenges of legal translation in the EU harmonisation of laws is for translators to produce a TT that reads like an original, yet preserving good inter-lingual concordance to prevent unintended ambiguity and misinterpretations.[15] One can say that the paradoxical relationship between language, translation and the autonomy of EU law strengthens the argument being made that EU law mirrors the *sui generis* nature of the European legal order. One can agree with Anne Lise Kjaer,[16] who argues that it is a challenge for practitioners of legal translation and calls for reflection on the part of translation scholars and lawyer linguists. She rightly argues that the real challenge in European law is not a translation in the narrow sense of the word, but translation in a broader sociological sense, that is, the transfer of the legal knowledge which is produced and developed by the interaction

---

[14] Kjaer, A., 'Theortical Aspects of Legal Translation in the EU: The Paradoxical Relationship between Language, Translation and the Autonomy of EU Law in Šarčević, S. (ed.) (2015), *Language and Culture in EU law – Multidisciplinary Perspectives*, Ashgate: Surrey, p. 97.

[15] Ibid., p. 105.

[16] Ibid., p. 105.

of lawyers and judges in the European institutions and at the European Courts as participants of discourse communities at the supranational level of the EU law. At the central level, the actors may well agree on the 'semantics' of the emerging European law and declare its 'semantic' independence from national law.

However, stating autonomy does not automatically result in autonomy. It still depends on the application of the text by the interpreter. Nevertheless stating the autonomy of European legal concepts does mark a shift in the legal discourse of European lawyers, also at a national level, and discourse can change what people believe is real. When European concepts are constructed as autonomous, people will increasingly treat them as such. Hence from this argument, one can appreciate the nature of EU legal translation and the contribution it makes to the harmonisation of law in the Internal Market.

3   MALTESE AS AN OFFICIAL LANGUAGE OF THE EU

Having discussed the importance of legal translation in the harmonisation of the EU Internal Market, one may ask how the least spoken official language in the EU play its role in the harmonisation of the EU's Internal Market.

3.1   *The Use of the Maltese Language in Maltese Law: Historical Background*

The national language of Malta did not always enjoy the official and fundamental status that it enjoys nowadays. Particularly noteworthy is the fact that the language used in the Maltese courts today is the result of a long historical struggle between various cultures, different civilisations and most of all, the political situation at the time, who all left a strong impact on our country.

The period of British rule in Malta stretched for a century and a half. However, even during this time of foreign rule, it was officially recognised that the official language which dominated the Maltese Islands was Italian. This was a time during which the island experienced many upheavals. Such a stronghold position of the Italian language was nonetheless upheld during this foreign rule, and the British did not interfere with the day to day spoken language- the Maltese language. The general perception was that the Maltese language a medium of communication used by the "common uneducated people" and the lower class and it was referred to as "the language of the kitchen".[17] It was predominantly spoken but was not at the time, the official language.

On the other hand, the Italian language was perceived as being the language of the learned, and also the language of culture and nobility. In fact, during the British reign, the elite sought to protect the Italian language from British influence. Even the language of the courts was Italian since many of the law practitioners at the time had pursued their studies in Italy. Thus, it was established that the Italian language was "the language of office and the educated".[18] It all revolved around the reality that the Italian language was strongly rooted in the daily lives of people, forming part of the various segments of society: *"Be they lawyers defending their domain in the Law Courts, merchants carrying on their business with nearby Italy, people who were sentimental about their historical and cultural connection with it or who just did not want to change their customs and habits, the ranks that bred politicians and gave them their seats, saw decided advantages in Italian over English"*.[19]

This meant that for some time, the status of Italian as an official language took precedence over the English language, even though Malta was under British rule. The British were not interested in taking over Malta and imposing upon such island their beliefs, culture and language. In this regard, even the Church was hesitant in accepting the English language since it associated it with the Protestant belief. At the time, the Church was still a strong entity, and it was very instrumental in maintaining the position of the Italian language as an official language, from being unchallenged.

The British had very narrowly defined interests in Malta, namely that of exploiting its strategic values.[20] This was because the island suited them perfectly as a military outpost, with their primary intention of creating "a world-class military base". However, this defence infrastructure necessitated the engagement of the workforce to work in this base. Moreover, the Maltese started to depend highly on the British to find jobs to earn their daily living. By the time the English language became instrumental in

[17] Aquilina Joseph, *Papers in Maltese Linguistics*, The Royal University of Malta, 1970.

[18] Fenech Dominic, *Responsibility and Power in Inter-War Malta, Book One: Endemic Democracy (1919–1930)*, Publishers Enterprising Group (PEG) Ltd, 2005, pg. 4.

[19] Ibid., p. 4

[20] Mallia-Milanes Victor, *The British Colonial Experience 1800–1964*, 1988, Mirev Academic Publications, pg. 165.

finding employment with the government. This mixture of cultures became evident when the English language began to be used along with the Italian language when civilian cooperation for work purposes became indispensable, and this intermixing of the Maltese people with the British was the spur which gave more strength to the English language.

The English language superseded the Italian language in the 1920s and 1930s when it began to spread very consistently. The 1921 Constitution was the source of significant power to the Maltese government. Throughout this period, Lord Strickland tried to push the English language in the education system and the courts, at the expense of the Italian language. Still, he had the drawback of the minority and the Senate.[21] However, the Italian language remained the language of the courts until 1933, because many lawyers have practised and studied in Italy during that time. The 1921 Constitution gave precedence to the English and Italian languages; "*the English language being the language of the British Empire and the Italian language being the language of records of our Courts*".[22]

It was only by Act XVI of 1929, *The Use of Maltese Language in Legal Proceedings Act, 1929*,[23] that the Maltese language was introduced into civil and criminal proceedings and given official recognition. A new paragraph was introduced after Article 409 of the Criminal Code, which was intended to remedy the situation at the time:

> *On the application of the person accused, or of any of the persons accused, the Court shall order that the proceedings in the cause shall be conducted in the Maltese language, and any decision or decree shall be delivered in any such case in Maltese, and it shall be registered in both the Italian and Maltese languages.*[24]

Moreover, another paragraph was inserted, which stated that:

> *When any of two or more persons accused should apply that the proceedings be conducted in the English language and any other one of the persons accused should apply that the proceedings be conducted in the Maltese language, the proceedings shall be conducted in English or in Maltese at the discretion of the*

---

[21] Mallia-Milanes Victor, *The British Colonial Experience 1800–1964: The Impact on Maltese Society*, Mireva Publications, 1988, pg. 65.

[22] Article 57(1), Letters patent 1921 in Laws of Malta 1921 Vol LIV, p. xxii.

[23] Laws of Malta 1929, Vol LXII, pg. 32.

[24] ibid.

Court, but in any case any sentence or decree shall be delivered in English and Maltese, and it shall be registered in English and Maltese, as well as in Italian.[25]

As stated earlier, the Italian language was the official language of the records of the Courts and having this possibility of allowing legal proceedings to be conducted in another language (English or Maltese), other than the Italian language, raised some questions at the time. Reference should also be made to a substituted provision in the 1921 Constitution which provided that: *"Whenever the only person accused or all the persons accused are or are Maltese-speaking, the Court shall order that all the oral proceedings in the cause shall be conducted in the Maltese language".*[26] The possibility of having proceedings conducted in the Maltese language as were available in the context of criminal proceedings did not apply in the same manner to civil proceedings. The *Laws of Organisation and Civil Procedure (Amendment) Act, 1932 (Act XI of 1932)* reiterated the fact that the language of the Courts was, in fact, the Italian language and if parties did not have sufficient knowledge of the Italian language, it was permitted that the English language was used by the judge, magistrate, advocate or legal procurator. Even when evidence was allowed in the English language, the Court would order that a translation be made into Italian, for the records of the proceedings.

In 1934, Maltese and English became the language of Maltese legislation. However, the influence of the Italian language nonetheless continued to maintain its status until 1939, when the new Constitution was enacted.[27] This was further emphasised in 1947, when *Malta (Constitution) Letters Patent*, under, upheld that the Maltese and English languages as the official languages of Malta.[28] This leads us to refer specifically to the language of the courts, which was clearly expressed in the Fifth Schedule, that the Maltese language was the official language of the Courts of Justice of civil and criminal jurisdiction and proceedings were to be conducted in Maltese. The rebuttable presumption is that every person is deemed to be Maltese-speaking unless proved to the contrary. The possibility of having

---

[25] ibid.

[26] Laws of Malta 1932, Vol LXV, pg. xx.

[27] Palmer Vernon V, *Mixed Jurisdictions Worldwide: The Third Legal Family*, Second Edition, 2012, Cambridge University Press, pg. 530.

[28] Article 46(1), Malta (Constitution) Letters Patent, 1947, MGG, 10 September 1947, pg. 975.

proceedings conducted in the English language have not been specifically excluded.

Additionally, the Maltese Language Act in its interpretative section states that: "*The Maltese language means the national language as prescribed by article 5 of the Malta Constitution*";[29] and that "*The Maltese State shall promote through all possible means the widest use of the Maltese language in education, broadcasting and the media, at the law courts...*".[30]

The Judicial Proceedings (Use of English Language) Act, came into force in 1965 to provide a remedy in certain exceptional cases where the use of the English language in judicial proceedings is allowed. The law states that the Court shall order that proceedings be conducted in English in cases when the parties to the suit are English-speaking. Furthermore, Maltese parties may consent that proceedings be conducted in the English language. Such use of the English language shall be used in all "*subsequent stages of the proceedings, unless the order is revoked by that court or any other court before which the proceedings are pending*".[31]

The Constitution of Malta states that: "*The language of the Courts should be the Maltese language: provides that Parliament may make such provision or the use of the English language in such cases and under such conditions as it may prescribe*".[32] Legislation shall be enacted in both the Maltese and the English language and gives prevalence to the Maltese language in the event of a conflict of interpretation.[33] On the other hand, the Maltese text prevails if promulgated after independence. Conversely, in cases attracting international confidence this rule is reversed: "*In case of any conflict between the Maltese and English text of any of the First, Second and Third Schedules to this Act, the English Text shall prevail*".[34] Reference to the language of the laws is laid down in the *Interpretation Act*, wherein it states that any Act of Parliament may only be enacted in the Maltese or the English language. If it is authorised to be enacted, it shall be published in any one of the said languages only.[35]

---

[29] Maltese Language Act, April 2005, Chapter 470 of the Laws of Malta, section 2.

[30] Maltese Language Act, April 2005, Chapter 470 of the Laws of Malta, section 3(e).

[31] Judicial Proceedings (Use of English Language) Act, September 1965, Chapter 189 of the Laws of Malta, Section 2(d).

[32] The Constitution of Malta, Chapter 1 of the Laws of Malta, September 1964, Article 5(3).

[33] The Constitution of Malta, Chapter 1 of the Laws of Malta, September 1964, Article 74.

[34] Arbitration Act, February 1998, Chapter 387 of the Laws of Malta, Article 77.

[35] Interpretation Act, February 1975, Chapter 249 of the Laws of Malta, Article 14.

Today the Maltese language and the English language are the two official languages though the Maltese is the national language.[36] However, Maltese is the language mainly used in the Courts. The use of other languages today has become an exception rather than the rule, and most of all, subject to the Court's discretion. However, notwithstanding that these are the official languages there are still traces of the Italian tradition reflected in the legal jargon still predominantly used by lawyers and the member of the Judiciary during court proceedings as well as in the preparation of the documents of the Court. When Malta joined the European Union in 2004, Maltese became one of the official languages of the European Union.

3.2 The Maltese Language in the EU Institutions

The Maltese language became an official language of the European Union immediately upon accession. This meant that from the point of accession on to the EU, all EU legislation and the judgements of the European Court of Justice had been provided to the Maltese language as per Regulation 1/58. However, although the vast majority of the *acquis communautaire* has been translated, the process had started since 2001, Malta was not yet equipped to start utilising the Maltese language immediately upon accession. In Malta, the language industry was very weak, and there were not enough human resources, i.e. translators and interpreters, to fulfil the requirements of the European institutions. As a result, the institutions found themselves recruiting Maltese translators to the point that action was needed to safeguard the legislative process and make sure that multilingualism is protected. As a result, the Council of Ministers adopted a derogation which was temporary regulation regarding the use of the Maltese language so that it could create a viable balance between multilingualism and efficiency in the operations of the institutions.[37] This derogation limited the use of the Maltese language to situations where it is only essential to use Maltese. However, this does not mean that Maltese was not used at all. Where resources were available translation into Maltese was still available. The derogation had a lifespan of three years with a

---

[36] Palmer Vernon V, *Mixed Jurisdictions Worldwide: The Third Legal Family*, Second Edition, 2012, Cambridge University Press, p. 530.
[37] Council Regulation (EC) No. 930/2004 of 1 May 2004 on temporary derogation measures relating to the drafting in Maltese of the acts of the institutions of the European Union, (OJ L 169, 1.5.2004, p. 1).

possible extension of another year. However, it was abandoned in 2007. The derogation did not affect the co-decision between the council and the European Parliament. The acts that were not translated still has to be translated at a later stage. It was facultative in the sense that the institutions could ignore it where it is necessary and, when resources were available, the derogation was not utilised.

Upon accession, the institutions and other applicable bodies of the EU established a Maltese unit responsible for translations into Maltese. The major institutions include the European Commission, the European Parliament, the Council of Ministers and the Court of Justice of the European Union. Not only translators and interpreters were employed but also lawyer linguists. The main task of lawyer-linguists is to ensure legal and linguistic consistencies in the translated texts. Within these units, personnel were appointed to take responsibility for consistent terminology to be applied not only within the institution itself but also among the other institutions. The use of the Maltese language increased drastically compared to the situation before accession, and the importance of the Maltese language both in Malta and in the EU institutions increased a lot.

One of the largest Maltese language units is that of the European Commission. While the European Commission is mainly based in Brussels, the Directorate for Translation, known as DGT, is for a considerable part based in Luxembourg. The Maltese unit is based in Luxembourg. DGT is responsible for the linguistic translations of the European Commission and is undoubtedly one of the largest language service providers in the world. DGT is divided into linguistic departments of the official language of the EU, including Maltese. The Maltese unit employs circa over 50 translators and several administrative assistance together it is responsible for the translation of around a hundred thousand pages of documents into the Maltese language. Most of the common subjects of translation include agriculture, transport, proposals for legislation, documents for consultation, information documents and the laws themselves, among others. Each document is attributed to a translator by the Head of Unit who after completion of the task, pass on the documents to an independent reviser within the unit. The reviser serves as an additional pair of eyes to ensure linguistic and terminological consistency. The DGT translators make use of various tools and resources they include computer-aided translations various reference documents Eurlex database and IATE. IATE (Interactive Terminology for Europe) is the EU's terminology database. It has been used in the EU institutions and agencies since summer 2004 for the collection, dissemination and management of EU-specific terminology. The project was launched in 1999 to provide a web-based infrastructure for all EU terminology resources, enhancing the availability and standardisation of the information. Maltese, initially proved to be a great challenge for the commission. Although Maltese spoken as an everyday language in Malta, it was never used as a language to describe highly technical descriptive terminology. As a result, the Maltese unit together with the units of the other institutions, was faced with the task of coining new Maltese words and finding a suitable way of creating new Maltese roles for technical texts.[38]

Another important unit is that of the European Parliament. The Maltese unit in the European Parliament, also based in Luxembourg is somewhat smaller than that of the Commission by around 50%. The EP unit also makes use of the same technical and linguistic resources and use the same translation procedures. However, the documents they translate are different. The vast majority of the documents are legal, and so the language is quite specific and used repetitively in the drafting of the laws. The subjects of the texts can be quite complex, ranging from agriculture and farming to railways transport, pharmaceuticals, matters of judicial interest, and other matters that fall within the legal basis of the European Union. The Maltese unit is also responsible for the translation of documents out of and into the 24 official languages of the European Union, thus providing all EU citizens with immediate access to European texts in their own language and the opportunity to communicate with the institutions in their own language. It supplies a translation service which ensures both quality and efficiency, keeping costs at an acceptable level. The Maltese unit also contributes to the development of the appropriate IT tools and terminology databases to aid translators and integrating them into the workflow and the revising of documents translated outside Parliament and monitoring the quality of external translations.[39]

Other important Maltese units include that of the Council of Ministers, the Court of Auditors, the unit of the Committees, the Translation Centre and that of the European Court of Justice that merits a sub-section in its own right in section 4 of this chapter.

---

[38] See http://ec.europa.eu/dgs/translation last accessed on 1 September 2020.
[39] See https://europarl.europa.eu/the-secretary-general/en/directorates-general/trad last accessed on 1 September 2020.

3.3   The Evolution of the Maltese Language as a Result of Malta's Accession to the EU

As it has been mentioned above, with accession to the EU, as an official language, Maltese started being used in contexts that were previously inconceivable. For example, as there are no railways in Malta, the Maltese language is very poor when it comes to railway technology. There is no use to create words in Maltese that are needed for the railway industry. The same can be said for many other subjects or policy areas. However, EU law requires that legislation in these fields is also provided in Maltese. This lead to a situation where Maltese linguists had either to choose to borrow words from other languages such as Italian, French and more often English. Sometimes this has also lead to either the coining of new words into the Maltese language or else the borrowing of vocabulary that became part of day to day Maltese. Maltese is a living and functional language which is used regularly by over 90% of Malta's half a million-plus population, and even without the impact of EU law, this was still an ongoing process. For example, many words in the IT sector or commerce were and are still being imported into the Maltese language. However, the use of Maltese language in the EU accelerated this process and led to a quicker evolution of the Maltese language. Maltese is no longer a language used for every day to day needs but a language suited for business, academia and the legal world.

Malta's accession to the EU led to the establishment of the Maltese Language Council. It was established in April 2005 with the enactment of the Maltese Language Act to promote the national language of Malta and to provide the necessary means to achieve this aim.[40] The Council was established to adopt and promote a suitable language policy and strategy for the Maltese islands and to verify their performance and observance in every sector of Maltese life, for the benefit and development of the national language and the identity of the Maltese people. Apart from this, the Council promotes the Maltese language both in Malta and in other countries by engaging actively to foster recognition and respect for the national language.

An important function of the said Council is to update the orthography of the Maltese Language as necessary and, from time to time, establish the correct manner of writing words and phrases which enter the Maltese Language from other tongues. In the execution of its functions and duties,

---

[40] Chapter 470 of the Laws of Malta, https://legislation.mt/eli/cap/470/eng/pdf last accessed on 1 September 2 2020.

the Council works to develop, motivate and enhance the recognition and expression of the Maltese language as well as to promote the dynamic development of such linguistic characteristics as identify the Maltese people. In consultation with the organs established by the Maltese Language Act, it adopts a suitable linguistic policy backed by a strategic plan, and ensure that the same are put into practice and observed in all sectors of Maltese life. The Council ensures that the language policy decided is put into practice to ensure its effective and faithful implementation. It evaluates and co-ordinates the work done by associations and individuals, in the Maltese language sector and to foster an atmosphere of co-operation through a consensual plan.

The Council draws the attention of all those who may contribute to the development of Maltese to work done in execution of the language policy and, where necessary, to advise the Minister of Education to commission any necessary assignment. It seeks to obtain financial resources locally and overseas to be able to strengthen its activities, especially such resources as are already accessible to local and international organisations for research purposes, the promotion of spoken languages by small nations, and other projects relating to the exchange of experts and research programmes. Finally, it co-operates with persons, bodies and organisations in various fields of life to increase and augment the recognition and appreciation of linguistic and cultural activities for the further advancement of the Maltese language and establishes a National Centre of the Maltese Language which, besides serving as the office of the Council, shall offer the necessary printed and audio-visual resources to members of Maltese language associations, institutions and other interested persons. The National Council for the Maltese Language maintains regular contacts with local, national and international organisations which have functions similar to or complementary to the functions of the Council and exchanges its views and resources with them.[41]

The EU's accession had a very positive impact on the Maltese language and as led to its updating to a more modern grammar and orthography suitable to the ends of today. If one were to look at the evolution of modern Maltese, the first rules were published in 1924. It took more than 60 years for the next two updates in 1984 and 1992 respectively. Since the EU's accession, there have been to major changes in what are known as Decisions I and II in 2008 and 2020 respectively.[42]

---

[41] http://www.kunsilltalmalti.gov.mt/legislation last accessed on 1 September 2020.
[42] See https://akkademjatalmalti.org/ir-regoli-tal-kitba/ last accessed on 1 September 2020.

Another example to see how the EU's accession is affecting the evolution of the Maltese language is through the introduction of eurojargon in Maltese. This paper is not meant to be a study of eurojargon, and the examples mentioned below are only intended as an example. They are by no means a comprehensive study of eurojurgan in the Maltese language.

Eurojargon can be analysed through two particular categories of eurojargon; 'creation of new words' and 'influence of other languages' are analysed to form a general idea of whether Maltese translators adopt a more conservative or liberal approach concerning the introduction of eurojargon into the Maltese language. Three words from each category are chosen; the definition as provided for by the glossary of eurojargon available on the europa website is included,[43] together with the most reliable Maltese translation as found in EU documents, ranging from directives, regulations and other internal documents as identified via the *Iate* database system.[44] The translations are recorded as follows (Tables 5.1 and 5.2):

Table 5.1   Creation of new words

Eurojargon	Definition	Maltese translation	Source of translation
Comitology	A committee through which authorities at national level supervise the implementation of EU law from a technical aspect	Komitoloġija	Council Directive 94/57/EC of 22 November 1994
Cross-border	Within the EU	(i) Transfruntier (ii) Transkonfinali (iii) Transnazzjonali	(i) Directive 2002/39/KE (ii) Regulation (EU) No 1316/2013 (iii) Council Decision 2016/0366(NLE)
Subsidiarity	A principle defined in Article 5 of the TEU. It upholds that decisions are taken and made as close as possible to the citizen.	Sussidjarjetà	Consolidated version of the Treaty of the Functioning of the European Union available at https://eur-lex.europa.eu/LexUriServ/LexUriServ.do?uri=OJ:C:2008:115:0013:0045:MT:PDF accessed 1 September 2020.

[43] European Commission (n 2).
[44] 'Iate' (*Iate.europa.eu*, 2018) https://iate.europa.eu last accessed 1 September 2020.

Table 5.2 Influence of foreign languages

Eurojargon	Definition	Maltese translation	Source of translation
Acquis communautaire	A French term used to mean the body of EU laws and rules which are binding on all Member States	Acquis communautaire	COM—Internal Document: AGRI-2005-64145-12-00
Enlargement	Refers to the concept of 'expansion' although it is probably a false friend from the French term 'englargissement.'	Tkabbir	Commission website http:// ec.europa.eu/enlargement/ index_mt.htm (accessed 1 September 2020).
Rapporteur	A person tasked with monitoring. The French language highly influences its use.	Relatur	Consolidated Version of the rules of procedure of the European economic and social committee CELEX:32010Q1209(01)/ MT

The following points can be gathered from the translations as listed above;

1. For the most part, intrusive techniques are utilised. The most obvious use of loan words is identified through the French term 'acquis communautaire' which is directly adopted into Maltese translations without any modification from the part of the translator. This stance, however, is not adopted for all French deriving terms; 'rapporteur' for example, is translated in most instances as 'relatur'.

2. Maltese-sounding neologisms are often preferred. Linked also the first point, one may notice that Maltese translators generally resort to borrowing foreign terms, as in the case of 'komitoloġija', and 'sussidjarjeta' however rather than importing loan words directly, Maltese-sounding neologisms were preferred.

3. Translations of eurojargon are not always fixed. It is also worth noting that Maltese translations of eurojargon are not always fixed, and are also subject to change and development in the search for the

most accurate and accepted term. This is made evident in the translation of 'cross-border' which is translated differently as 'Transfruntier', 'transkonfinali' and 'transnazzjonali' in separate official EU documents.

4   THE MALTESE LANGUAGE AND THE EUROPEAN COURT OF JUSTICE OF THE EU

The legal translation service, shared between the two jurisdictions (Court of Justice and General Court), comprises two directorates, between which the language units are apportioned. The directors share responsibility for 23 language units (Bulgarian, Croatian, Czech, Danish, Dutch, English, Estonian, Finnish, French, German, Greek, Hungarian, Italian, Latvian, Lithuanian, Maltese, Polish, Portuguese, Romanian, Slovak, Slovenian, Spanish and Swedish).

The Court's translations are established per mandatory language arrangements and include all the combinations of the official languages of the European Union. The volume of pages to be translated currently exceeds 1,100,000 pages per year. The texts to be translated are all highly technical legal texts. To accomplish that task, the service employs only jurists who have completed their education in law and who have a thorough knowledge of at least two languages other than their mother tongue.[45]

The Maltese Linguistic Unit was established in October 2003 and started its official functioning on the 1 May 2004. Its main role and responsibility are to translate all CJEU legal instruments and documents into the Maltese language. At the beginning its role was limited in the translating and revising of few judgments, however, nowadays its functions extended to translating and revising all Court of Justice and General Court's judgments, the Advocate General's opinions, judgments summaries, Official Journals notices, annual report, budget's report, historical jurisprudence, press and internet sites. The Maltese translation unit of the Court of Justice of the European Union's job of translating from mainly French to Maltese is one of the most remarkable work ever done by a Maltese linguistic unit. Another significant achievement of this linguistic

---

[45] See https://curia.europa.eu/jcms/jcms/Jo2_10744/en/ last accessed on 1 September 2020.

unit is the preparation and publication of the CJEU collection of jurisprudence translated in Maltese since 1 May 2007 the day in which the temporary waiver in favour of Maltese ceased to apply. All the advancements mentioned above where possible because of the hard-working team of circa twenty-five lawyer linguist, a few proofreaders, an administrative assistant and a small number of secretaries under the lead of the Maltese Linguistic Unit's Head.

The translation and reviewing of the Court of Justice's documents must be of a high-quality level. To do so, the Court of Justice employs lawyer-linguists, well versed into their national laws and mother tongue language. In the case of Malta, lawyer-linguists have to be lawyers, notary publics or legal procurators. Indeed, these legal professions listed have to be very knowledgeable of the Maltese language, together with sufficient knowledge of the French language, the internal language of the CJEU and also knowledge of another EU language. Lawyer-linguists are recruited and selected as officers through a very tough competition organised now and then by the European Personnel Selection Office (EPSO). Candidates who successfully pass through all the exams will be listed on the reserve list and subsequently offered a job with the CJEU according to vacancies. The CJEU also offers definite work contracts to lawyer linguists when there is an immediate need or when the number of candidates passing the EPSO exams was not enough to fill in all the vacancies, as had happened when the Maltese Linguistic Unit was established.

The CJEU issues documents which may be categorised as legal texts being highly technical and complex on various subjects. Thus, translation of these documents requires detailed research of both EU and national legislation, relevant jurisprudence and also the proceedings of the case in question. The research involves a linguistic perspective where the lawyer-linguists try to come up with the exact terminology to translate the particular legal concept in the best possible way especially when no ordinary concept is found in the national language. This, in-depth research ensures that the final result precisely reflects the original document's text. Nonetheless, due to the high workload, the lawyer-linguists have to work under pressure and short deadlines, with the risk that their quality of work is undermined. A balance needs to be found between the quantity and quality of translation. Thus the main priority of the linguistic units is to provide a good translation within the established time frame.

The Maltese linguistic unit is subdivided into smaller groups made of lawyer-linguists and proofreaders directed by a coordinator in an attempt to address the challenges. This informal system help lawyer linguists work closely together for better results. The coordinator's role is to address the difficulties related to terminology. Therefore, the coordinators meet regularly together with the Head of the Unit to further discuss difficulties and to slowly continue adding to the internal glossary of terminology. This glossary ensures uniformity and precision in the terminology used, thus establishing a president. It also serves as a tool in the hands of a lawyer-linguists allowing them to be more efficient. During the publication stage of jurisprudence, a higher threshold is set on uniformity and precision in translation. Indeed, after translation, reviewing and proofreading, the terminology group reviews the main parts of the judgements for double-checking. Subsequently, the judgements and their summaries together with related opinions are reviewed once again by a proofreader.

If Maltese is used as a language in litigation, the Maltese Linguistic unit appoints one Maltese lawyer-linguist is appointed as a person of reference; his/her role is to translate all the acts and documents in Maltese into another language generally in English. Furthermore, s/he also has to assist lawyer-linguists of other linguistic units which can translate from Maltese, in clearing any possible doubts they might have when it comes to Maltese legal concepts. One the other hand, when a Maltese court refers to a preliminary decision, a Maltese lawyer-linguist is required to translate the request for a preliminary decision and Maltese court's queries from Maltese into another language generally to English. Every time the case language is in Maltese, translation is necessary of the report of the sitting from French into Maltese. The simple fact that the case language is in Maltese means that the authentic version of the judgment is that in Maltese and thus the Maltese version acquires the binding force.

The quality of Maltese in the CJEU's judgments is much better than that of judgments given by the Maltese courts in Valletta. In a way, the CJEU's Maltese language unit has done an impeccable job over the past years, and its work practices should be adopted by other Maltese domestic institutions, including the Maltese courts. The use of Maltese at CJEU lead to the elevation of status and quality of legal Maltese in general.

5   CONCLUSION

From the above, it is clear that while EU legal translation is an essential tool for the continuance participation in the European Union, the smallest Member State of the EU has so far managed successfully to make one of the least spoken languages in Europe as an official language in the European Union, at par with most more widely spoken languages such as Portuguese and Polish.

On the one hand, EU legal translation in Maltese is perhaps a reflection of the tendency of Maltese translators to obtain a balance between a more liberal and conservative approach, while aiming to achieve the most precise meaning possible. This exercise has given rise to several neologisms in the Maltese language, whereby words have a specific 'European Union' meaning is introduced within the Maltese vocabulary, thereby expanding it through the creation of technical words, but perhaps at the cost of rendering the Maltese text less accessible to the general public. Unfortunately, many Maltese professionals, including lawyers and judges, are taking too many short cuts and prefer to use English EU legal translation rather than Maltese EU legal translation. On the other hand, Maltese as a language has adapted well to EU legal jargon and has proven to be an even better success than the use of the Maltese language in the domestic legal circles. Hopefully, by time and through the new generation of lawyers, the success of the Maltese language in the European Union's institutions, in particular, the very great success and excellent level of Maltese attained by the MT unit of the CJEU will by time be replicated locally. Legal Maltese in EU law has proven to be a bar setting experience which the local Maltese institutions and professions need to learn from and follow in their daily activities domestically.

CHAPTER 6

The Transposition of the EU Consumer Protection Directives in Maltese Law: A Study Under Twenty Headings

David Fabri

1 INTRODUCTION AND SCOPE

When Malta applied for membership in 1990, both EU consumer law and Maltese consumer law were in their infancy and in a state of evolution. In late 1998, the European Commission allowed Malta to re-ignite its accession application, which had been suspended by the new incoming Labour party government in 1996. As a result, Malta had to start in earnest and haste the negotiation and transposition of an extensive compendium of Directives, decisions and other measures comprised in 29 of the 32 chapters into which the *acquis communautaire* was conveniently arranged for accession purposes. The other three chapters were institutional and were not negotiable or transposable. A chapter of EU law dealt with consumer protection, and most of the measures were in the form of minimum

D. Fabri (✉)
University of Malta, Msida, Malta
e-mail: david.fabri@um.edu.mt

© The Author(s), under exclusive license to Springer Nature
Switzerland AG 2021
I. Sammut, J. Agranovska (eds.), *The Implementation and Enforcement of European Union Law in Small Member States,*
https://doi.org/10.1007/978-3-030-66115-1_6

135

directives.[1] New important measures were being adopted at Union (at that time Community) level even while the island's accession procedures were slowly progressing. The directives which required transposition by Malta before accession are listed in Table 6.1 below. While retaining its primary focus on the measures comprised in this Consumer Protection chapter of EU law, this study makes several references to other consumer measures which might arise from other parts and chapters of the *acquis*. The reference to Metrology under section 15 of this chapter is a case in point.

This chapter is constructed under twenty headings (sections) which collectively go a long way in explaining how Maltese consumer law and policy developed from the date of Malta's application to join the EU in 1990 to subsequent membership in 2004. These years marked the formative years both of Malta's relationship and ever closer ties with the then Community and of the Union's own increasing interest in pursuing consumer protection policies and legislation. The Accession-related transpositions are the main interest of this chapter. However, it also examines some relevant developments post-membership. Indeed, the new Consumer Rights Omnibus Directive came into force on 7 January 2020. This new Directive[2] amended several EU consumer protection legislation, namely: Directive 93/13/EEU (unfair contract terms), Directives 98/6/EU (price indications), 2005/29/EU (unfair commercial practices) and 2011/83/EU (consumer rights).[3]

These twenty different headings highlight a series of circumstances, events, pressures, difficulties, weaknesses and other factors which have influenced the transposition of this chapter and other consumer measures. Together they offer a useful case-study from both academic and practical perspectives, of potential interest to students and academics from the other Member States and especially from new candidate countries. This study may also prove useful for students undertaking small-island studies, especially in the fields of law-making and policymaking.

---

[1] The current *acquis* is today divided in 35 Chapters. As part of the Accession programme, Malta was required to screen and transpose the Consumers and Health Protection Chapter, then Chapter 23 of the *acquis*. Currently the consumer chapter is designated as Chapter 28.

[2] EU/2019/2161.

[3] https://www.ethics-compliance.ch/2020/01/24/consumer-rights-enhanced-by-new-directive-of-the-european-union/; https://globalcompliancenews.com/get-ready-for-the-new-deal-consumer-rights-enhanced-by-the-omnibus-directive/ last accessed on 1 February 2020.

Table 6.1 The EU Consumer Directives which Malta was required to transpose before accession

1. Council Directive 84/450/EEU of 10 September 1984 relating to the approximation of the laws, regulations and administrative provisions of the Member States concerning misleading advertising, (amended by Directive 1999/34/EU of the European Parliament and of the Council)

2. Council Directive 85/374/EEU of 25 July 1985 on the approximation of the laws, regulations and administrative provisions of the Member States concerning liability for defective products

3. Council Directive 85/577/EEU of 20 December 1985 to protect the consumer in respect of contracts negotiated away from business premises;

4. Council Directive 87/102/EEU of 22 December 1986 for the approximation of the laws, regulations and administrative provisions of the Member States concerning consumer credit, amended by Council Directive 90/88/EEU and by Directive 98/7/EU of the European Parliament and of the Council

5. Council Directive 90/88/EEU of 22 February 1990 amending Directive 87/102/EEU for the approximation of the laws, regulations and administrative provisions of the Member States concerning consumer credit

6. Council Directive 90/314/EEU of 13 June 1990 on package travel, package holidays and package tours

7. Council Directive 92/59/EEU of 29 June 1992 on general product safety (which was replaced by Directive 2001/95/EU of the European Parliament and of the Council of 3 December 2001)

8. Council Directive 93/13/EEU of 5 April 1993 on unfair terms in consumer contracts

9. Directive 94/47/EU of the European Parliament and the Council of 26 October 1994 on the protection of purchasers in respect of certain aspects of contracts relating to the purchase of the right to use immovable properties on a timeshare basis

10. Directive 97/7/EU of the European Parliament and of the Council of 20 May 1997 on the protection of consumers in respect of distance contracts, amended by Directive 2002/65/EU of the European Parliament and of the Council

11. Directive 97/55/EU of European Parliament and of the Council of 6 October 1997 amending Directive 84/450/EEU concerning misleading advertising so as to include comparative advertising

12. Directive 98/6/EU of the European Parliament and of the Council of 16 February 1998 on Consumer Protection in the indication of the prices of products offered to consumers

13. Directive 98/7/EU of the European Parliament and of the Council of 16 February 1998 amending Directive 87/102/EEU for the approximation of the laws, regulations and administrative provisions of the Member States concerning consumer credit

14. Directive 98/27/EU of the European Parliament and of the Council of 19 May 1998 on injunctions for the protection of consumers' interests

15. Directive 99/34/EU of the European Parliament and of the Council of 10 May 1999 amending Council Directive 85/374/EEU on the approximation of the laws, regulations and administrative provisions of the Member States concerning liability for defective products

16. Directive 99/44/EU of the European Parliament and of the Council of 25 May 1999 on certain aspects of the sale of consumer goods and associated guarantees

17. Directive 2001/95/EU of the European Council and of the Council of 3 December 2001 on general product safety

18. Directive 2002/65/EU of the European Parliament and of the Council of 23 September 2002 concerning the distance marketing of consumer financial services and amending Council Directive 90/619/EEU and Directives 97/7/EU and 98/27/EU

2   SETTING THE SCENE

The history of consumer law in Malta is a recent one. To some degree, it has been a peculiar story comprising highs and lows, with short periods of initiatives followed by bouts of indifference and inconsistencies. When Malta had applied to join the European Union in 1990, Maltese consumer law was at best patchy, and a few unsatisfactory pieces were all that had been produced. The administrative set-up was equally inadequate, and few public resources were dedicated to Consumer Protection. For many, the adoption of the Trade Descriptions Act in 1986[4] coupled with the extensive and restrictive price control regime that had been in place and regularly refined since the Second World War constituted sufficient guarantees for the safeguarding of the vital interests of consumers. It was felt that these two measures provided a sufficient safety-net for Maltese consumers and that little else was needed. Two events then intervened. First, the new Nationalist Government elected into office in 1987 published the first-ever official consumer policy and strategic document.[5] Later, as an applicant country, Malta was handed a list (and a copy) of the EU consumer Directives which it was required to transpose into national law and to ensure their effective enforcement, as soon as possible. The two projects had to be merged and integrated into one coherent roadmap. Overall, at that stage, the local consumer protection position fared poorly when compared to the EU framework, which was then largely composed of so-called Minimal Directives on a variety of consumer concerns. These directives, one must clarify, did not amount to a complete and comprehensive framework of consumer law; that was not their objective. They represented the extent of the political consensus that could be reached between the Member States at that moment in time.

The European Commission's regular reports on Malta's application starting from 1993 onwards repeatedly highlighted the substantial lacunae and weaknesses in Maltese consumer law, at least in comparison with EU law.[6] Accession added significant fresh impetus and unexpected challenges to Maltese consumer law. The obligation to transpose the EU directives

---

[4] Chapter 313 of the Laws of Malta.

[5] White Paper, Rights for the Consumer, Department of Information, August 1991.

[6] Commission, Opinion (Avis) on Malta's Application for Membership (Bulletin of the European Communities) Supplement 4/93, June 1993. Subsequent to the original 1993 Avis, the full list of Commission Reports on Malta's application to join the EC leading to the Treaty of Accession reads as follows:

specifically helped to shore up national consumer law development to a significant level, and Maltese consumer law probably reached its highest point in the years 2000–2001 when important new consumer laws were adopted.[7]

In this present context, it must be noted that 1994 was a very productive and valuable year in Maltese law-making, including a new Consumer Affairs Act[8] and the first-ever Competition Act.[9] Both laws had been originally launched in the 1993 White Paper "Fair Trading—the next step forward".[10] 1994 also saw the introduction of new laws on banking, investment services and other modern financial laws. In their own way, these laws boldly reformed and strengthened the regulation of financial services in Malta and added new structures and remedies for consumers in that sector. Notwithstanding the importance of financial services regulation and oversight for consumers, particularly small depositors and investors, this chapter does not examine this part of the subject, primarily for manageability and space reasons. Another reason is that these measures fell outside the Consumer Protection directives that had to be transposed and were instead largely classified under the chapters dealing with the freedom to provide services and freedom of establishment.

3 UNPREPAREDNESS

In 1990, and for several years thereafter, Malta was unprepared for membership and for the massive transposition requirements this project would entail. Lack of training and expertise was only too evident both in the public service as well as in the private sector. The European Union was still viewed as a foreign and distant institution largely disconnected to Maltese

Commission Report [COM(1999)69 final]
Commission Report [COM(1999)508 final]
Commission Report [COM(2000) 708 final]
Commission Report [SEC(2001) 1751]
Commission Report [COM(2002) 700 final]
Commission Report [COM(2003) 675 final—SEC(2003) 1206]

These Reports were not published in the Official Journal.
[7] Act XXVI of 2000 effected various significant amendments to the Consumer Affairs Act 1994 which were largely but not exclusively Directives-derived.
[8] Chapter 378 of the Laws of Malta.
[9] Chapter 379 of the Laws of Malta.
[10] White Paper, Department of Information, November 1993.

affairs. 'Experts' were lacking. This meant that, out of necessity, learning by doing became the normal practice. No time was available for study and research. Officials dealing with the transpositions were learning the Directives in the course of implementing them. Persons in Malta formally qualified in European law studies were very few and were in any case engaged in other areas of the huge *acquis*. The adoption of the consumer *acquis* was not preceded or supported by any substantive studies and preliminary report and research.

Another peculiar feature was that while one section the Commission was chasing the Maltese side to transpose the Directives, another division of the Commission was busy changing them and seeking to add new ones. This made the task more complicated and difficult to manage to see the transpositions were required with some urgency. The EU's *acquis* became a moving target and continued to evolve and change while Malta and the other candidate countries were still struggling to understand it and implement it. By 1996, Malta had done little by way of transpositions and aligning to structures and expectations. A blow to aspiring membership was delivered when the anti-membership Labour Party, freshly elected to govern in 1996, immediately took steps to suspend Malta's application. The position was only restored in late 1998, at a stage when other candidate countries had already embarked on negotiating and closing various chapters of the *acquis*.

The Commission's experts made it repeatedly clear to the Maltese authorities that it was not enough to show a willingness to transpose the required measures. Still, they had to show also that they understood the *acquis* and were capable of effectively implementing it. They seemed particularly concerned by the lack of any legislation or structure that could prevent unsafe products from coming to, or remaining on, the market.

4   An Easy Chapter

When Malta's accession process with the Commission's Enlargement experts finally started in earnest in 1999, the Maltese Government tried its best to catch up with the other candidate countries which had enjoyed a head start and had already closed some chapters on their way to eventual membership. Malta had fallen way behind as a result of the suspension of its application between 1996 and 1998. To make up for this delay, the Maltese accession negotiating team tried to identify which were the possibly easy chapters that could be concluded relatively fast, thereby creating the perception of a successful momentum to the process. They identified the consumer protection chapter as one of a few that appeared potentially easier to negotiate and close, compared to some other chapters which presented difficulties or complications. It helped that in this context agreement was secured at an early stage with the local experts that no transitional arrangements would be requested from the Commission for any of the transposable directives. This meant that the Maltese Government was formally committing itself that at the date of eventual membership, should this happen, the consumer Directives would have been fully transposed and implemented. This approach ensured that the chapter was among the first to be successfully screened and negotiated. The EU Commission's Enlargement officials had warned the Maltese Government's negotiators that any transitional arrangements or exemptions requested by Malta would delay the negotiation and accession processes and might probably cause Malta to miss out on the next following enlargement.

Just for the sake of comparison, Company law was another chapter which too had been correctly deemed easier to negotiate. This was the case because the Companies Act of 1995 had more or less transposed the entirety of the company law directives in advance. Indeed, it was one of the very first chapters to be successfully negotiated and 'closed.'[11]

The assertion that a particular chapter was 'easy' was predicated on at least four assumptions: (a) that the Directives in question would not present conceptual or legal difficulties; (b) that the drafting of the necessary transposition measures would be a straightforward process from a technical angle; (c) that the draft legislation and its passage through Parliament would be uncontroversial and uncomplicated, and (d) that the Maltese authorities would request no transitional arrangements or derogations.

5   Trade Lobbies Try to Delay Transpositions

Several trade associations lobbying for different vested interests too were caught unprepared to master and comprehend the massive *acquis* that the country was rushing to transpose. Many Directives affected their members' interests, but it was not always immediately clear to them how this would play out. It would have been a daunting task even had the transposition been carried out at a gentler pace. Two of the consumer Directives

[11] See *Government satisfaction at opening of nine Chapters*, front page, The Malta Independent, Malta, 6 July 2000.

raised particular concerns and objections. The banks forcefully attacked the swift implementation of the Unfair Contract Terms Directive arguing—whenever the opportunity presented itself—that their standard consumer contracts and terms needed years of study and examination before they could be brought into line with the Directive. They also clamoured for a ten-year transitional delay for the introduction of a Bank depositor compensation scheme which fell outside the consumer chapter but was a pro-consumer measure. On their part, the General Retailers and Traders Union, one of the leading trade associations on the island, primarily directed its hostility and objections in the direction of the Product Liability Directive arguing in panic mode that the measure would put many Maltese retailers out of business. It insisted on an impact assessment which Government conceded to carry out—with no apparent advantage to anyone. The transposition of the consumer Directives was mostly carried out in time, and the measures received the Commission's approval except on a few inconsequential matters of detail. Both measures were in force on the date of Malta's official date of entry into the EU, and it is safe to say that neither the unfair terms rules nor the product liability measures led to any business failures.

By and large, the trading community held the view that competition was the best form of consumer protection and that no scope existed for additional specific statutory protection for consumers. Traders repeatedly insisted that the consumer directives should be applied in the most minimal manner possible and that more favourable rights should not be introduced. Seeing they were largely in favour of EU membership, they gradually and rather grudgingly accepted the consumer directives as a kind of necessary evil. This price had to be paid in order to enjoy the undoubted benefits of membership.

6   THE OPPOSITION IN PARLIAMENT

The Labour Party in opposition during the accession period was vehemently opposed to EU membership and favoured other less intensive association arrangements with the EU. The Labour Government in power between 1996 and 1998 suspended Malta's application to join the EU. After 1998, it persisted in raising negative and alarmist objections to EU membership. Nonetheless, one notes that in Parliament it offered only weak opposition to the extensive adoption of transposition measures in Maltese law. In this particular field under review, the Labour Party spokesmen generally argued that consumer protection measures being transposed would have been welcome even if they were not linked to EU membership. They criticised the Nationalist Government for slavishly copying what came out of Brussels, and for failing to consider consumer protection models originating outside the EU. During the relative parliamentary debates, the laws transposing the EU directives largely passed without any dissenting vote.

Overall, the Labour Party in Opposition played a mainly negative role in the accession process and did not provide much constructive input into the extensive transposition exercises. Its representatives refused to participate in the official structures and mechanisms established by the government to coordinate the transposition and accession process and thereby to forfeit the opportunity to make a constructive contribution to the vast law-making exercise. For several years after Malta's accession, the Malta Labour Party remained steadfast in its opposition to EU membership. It was only in the months leading to the 2013 general elections that the party finally shed its objections and formally accepted that EU membership was there to stay. At that juncture, the Labour Party started supporting Malta's EU membership.

7   Some Bright Spots

The Commission's reports on Malta's application up to 1999 were never flattering about Malta's level of adherence to the EU's consumer *acquis* and the credibility of its practical implementation. Before 1994, consumer law in Malta was in dire straits. Nonetheless, the Commission did find some bright spots which facilitated the eventual implementation of the relevant directives, most of which were till then unrepresented in Maltese law. The positive elements that the Commission found were (a) that the Maltese Government had addressed consumer protection policy some years earlier in a White Paper published in 1991 which was updated in 1993; (b) that, as a result, the Government had passed a Consumer Affairs Act in 1994; and (c) that the Government had in 1992 established a new department solely dedicated to the promotion and protection of consumer rights and interests and tasked with oversight of consumer law. The Commission was positively impressed that national policy and a national legal and administrative framework already existed and had been in operation for several years. These factors also meant that a cadre of expertise in the area was developing and that the Maltese side was not starting from scratch, as was the case with various East European candidate countries. The Commission admitted that at that time, even within the EU itself, very few Member States if any, had a publicly funded agency dedicated to protecting consumer interests similar to the Maltese model. These encouraging developments may have had no direct bearing on the EU directives, but they certainly supported and facilitated the competent and timely transposition of the Directives, especially from 2000 onwards.

Clearly, on a more general level, some factors worked subtly in Malta's favour as compared to the position in certain other candidate countries. The fact that in Malta, English was widely known and spoken was an advantage that accelerated the accession processes. Others were not so lucky and relied on time-consuming translators and interpreters. Further, Malta had already, before the start of the accession procedures, addressed consumer protection policy and had already implemented some home-grown legislative proposals. This fact certainly helped the EU negotiators develop a more positive perception of the island as a potential Member State. The knowledge probably enhanced that image that since 1994, Malta had also had a comprehensive competition law framework, a relatively sophisticated financial services regulatory framework and modern company legislation based on the latest UK model. This was far from being the case in certain other applicant countries, a few of which did not make it to the 2004 enlargement.

8   The EU Consumer Law Task Force

The Maltese Government found itself obliged to establish procedures and teams to organise, handle and transpose the massive *acquis* that the EU had developed over more than twenty years. In the consumer protection field, the government chose not to rely on the ability and competence available within the Department of Consumer Affairs which it found unconvincing. It instead opted to appoint a team from outside the department. These included persons who had proven experience in the law and practice of consumer protection. As the focal point for the transposition of this chapter, the Task Force organised several consultations and information meetings for different sectors of society, including the business sectors, about the EU policies towards consumer protection and explaining the various directives. In this exercise, perhaps the most difficult to explain and get across were the Consumer Credit Directives.

The responsibility for the transposition of certain directives fell outside the Task Force's remit. Product Safety was delegated to the Malta Standards Authority, while the Timeshare and Package Tours Directives fell under the direct responsibility of the newly established Malta Tourism Authority in 1999.[12] The Task Force headed the so-called Screening Meetings for Chapter 23 with the Commission in Brussels on 7–8 October 1999 on behalf of the Maltese Government.[13]

9   THE EFFECT ON THE CODES

It is remarkable that in a jurisdiction, which nominally had a continental codified system of law, the transposition of various consumer Directives of a private law nature, such as guarantees in the sale of goods and unfair contract terms, were adopted in their entirety in a special law and no reference to it was made in the Civil Code[14] which still contained the bulk and the core of private law rules in Maltese law. Even today the Civil Code does not refer to the various matters of private law interest adopted since at least 1999.

The Consumer Directives were a great addition to national consumer legal remedies, and it is a pity that no reference is made to them in the Civil Code. But then even significant strides in competition law and sectoral pillars of the economy like financial services and gaming, which entail multiple contracts and investor and player concerns, remain unacknowledged in the Code. As a result, the Code seems increasingly insulated, if not isolated, from all recent modern legislation adopted during these last forty years.[15]

[12] See the Malta Travel and Tourism Act, 1999, Chapter 409 of the Laws of Malta.

[13] Fabri David, *From application to accession: the Interplay between the EU. Consumer Directives and Selected Areas of National Consumer Law and Policy – a case study from Malta (1990–2004)*, Ph.D. thesis, University of Malta (2015), A copy of the minutes of these meetings were reproduced in Appendix 4.

[14] Chapter 16 of the Laws of Malta.

[15] Fabri David, *From application to accession: the Interplay between the EU. Consumer Directives and Selected Areas of National Consumer Law and Policy – a case study from Malta (1990–2004)*, Ph.D. thesis, University of Malta (2015). A copy of the minutes of these meetings were reproduced in Appendix 4. A detailed examination of the continued relevance of the Codes is found in Chapter 5 of the 2015 Thesis.

10   CONSUMER CREDIT

The Directives dealing with consumer credit were the last to be transposed.[16] The transposition measures were introduced in 2005. Why is this significant? It is significant because, contrary to what the Commission had been constantly promised, the transposition was finalised late and only after the date of membership.[17] The relative regulations were adopted a year after membership. Their late implementation finalised the transposition of Chapter 23, then comprising the consumer protection *acquis.* The regulations were extended to apply to home loans, which was not a directive requirement.

The very topic of consumer credit was probably the least familiar to the Maltese side, and they decided to leave it for last. Interest in the subject was weak both before and indeed also after transposition, and the enforcement of this measure lacks any enthusiasm and is practically absent even today. It may be suggested that consumer credit is the area where the consumer *acquis* has been the least effective. Awareness and enforcement of these regulations remain low and problematic to this day.

11   TIMESHARE

Since the Seventies, timeshare had gradually become a fast-growing subsector of the tourism industry in Malta. Careful lobbying ensured that no new law specifically regulated this complex subject. Operators deliberately made the timeshare arrangement as complex as possible to discourage consumers from exercising their rights or pretensions. The arrangements often included trusts constituted overseas and proper foreign laws, foreign arbitration clauses and the like. These placed the often unwary consumers at huge disadvantages.

Within this lucrative and unregulated business, an army of well-drilled timeshare touts descended on the more popular local tourist resorts to push or pull or otherwise entice unsuspecting tourists to make their way to timeshare resorts where trained salesmen badgered them into signing contracts they did not need, desire or afford. They were inevitably subjected to pressure and unfair treatment. No law on the subject as ever

---

[16] Indeed the transposition was carried out after accession and membership had already been achieved.

[17] Consumer Credit Regulations, Legal Notice 84 of 2005.

introduced. Several reasons explain why this did not happen: (a) the industry was bringing in foreign income and served to push up the tourism figures; (b) there was no local outcry at this abuse seeing that at that time timeshare touts principally targeted foreigners, especially older couples coming from the UK; (c) the timeshare purchasers were unorganised and isolated, and some were too old to complain or take action in any systematic manner. The legislators, therefore, failed these people.

Incredibly the only regulation of the timeshare agreement, and the way it may be sold, are still largely derived from the timeshare Directives emanating from Brussels. The timeshare Directive only became part of national law as a requirement of EU membership. No other regulation exists. Thus rather than harmonising Maltese law with EU law, the transposition helped to introduce new law where none previously was in place.

12   Product Safety

This section argues that the transposition of the Product Safety Directives in Maltese law is a useful lesson in how transpositions can be carried out badly and how they can be undertaken successfully. The adoption of a product safety law was earmarked 'for end of 1999', but this did not happen. The first draft submitted to the Commission experts was deemed unsatisfactory and of poor quality. In its review, the Commission experts expressed the view that it failed to focus sufficiently on the core safety issue. They recommended that rather than try to salvage it through amendments, the drafting exercise should be started newly. It was unfortunate evidence that the cliché 'haste makes waste' still held true.

The law eventually adopted in 2001 by the Maltese Parliament managed to transpose in advance the revisions to the original directive on the subject.[18] It also ably merged the new rules on product safety with the main body on consumer law which had been reformed just a year earlier, in 2000. The proper regulation of the safety of consumer goods filled one of the most significant gaps in Maltese law up till 2001. Before then, the matter had relied largely on self-regulation, and no proper supporting and enforcement legal structures existed—a grave dereliction by the authorities for so many years. Fortunately, the transposition obligations forced the Maltese authorities to address the issue and adopt the comprehensive

---

[18] Directive 2001/95/EC of the European Parliament and of the Council of 3 December 2001 on general product safety [2001] OJ L11/4.

and sophisticated EU framework. The relevant law was finally adopted by the Maltese Parliament in 2001, transposing not one but two directives in the process.[19]

13   UNINTENDED CONSEQUENCES

Perhaps the worst unintended consequence of EU membership was the complete absence of any further interest or initiative by the Maltese authorities in the consumer protection field in the years following membership up till the present day. EU membership seems to have offered a false sense of security and completeness, and Government officials were found only too willing to claim, falsely, that Malta should henceforth only follow what comes out from Brussels and should not try to be 'holier than the Pope' or 'more European than the Europeans'. After the extensive beneficial reforms that came with accession, Maltese national consumer law development fell into a rut and effectively ceased. Although accession initially produced undoubted benefits for consumers in this new Member State, post-membership indigenous consumer law and policy has struggled and has indeed largely failed to survive the advent of ever more European directives.

14   EARLY CASUALTIES

The transposition of the consumer directives had another unfortunate consequence as Government, rightly or wrongly, repealed useful original national consumer Protection rules on the ground that they were incompatible with EU law. No study was ever drawn up or presented. The rules that were sacrificed in this way are the Trade Descriptions Act of 1986, and the rules prohibiting pyramid schemes and controlling gift offers that had been inserted in the Consumer Affairs Act of 1994 as amended in 2000. It was thought that these, had been superseded by the transposition of the Unfair Commercial Practices Directive in 2008. The Doorstep Contracts Act adopted in 1987[20] was repealed following the

---

[19] The rather turbulent history of the Product Safety Act is described in Chapter 6 of the 2015 Thesis, which also analyses its provisions and how these co-exist with the Consumer Affairs Act.

[20] Chapter 317 of the Laws of Malta.

implementation of the Consumer Rights Directive,[21] which is considered further under heading number 17.

15 THE STRANGE TALE CONCERNING METROLOGY

Protecting shoppers from false or deceptive weights and measures is one of the earliest consumer protection safeguards known in history. The condemnation of false weights and measures is repeatedly condemned in the Old Testament evidence that sharp, practice was as rampant as it was abusive even in those early days. The need to have nationally established standard weights and measures are specifically mentioned in the Magna Carta and in the US Constitution, which is partly inspired. Malta had an old law on the matter since 1910 called the Weights and Measures Ordinance.[22] When Malta was negotiating its entry into the EU, it was found that the Ordinance was no longer adequate and did not fit with the quality of the rules, expectations and principles that EU membership would imply, especially in the retail trading sector. EU law on the matter was quite detailed and sophisticated.[23] Malta obliged itself to update its legislation on the matter through a new and modern Metrology Act.[24]

Although a law was passed, it took years for the authorities to bring it into effect, partly due to obstruction from vested interests and to Government's lack of will to enforce this new framework and a reluctance to impose new burdens on the business sector. The law was only brought into effect on the 15 September 2006.

16 PRICE CONTROLS PROVE RESILIENT

For many in authority in Seventies and Eighties Malta, strict price control on practically every commodity was the be-all and end-all of consumer protection. A closed market suffocated by importation restrictions, bulk-buying by government and import substitution contributed to a generally

---

[21] Act No. VI of 2014 repealed the Trade Descriptions Act and the Doorstep Contracts Act.
[22] Chapter 39 of the Laws of Malta.
[23] See Regulation (EC) No 765/2008 of the European Parliament and of the Council of 9 July 2008 setting out the requirements for accreditation and market surveillance relating to the marketing of products and repealing Regulation (EEC) No 339/93 (Text with EEA relevance). This was deemed to more relate to free movement of goods rather than to consumer protection.
[24] See the Metrology Act, 2002, Chapter 454 of the Laws of Malta.

low standard of living. Competition, choice, safety and quality were not priority concerns. It was painful to observe and more painful to experience.

Price control meant that every item which was to be offered on the Maltese market to retail customers had to have its price fixed by the authorities. Most items had a fixed price which was published in the Government Gazette.[25] These ranged from soft drink bottles to toilet papers to cars. Where no fixed price was published, the retailer could not charge beyond a pre-established fixed percentage of profit. During the accession negotiations, the Maltese authorities acknowledged that these extensive price controls were incompatible with the EU freedom of goods and liberalisation of the markets policy and promised to reform the sector. An attempt was made to considerably reduce these controls and to restrict them to a few sensitive and essential goods which were considered necessary for the well-being of the Community, where competition is inexistent or is found to be ineffective in that particular area. Parliament passed a new law to this effect through all its stages, but incredibly it has never been brought into force and remains in abeyance, seemingly forgotten. What is surprising here is that the whole framework of price controls has remained in place even after EU accession, but it is not being enforced except on a selective basis.[26]

17   THE TRANSPOSITION OF THE CONSUMER RIGHTS DIRECTIVE OF 2011/83/EU

The Consumer Rights Directive came into force on the 12 November 2011 and EU member states had until 13 December 2013 to implement the Directive. The Directive was transposed into Maltese law through ministerial regulations, namely LN 439 of 2013 which were issued under the Consumer Affairs Act. The regulations are called the Consumer Rights Regulations and came into force on 13 June 2013. The regulations

---

[25] See especially the Sale of Commodities (Control) Regulations, Legal Notice 117.15 of 1972, issued under the Supplies and Services Act, Chapter 117 of the Laws of Malta.

[26] See generally David Fabri, A Decade After EU Membership: Price Control Law in Malta Revisited, https://www.um.edu.mt/library/oar/bitstream/123456789/18762/1/David%20Fabri%20(1).pdf; Reflections on a Decade of EU Membership website: http://www.um.edu.mt/europeanstudies/projects/reflections_on_a_decade_of_eu_membership_expectations,_achievements,_disappointments_and_the_future   last   accessed   on   1 February 2020.

faithfully transpose the Directive.[27] Later, in 2016, through LN 124 of 2016, the local regulations were amended to effect a few corrections. As a result of this transposition, the Distance Selling Regulations of 2001 were repealed. This was done by Article 28 of the 2013 regulations. The 2001 regulations had been issued under this same Act and had implemented the Distance Selling Directive. Following the adoption of the 2013 Regulations, the Doorstep Contracts Act of 1987 was also repealed. Act No. VI of 2014 did away with this pioneering piece of local consumer law on the ground that it was no longer compatible with the Consumer Rights Directive, a maximal harmonisation measure.

The writer is not aware of any judicial decisions regarding the implementation of the Consumer Rights Directive or how effectively the transposing regulations are being enforced by Malta's leading national central consumer authority, the Malta Competition and Consumer Affairs Authority (MCCAA).[28]

18   THE TRANSPOSITION OF THE REVISED PACKAGE TRAVEL DIRECTIVE OF 2015

Directive 2015/2302/EU of the European Parliament later amended Directive 2011/83/EU and of the Council of 25 November 2015 on package travel and linked travel arrangements, amending Regulation (EU) No 2006/2004 and repealing Council Directive 90/314/EEU. This repealed Directive was Council Directive of 13 June 1990 on package travel, package holidays and package tours (90/314/EEU) which were repealed with effect from 1 July 2018 and the Member States had until that same date to apply these measures. This meant that the original package travel transposition regulations introduced in Maltese law before accession was repealed in 2018.

The original Package Travel, Package Holidays and Package Tours Regulations were introduced on 1 November 2001 by LN 157 of 2000, as amended by Legal Notices 258 of 2001, in good time before accession in 2004. These ministerial regulations were issued in terms of the Malta Travel and Tourism Services Act. They were eventually repealed by LN 94

---

[27] file:///C:/Users/University%20User/Downloads/document%20(5).pdf last accessed 1 February 2020.

[28] See the Malta Competition and Consumer Affairs Act 2011, Chapter 510 of the Laws of Malta; and https://mccaa.org.mt/ last accessed 1 February 2020.

of 2018, by the Package Travel and Linked Travel Arrangements Regulations, 2018. Additionally, one should note the Package Travel Insolvency Funds Regulations which came into effect on the 4 October 2016 through LN 315 of 2016. Regulation 2 stated that the objective of these regulations was "to partially transpose the provisions of the Directive (EU) 2015/2302 of the European Parliament and of the Council of 25 November 2015 on package travel and linked travel arrangements, amending Regulation (EU) No 2006/2004 and Directive 2011/83/EU of the European Parliament and the Council and repealing Council Directive 90/314/EEU."

19   PUBLIC STATUTORY ADMINISTRATIVE AUTHORITIES

When in 1990 the Maltese Government embarked on a wholesale review of the state of consumer protection in Malta, it was rightly advised that it would not be sufficient to pass substantive consumer law unless a publicly-funded efficient administrative agency tasked with overseeing and enforcing them was also in place. The independent Consumer Protection Agency envisaged in the 1991 White Paper was not set up, and instead, a new Government department was established in 1992 for roughly those same purposes. The status and functions of this department were in due course specifically recognised and confirmed in the Consumer Affairs Act of 1994. Contrary to the proposal contained in the Molony Committee Report on Consumer Protection presented to the UK Parliament in 1962, the local department was charged with meeting consumers and provide them with advice and information and to assist them with their grievances against traders.[29]

Before the 1994 Act, the only administrative entity which played a generic consumer protection role was a little-known section within the Department of Trade which was broadly responsible for the administration of the Trade Descriptions Act and the then Door-to-Door Salesmen Act. Its resources were thin, its level of enforcement was unsatisfactory, and it kept a very low profile largely detached from the public. The 1991 White Paper kick-started interest in improving the institutional framework. Apart from the new department, the 1994 Act also created two new

---

[29] See Final Report of the Committee on Consumer Protection, presented to Parliament by the president of the Board of Trade by Command of Her Majesty: Board of Trade (Cmnd 1781, 1962).

structures: a Consumer Affairs Council conceived as a permanent advisory and policy think-tank, and a new Consumer Claims Tribunal. In 2011 the Malta Competition and Consumer Affairs Authority was established. This new authority has suffered from a chronic lack of expert resources and may have suffered from internal conflicts and political interference. It has yet to leave its mark on the development or growth of a national policy and legislative initiative in the consumer protection field.

20   FINAL NOTE: POST-ACCESSION

Post-accession Malta has so far had no problem in transposing EU consumer directives in a largely correct and timely fashion. Regrettably, recent transpositions have proved no more than faithful cut-and-paste exercises.

The immediate post-accession years also witnessed the demise of two remaining consumer laws from the Eighties, namely the laws on doorstep contracts and trade descriptions. This process has already been analysed elsewhere. The two laws were repealed as they deemed to be incompatible with the new EU directives on consumer rights and unfair business practices. As a result, the three original pioneering consumer statutes, namely the poor Consumers Protection Act of 1981, the unoriginal Trade Descriptions Act of 1986 and the more effective Doorstep Contracts Act of 1987 have all been repealed. In this context, it is also useful noting that the use of criminal law in support of consumer rights has proved ineffective. The Trade Descriptions Act hardly saw one successful prosecution in its 30-year existence and the criminal offences created under the Doorstep Contracts Act, as later amended, remained on paper. The authorities have generally demonstrated very little appetite for pursuing business wrong-doers through the criminal process.

Two recent post-membership consumer mechanisms may be highlighted at this point. One measure, the Collective Proceedings Act of 2012[30], set out a formal procedure allowing aggrieved consumers to initiate class actions, provided their claim arose from the Consumer Affairs Act, the Product Safety Act or the Competition Act, but not from any other law. Luckily, the first law mentioned is very substantial and comprises the bulk of the consumer Directives transposed to date. Later, 2016 saw a new consumer protection mechanism through the establishment of the Office of the Arbiter for Financial Services, an inexpensive and

[30] Chapter 520 of the Laws of Malta.

consumer-friendly mechanism for the benefit of consumers who had grievances against financial services operators including banks, investment services advisers and insurance companies.[31] The majority of decisions taken
by the Arbiter have related to mis-selling of financial products. This measure was not strictly related to EU law, but it introduced an alternative
dispute mechanism in terms of the recent Directive.[32]

Whereas EU law has heavily influenced the direction and content of
Maltese consumer law and will continue to do shortly, Maltese law has
failed to influence the development of EU consumer law and policies.
Original national measures and solutions to enhance local consumer wel-
fare are absent. The position today is that purely domestic consumer law
and local creative policy initiatives remain in hibernation, seemingly abandoned. In pro-business Malta, consumer associations have remained weak.
They are often ignored as consumers fail to recognise the long-term benefits of pursuing collective interests through a well-supported bargaining
and representative entity.

The EU does not provide consumers with a comprehensive fool-proof
protection system, and this admittedly was never its intention. The
Commission continues to monitor the status and effectiveness of its consumer measures. Indeed, in recent years, it has taken a series of initiatives
to update and improve legal protection for European citizens.[33] Steps have
also been taken to measure public opinion on how directives may be made
more relevant and effective.[34] Improvements started being considered in
various fields which include class actions, unfair contract terms, product
safety, unfair commercial practices and price indications. It also planned to
amend the recent Consumer Rights Directive of 2011. On 11 April 2018,
the Commission adopted the New Deal for Consumers package composed
of two proposals for Directives and a Communication.[35] At the time of
writing, the Commission has just finalised and published a new so-called

[31] See The Arbiter for Financial Services Act 2016, Chapter 555 of the Law of Malta.
[32] See Annual Reports 2106–2019 published by the Office of the Arbiter for Financial
Services.
[33] https://ec.europa.eu/info/law/law-topic/consumers/review-eu-consumer-law-new-
deal-consumers_en last accessed 1 February 2020.
[34] https://ec.europa.eu/info/sites/info/files/summary_main_results_public_consulta-
tion_eu_consumer_law_1.pdf last accessed 1 February 2020.
[35] https://www.consilium.europa.eu/en/press/press-releases/2019/03/29/eu-to-
modernise-law-on-consumer-protection/ last accessed 1 February 2020.

Omnibus Consumer Directive, the impact of which will only become clear in the future.

All these measures and relative documentation are all conveniently documented and reproduced on the Commissions Europa website and may be consulted there. Another useful examination of the state of fitness of EU consumer law is found in a study published in 2016 by BEUC, the international consumer association.[36] This study addressed each Directive individually and highlighted perceived weaknesses and scope for improvements. Interestingly, BEUC here also addressed the Volkswagen diesel engines abuse case, remarking critically that individual court cases against the big German company have proved "expensive, complicated, time-consuming and intimidating for many, and even more so in cross-border cases". It argued in favour of the introduction of collective redress mechanisms in EU consumer law which would have made it easier for consumers to obtain compensation for the loss suffered as a result of Volkswagen's unlawful practices.

Despite the undoubted developments and improvements in EU consumer law over these past thirty years, the consumer remains in many ways vulnerable and subject to the good faith and care, sometimes lacking, of the corporate world. One need only consider the dicey ingredients that often make up the products that we eat, the cheating and fraud perpetrated on hundreds of thousands of consumers by Volkswagen, and the unexpected failures by Boeing which occasioned the death of hundreds of passengers, to realise just how much the consumer is no king at all, but is still very much a stranger abroad. Despite the various Directives, consumers often find it difficult to enforce their rights efficiently, swiftly and inexpensively. With business still holding the upper hand, its continued regulation is thoroughly justified and accordingly, the continued relevance of consumer protection measures and the need for constant vigilance and the active pursuit of consumer interests remain high.

---

[36] https://www.beuc.eu/publications/beuc-x-2016-081_csc_fitness_check_of_eu_consumer_law_2016_beuc_position.pdf last accessed on 1 February 2020.

CHAPTER 7

EU Company Law & Malta

Ruth Vella Falzon

1 Introduction

The Companies Act, Chapter 386 of the Laws of Malta came into force on the 1st of January 1996 and replaced the Commercial Partnerships Ordinance of 1962. The Companies Act built on the existing rules and broad structures of the Commercial Partnerships Ordinance; however it reflected the ever changing financial and commercial environment. Modernisation of the Act was carried out in a twofold manner, firstly through an upgrade of the existing provisions, secondly by the introduction of the principles and standards established in the Company Law Harmonisation Directives of the European Union.[1]

---

[1] Malta Financial Services Authority Summary of the Companies Act: https://www.mfsa.com.mt/pages/readfile.aspx?f=/files/LegislationRegulation/legislation/CompanyLaw/summarycompaniesact.pdf.

R. Vella Falzon (✉)
University of Malta, Msida, Malta
e-mail: ruth.vella-falzon@um.edu.mt

© The Author(s), under exclusive license to Springer Nature Switzerland AG 2021
I. Sammut, J. Agranovska (eds.), *The Implementation and Enforcement of European Union Law in Small Member States*,
https://doi.org/10.1007/978-3-030-66115-1_7

The Act was primarily shaped on the UK Companies Act 1985/1989, essentially meaning that where up to that point the UK had implemented the EU Company Law Harmonisation Programme, the same happened in Malta. The inverse was also the case, i.e. where the UK did not implement, Malta did not either. However, another major factor which had a direct influence on the shaping of the Maltese Companies Act was Malta's impending EU membership. It had become imperative to harmonise Malta's company law regime with EU standards. As Professor Andrew Muscat argues, some of the reforms were motivated by a wish which eventually turned into an obligation to ensure that Malta was in line with EU laws in order to successfully join the Union.[2] The wish to attract foreign investment by ensuring that Maltese company laws were in line with the EU corporate programme could also be felt.

The 1995 reform which led to the birth of the Companies Act was a window of opportunity to implement the EU Company Law Directives, irrespective of Malta's future accession to the Union. The common perception is that the Act is built in totality on the UK Companies Act, whilst this is not entirely untrue; the influence of the EU Company law harmonisation Directives was major. The assumption generally is that the company law harmonisation programme had/has minimal effect on Maltese Company law, but on the contrary the EU Directives literally shaped the Companies Act. This was confirmed by Dr. Joe Borg (heading the drafting team of the Companies Bill) when interviewed by Dr. Michael Camilleri as part of his research for his thesis entitled 'The Commercial Partnerships Ordinance, 1962 and the Companies Act, 1995 A History, 1954–2000'.

In that interview, Dr. Borg had stated that in the 1960s when the Commercial Partnerships Ordinance was being enacted there was at the time only one EU Company law Directive. By the 1980s there were twelve Directives; therefore the need to have a Companies Bill in line with EU company law harmonisation programme was more pressing. Dr. Borg also stated that the feeling of being left behind by Malta's industrial partners who were harmonising their laws was independent of Malta's accession to the EU. The UK had brought its Companies Act in line with the EU

---

[2] Dr. Joe Borg (heading the drafting team of the Companies Bill) when interviewed by Dr. Michael Camilleri as part of his research for his thesis entitled 'The Commercial Partnerships Ordinance, 1962 and the Companies Act, 1995 A History, 1954–2000'.said that reforms had nothing to do with the P.N government's policy of EU membership (see n.3).

Directives so being that Malta always followed the UK, it was felt that this was the time to follow suit.[3]

Dr. Borg in his interview confirms that the models of the Companies Act were mainly the EU Company Law Harmonisation Directives. With regards to mergers and divisions, Dr. Borg confirmed that the EU directives were used almost exclusively as the sole models. It is reported that Minister John Dalli (Ministry of Foreign Affairs) had instructed the Attorney General to incorporate all the provisions of the EU Company law Directives (from the 1st to the 12th) in the Companies bill.

The main bulk of Title I of the Companies Act (articles 67–214) is largely modeled on the EU Directives.[4] The Directives which had the biggest influence being the 1st, 2nd, 6, 12th, 4th, 7th, 10th and 11th. The change to corporate law in Malta was less drastic than in other member states such as Germany or France because the changes in the Maltese company law were introduced upon the inception of the Act itself ahead of accession. As opposed to those countries that had to radically change their long-standing corporate laws to implement the harmonisation Directives.

Malta has been declared to be fully complaint with the *acquis* almost a decade prior to its membership to the European Union: "*In the field of company law as such, Maltese legislation is essentially in line with the acquis. Transposition of the new acquis concerning involvement of workers in the European Company and information and consultation of workers is foreseen after accession*".[5]

In 1999 the Commission February report stated that Malta had achieved "*a fairly good degree of compliance with the acquis in the field of company law. No further progress is to be reported in this area*"[6]

The following year, the Commission established that Maltese Company law incorporates most of the requirements of the EU Directives:[7]

---

[3] Camilleri Michael, 'The Commercial Partnerships Ordinance, 1962 and the Companies Act, 1995 A History, 1954–2000', (LL.D. Thesis, University of Malta 2003).

[4] The UK Insolvency Act was used for winding up provisions.

[5] Comprehensive monitoring report on Malta's preparations for membership {COM(2003) 675 final} /* SEC/2003/1206 final *http://ec.europa.eu/development/body/organisation/docs/CMR_MT.pdf.

[6] https://ec.europa.eu/neighbourhood-enlargement/sites/near/files/archives/pdf/key_documents/1999/malta_en.pdf.

[7] Regular Report on from the Commission on Malta's Progress Towards Accession, 8 November 2000, COM (2000) 708 final. http://aei.pitt.edu/44582/1/Malta_2000.pdf.

> *Since the last Regular Report, Malta has made substantial progress in this area*
> *Following recent progress, <u>Malta has achieved high level of alignment in the</u>*
> *<u>area of company law</u>. However, the administrative capacity needs to be strength-*
> *ened. <u>The 1995 Companies Act incorporates most of the requirements of the EC</u>*
> *<u>Directives on Company law</u>.*
> *With a staff of 25 people, the Registry of Companies is fully computerised*
> *and <u>the existing administrative structure should be adequate to implement</u>*
> *<u>and enforce the acquis. The same assessment is valid for accounting law, where</u>*
> *<u>Malta's legislation is already to a large extent in line with the acquis,</u> but*
> *minor adjustments are still needed, inter alia, as regards consolidated accounts,*
> *voting rights and disclosure requirements for branches.*[8]

In the same year (2000) the Ministry for Foreign Affairs Malta[9] confirmed that the Companies Act was broadly in line with EU company law
harmonisation Directives, in particular it listed: public disclosure requirements, mergers, divisions, single member company, the Second Company
Law Directive and the accounting principles in line with the Accounting
Directives. By this time the only recorded exception was Directive 78/855
and 82/891 on the protection of employees in a transfer of companies.
The Ministry had also confirmed that the EEIG Regulation will be
adopted.

These annual reports by the Commission on Malta's progress show
that the Maltese legislative framework and administration was set up and
well in place. Malta was in a position to implement the company law chapter of the *acquis* as early as late 1999. The biggest change came in 1995
with the coming into force of the Act itself, but we have seen some changes
along the years owing to the implementation of various Directives.

It is beyond the scope of this chapter to examine the transposition into
Maltese law of each of the EU Company Law Directives since in general
most of the Directives forming part of the EU Company law Harmonisation
Programme have been fully transposed into Maltese Law in a minimum
implementation manner with nothing irregular which renders a discussion.[10] Whilst all the Directives have in one way or another shaped Maltese
Company law, this chapter will discuss those noteworthy elements within

---

[8] Emphasis added.
[9] The Malta National Programme for the Adoption of the Acquis, Ministry of Foreign
Affairs Malta, 1 September 2000, circulated by Malta – EU Information Centre.
[10] For e.g. the Accounting Directives, the Merger, Division and Cross-border Merger
Directives and the EEIG Regulation.

a number of several Directives which have either not been implemented; which raise a number of questions, or which have changed the face of Maltese Company law drastically.

2 THE FIRST COMPANY LAW DIRECTIVE[11]

The First Company Law Directive on co-ordination of safeguards which, for the protection of the interests of members and third parties, are required by Member States of companies with a view to making such safeguards equivalent throughout the Community was enacted in 1965. The Directive deals with three major issues: publicity requirements, validity of company transactions; and nullity of companies. This Directive has now been incorporated into Directive 2017/1132 relating to certain aspects of company law (codification Directive) as part of a simplification and codification exercise carried out in 2017.

Elements of publicity (disclosure) requirements and validity of company acts were to be found in the Maltese Commercial Partnerships Ordinance (1962), but the drafting of the Companies Act saw the inclusion of the First Company Law Directive provisions. A number of elements within the Directive, such as the ultra vires rules were already existent but these have been clearly established following the inclusion of the Directive provisions.

Whilst the provisions related to publicity and validity of company transactions have been successfully implemented, the same cannot be said to nullity provisions.

Nullity provisions are now Article 11 of Directive 2017/1132. This lays down that:

> *The laws of the Member States may not provide for the nullity of companies otherwise than in accordance with the following provisions: (a) nullity must be ordered by decision of a court of law; (b) nullity may be ordered only on the grounds: (i) that no instrument of constitution was executed or that the rules of preventive control or the requisite legal formalities were not complied with; (ii) that the objects of the company are unlawful or contrary to public policy; (iii) that the instrument of constitution or the statutes do not state the name of*

---

[11] First Council Directive 68/151/EEC of 9 March 1968 on co-ordination of safeguards which, for the protection of the interests of members and others, are required by Member States of companies within the meaning of the second paragraph of Article 58 of the Treaty, with a view to making such safeguards equivalent throughout the Community.

> *the company, the amount of the individual subscriptions of capital, the total amount of the capital subscribed or the objects of the company; (iv) of failure to comply with provisions of national law concerning the minimum amount of capital to be paid up; (v) of the incapacity of all the founder members; (vi) that, contrary to the national law governing the company, the number of founder members is less than two. Apart from the grounds of nullity referred to in the first paragraph, a company shall not be subject to any cause of nonexistence, absolute nullity, relative nullity or declaration of nullity.*

The provisions stipulated in Articles 11 and 12 regarding the conditions and consequences for nullity are not found in the Maltese Companies Act. Malta is thus not fully compliant with the First Company Law Directive. The only Article which might have been inserted to combat the nullity provisions in the Companies Act is Article 77(2) which stipulates that a registration certificate is conclusive evidence *that the requirements of this Act in respect of registration and of matters precedent and incidental to it have been complied with and that the company is duly registered as a public or private company under this Act.*

This Article creates a number of ambiguities.[12] Is it, in an unclear manner implementing Article 11 of the Directive? On the contrary, could it be stating that once a registration certificate is issued by the Registry of Companies, there could be no such occurrence during a lifetime of a company that would render the company to be declared null? The irony is that Annex II of the Directive indicates that the nullity provisions are applicable in Malta to both public and private companies, despite the fact that neither the concept of nullity nor the nullity provisions are found in the Companies Act. Malta missed its chance of rectifying its position when transposing Directive 2017/1132 in 2017; in fact no measures are reported to have been implemented with regards to nullity.[13] Nullity provisions should be implemented and clarity provided *vis a vis* Article 77(2) so as to avoid infringement proceedings against Malta.

It seems that the only provisions which were introduced to implement Directive 2017/1132 in Malta were those related to Article 16 regarding

---

[12] See also Principles of Maltese company law, Andrew Muscat, Malta university press, 2007, (pg. 97).

[13] See National transposition measures communicated by the Member States concerning: Directive (EU) 2017/1132 of the European Parliament and of the Council of 14 June 2017 relating to certain aspects of company law (Text with EEA relevance.) https://eur-lex.europa.eu/legal-content/en/NIM/?uri=CELEX:32017L1132.

the interconnection of central, commercial and companies' registers.[14] The new measures for the interconnection of registers were introduced in Malta through the Companies Act (Register of Beneficial Owners) Regulations, 2017.[15] With the introduction of this new system Maltese registered companies feature in the central register. Apart from the basic information as already disclosed through the disclosure requirements, the central platform features information such as winding up or insolvency proceedings and cross-border mergers. Likewise, Maltese citizens and business may access the platform to gather information on individuals/companies in other Member States[1617]

Another Directive which has had an effect on disclosure requirements in Malta is Directive (EU) 2015/849 on the prevention of the use of the financial system for the purposes of money laundering or terrorist financing[18] which has been transposed into Maltese law through the Companies Act (Register of Beneficial Owners Regulations).[19] This is a financial services Directive aimed at curbing money laundering and does not fall within the EU Company law harmonisation programme. However, as a result of this Directive, the disclosure documents required for the registration of a new company are to include a declaration, containing information on the

---

[14] See also Directive 2012/17/EU of the European Parliament and the Council of 13 June 2012 amending Council Directive 89/666/EEC and Directives 2005/56/EC and 2009/101/EC of the European Parliament and of the Council as regards the interconnection of central, commercial and companies registers.

[15] Legal Notice 202 of 2017. http://www.justiceservices.gov.mt/DownloadDocument.aspx?app=lp&itemid=28613&l=1.

[16] https://e-justice.europa.eu/content_find_a_company-489-en.do?m=1, last accessed on 1 February 2020.

[17] *The interconnection of company registers will ensure cross-border exchange of information between registers and will facilitate EU-level access for citizens and businesses to data on companies, thus improving legal certainty in the business environment in Europe.*Brussels, 26.6.2014 COM(2014) 367 final 2014/0185 (COD) Proposal for a DECISION OF THE EUROPEAN PARLIAMENT AND OF THE COUNCIL establishing a programme on interoperability solutions for European public administrations, businesses and citizens (ISA2) Interoperability as a means for modernising the public sector.

[18] Directive (EU) 2015/849 of the European Parliament and of the Council of 20 May 2015 on the prevention of the use of the financial system for the purposes of money laundering or terrorist financing, amending Regulation (EU) No 648/2012 of the European Parliament and of the Council, and repealing Directive 2005/60/EC of the European Parliament and of the Council and Commission Directive 2006/70/EC.

[19] Subsidiary Legislation 386.19, Companies Act (Register of Beneficial Owners Regulations).

beneficial owners of the company.[20] Companies formed and registered before the coming into force of the rules had six months to comply.

3   THE SECOND COMPANY LAW DIRECTIVE[21]

The Second Company Law Directive which has now also been consolidated into the Codification Directive (EU) 2017/1132, dealt with capital on formation; maintenance and alteration of capital and creditor protection. Its provisions were inserted in the Maltese Companies Act during the drafting stage of the Act.

Whilst certain levels of share capital measures were present in the 1965 Commercial Partnerships Ordinance, the Second Company Law Directive shaped the Maltese rules on capital maintenance and protection of shareholders in the Companies Act. One example is Article 88 on the offering of shares to shareholders on a pre-emptive basis when the capital is being increased by consideration in cash.[22] This was not previously found in the Commercial Partnerships Ordinance and was not made applicable to private companies; it was clearly inserted to abide by the terms of the Directive. Other provisions which were not previously found in the old ordinance include Article 73 (1) based on Article 46 of the Directive providing that subscribed capital may be formed only of assets capable of economic assessment. However, an undertaking to perform work or supply services may not form part of those assets; and Article 73 (2) based on Article 48 stipulates that, where shares are issued for consideration other than in cash at the time the company is incorporated or is authorised to commence business, the consideration shall be transferred in full within five years of that time.

As is (unfortunately) customary in Maltese transposition of EU Directives, the second company law Directive was transposed *ad verbatim* into the Companies Act. The result is one where it seems that

---

[20] See MFSA Notice The Companies Act (Register of Beneficial Owners) Regulations, 2017. Registration of new companies as from 1st January 2018.

[21] Second Council Directive 77/91/EEC of 13 December 1976 on the coordination of safeguards which, for the protection of the interests of members and others, are required by Member States of companies in respect of the formation of public limited liability companies and the maintenance and alteration of their capital, with a view to making such safeguards equivalent.

[22] Article 72 of Directive 2017/1132, previously numbered article 29 in the second Directive.

cumbersome and vague provisions have just been re-produced without much thought into the clarity or applicability of that particular provision. One example is Article 88 (10) of the Companies Act which reproduces Article 72 (7) of the Directive regarding increase in capital by consideration in cash when shares are issued to banks or other financial institutions with a view to their being offered to shareholders of the company.[23] The provision in the Directive is far from clear and its counterpart in the Companies Act does not offer any insight or clarity.

Having said this, there are cases were some provisions seem to have been thoughtfully implemented rather than just being reproduced. One case is the minimum share capital, whereby the Directive sets it at EUR 25 000, which has been a consistent point of debate since the inception of the Directive. The main contentions are that such a minimum amount does not truly offer any credit protection. The Maltese Companies Act sets the minimum share capital for public companies at EUR 46,587.47, 25% of which must be paid up on the signing of the memorandum in what seems to have been the legislator's wish to offer higher creditor protection than that afforded in the Directive.

Furthermore, we do note that in certain cases, contrary to the implementation of the Second Company Law Directive in the UK Companies Act, some provisions of the Directive were made applicable even to private companies in Malta. Bearing in mind that the Directive is applicable to public limited liability companies. These include Article 88 (offering of shares on pre-emptive basis).

On the contrary, we then find provisions which could prove to be useful for both private and public companies alike but which have been kept applicable only to public companies, such as Article 104 on the duty of directors to call a general meeting in the event of a serious loss of capital. An interesting twist is noted in the provisions on financial assistance by a company for acquisition of its shares by a third party. The Member States were given the option of permitting a company to, either directly or indirectly, advance funds or make loans or provide security, with a view to the acquisition of its shares by a third party.[24] This was not made permissible

---

[23] *The right of pre-emption is not excluded for the purposes of paragraphs 4 and 5 where, in accordance with the decision to increase the subscribed capital, shares are issued to banks or other financial institutions with a view to their being offered to shareholders of the company in accordance with paragraphs 1 and 3.*

[24] Article 64 of the Codification Directive 2017/1132.

in Malta for public companies[25] but it was made permissible for private companies.[26]

Then there are those provisions which do not stipulate whether the provision is applicable to a private or public company. The wording used is simply "company" which refers to both types in the Companies Act, thus the inference might be that these provisions have also been made applicable to private companies. Such as Article 106 (conditions in which a company may acquire its own shares) whereby the provisions are those found in Article 60 of the Directive. In cases where the legislator wanted to differentiate between public and private companies—such as in the case of pledging of securities[27]—this was made clear.

One begs to ask was this haphazard applicability to private companies in some provisions done intentionally? Were those particular provisions deemed to be of specific value to private companies? Or was this done unintentionally during the process of the ad verbatim implementation of the Directive? Would this mean that in those cases where the Companies Act refers to "public companies", the legislator felt that the particular provision has no value to private companies? Finally, could it be that wherever the Companies Act uses the term "company" the intention was that those provisions would be applicable to private and public companies alike? It is the opinion of the author that a clarification exercise should be carried out by the legislator in a bid to provide a clear understanding of which provisions are applicable to the respective company form.

4   THE EUROPEAN COMPANY REGULATION AND ACCOMPANYING DIRECTIVE

The European Company also referred to as *Societas Europeas* (SE) was adopted by Regulation (EC) No 2157/2001 on the Statute for a European Company. It is accompanied by Directive 2001/86/EC of 8 October 2001 supplementing the Statute for a European Company with regard to the involvement of employees. The EU Commission promotes the European

---

[25] Except in the case of assistance for the acquisition of shares by or for a company/group employees and in the case of provision of financial assistance by an investment company with fixed share capital for the purpose of or in connection with the acquisition of its fully paid up shares by another undertaking.

[26] Article 110 of the Companies Act, Chapter 386, Laws of Malta.

[27] Article 122 of the Companies Act, Chapter 386, Laws of Malta.

Company as "*a simpler way to run your business if you are active in more than one EU country*". In essence this is a legal structure that allows a public limited liability company to operate in different EU countries under a single statute, as defined by the law of the Union and common to all EU countries.

As reported in the European Company Prospects for Worker Board— Legal Participation in the Enlarged EU: "*Of the 22 states which had transposed the Directive by the start of December 2005 only two, Italy and Malta, appear not to have introduced detailed legislation to adapt their national systems to the new requirements of the Regulation*[28]".

Therefore EU Council Regulation 2157/2001 of 8 October 2001 on the Statute for a European Company is directly applicable. The European Company Database reports that there are 3334 SEs registered by September 2020. One appreciates that this a minimal number, and there are even fewer SE companies registered in Malta. With regards to the accompanying Directive, this was transposed in Malta in 2004 as Legal Notice 452 of 2004 entitled Employee Involvement (European Company) Regulations 2004 *(Regolamenti ta'l-2004 dwar Involviment ta'l-Impjegati (Kumpannija Ewropea)*.

There are no worker participation rules in Malta but we find some minimal representation rights in the European Works Council Regulations;[29] in the European Works Council (Further Provisions) Regulations[30] and in the Employee Information and Consultation Regulations.[31] Any worker participation is practically introduced voluntarily by companies.

Due to socio-historical reasons, Malta has always followed the British style of employment legislation closely. There is thus no tradition of employee representation except through trade unions.[32] Employee board level representation is close to none except for a few-state owned and/or

---

[28] The European Company – prospects for worker board-level participation in the enlarged EU edited by Norbert Kluge and Michael Stoll, Social Development Agency and European Trade Union Institute for Research, Education and Health and Safety, Brussels 2006 – published with the financial support of the European Commission.

[29] Subsidiary Legislation 452.86, European Works Council Regulations.

[30] Subsidiary Legislation 452.107, European Works Council (Further Provisions) Regulations.

[31] Subsidiary Legislation 452.96, Employee Information and Consultation Regulations.

[32] Saviour Rizzo, "NOT QUITE THERE: EUROPEANISING MALTA'S INDUSTRIAL AND EMPLOYMENT RELATIONS" https://www.um.edu.mt/europeanstudies/books/CD_CSP5/pdf/srizzo.pdf. Saviour Rizzo "Corporate Governance and Workers' Participation" https://www.um.edu.mt/europeanstudies/books/CD_CSP3/pdf/tmsitbc-srizzo.pdf.

privatised companies.[33] Unfortunately, feedback during the consultation period of the SE Directive was close to none and as a result there seems to have been no public debate on the European Company.[34] It has been reported by Lionel Fulton[35] that there was a lack of interest in the transposition of the Directive in Malta. Fulton does not blame this solely on the lack of workers participation in employment history but also on the lack of larger Maltese-owned companies with operations across Europe, and the range of other EU legislation which Malta transposed at the same time.

Unfortunately for the employee representation situation in Malta, the legal notice which transposed the SE Directive left quite a lot to be desired. For instance, it does not include national rules for the choice of employee board-level representatives. It merely deals with the overall situation, where it repeats some of the wording of the Directive and states that it is for the representative body to decide on the way in which *"the SE's employees may recommend or oppose the appointment of the members of these [board-level] bodies.*[36]

Another area where the legal notice is silent is on the misuse of procedures. The Directive lays down that *"Member states shall take appropriate measures in conformity with Community law with a view to preventing the misuse of an SE for the purpose of depriving employees of rights to employee involvement or withholding such rights"*. The only reference which we find to this regard is Article 14 stating that *"no person shall use an SE for the purpose of depriving employees of rights to employee involvement or withholding any such rights"*. There is no definition of misuse, by way of interpretation of Article 14 the only definition is that misuse amounts to depriving employees of their right to involvement. How does Article 14 protect the employees? What happens if there is a misuse of the SE as stipulated in Article 14? The legislation does not state that in such circumstances negotiations should be reopened.

Similarly, there is no provision for an automatic right to renegotiate the agreement if there are changes in the structure of the SE. The Directive leaves it up to the Member states to include cases where the agreement should be re-negotiated and to prescribe the procedure which should be

---

[33] Aline Conchon, Board-level employee representation rights in Europe Facts and trends, Report 121, European Trade Union Institute.

[34] Lionel Fulton just reports that the Directive was only discussed in the employment relations board.

[35] www.worker-participation.eu.

[36] Clause 4 (b), Schedule to the legal notice.

followed in such a case. The Maltese legislator did provide for safeguards by providing that the agreement should include "*the duty to renegotiate on changes in worker involvement whenever a substantial change in the structure of the SE is foreseen, and the procedure for its renegotiation*"; however, the procedure is left to the agreement.

Another part where the Maltese legislator left much to be desired was the fallback position when the negotiations between management and the special negotiating body (SNB) fail to reach an agreement. The Directive includes a set of standard rules. A 2005 report[37] notes that Latvia and Malta have not drawn up detailed national rules on this issue but have essentially repeated the generalised wording of the Directive. Another area where the Maltese law is silent are provisions regarding the choosing of employee representatives wherein Malta[38] did not provide for a national method for making the choice, but left the selection in the hands of the representative body in the European Company.

We can safely conclude that the European Company Directive was successfully implemented in Malta but in a somewhat abrupt manner. *De jure* the Directive was implemented but *de facto* a number of features lack. This could be owing to the fact that the culture of employee involvement and/or representation is not predominant in Malta, mostly as Maltese industrial relations law has always followed the British system.[39] It cannot be a coincidence that where the UK did not implement EU provisions, Malta did not either. It has also been reported that both employers and employees alike were limitedly interested in the debates leading up to the SE Directive.

The implementation of the Directive could have been an opportune moment to re-visit the Maltese industrial relations law and break ties from the British system. Did we miss the boat? Could the implementation of the SE Directive have been an opportunity to introduce board-level representation provisions?[40] Once again, could this have been the time to consider the introduction of a two-tiered board level system? Yet again, such a change would have required a sociological cultural and historical

---

[37] Worker board level representation in the new EU member states: country reports on the national systems and practices. edited by Social Development Agency and European Trade Union Institute for Research, Education and Health and Safety Brussels, 2005.

[38] Together with Hungary, Italy, Latvia and the UK.

[39] The main elements of industrial relations in Malta consist of collective bargaining through trade unions and conflict and negotiations.

[40] There are currently only minimal provisions relating to board representation in state owned enterprises.

change in Malta and corporate governance in Malta would have been rocked. The SE is quite unpopular[41] on a general level in the EU, thus hoping that an SE Regulation and Directive would have brought about employee participation and involvement in Malta could have been too optimistic.

5   THE TAKEOVER BIDS DIRECTIVE: 13TH COMPANY LAW DIRECTIVE[42]

This is probably one of the areas where the EU company law harmonisation's influence in the Maltese corporate system was mostly felt because prior to the Takeover Directive, Maltese legislation was almost silent on takeovers. As declared by the Malta Financial Services Authority (MFSA), legislation in this field was required from scratch and the Directive has introduced significant changes to Maltese company law. The Directive was implemented by means of Chapter 11 of the MFSA Listing Rules.[4344]

The applicability of the Directive as implemented by the Maltese Listing Rules creates some ambiguities. The Directive is clearly applicable to both mandatory and voluntary bids. On the contrary, the Maltese Listing Rules lay down that *"the provisions of Chapter 11 of the Listing rules apply to both Voluntary and Mandatory Bids, but with only a specific set of the Listing Rules relating to Mandatory Bids*[45]*"*.

Once again here we see that in certain parts of the Rules, implementation was carried out *ad verbatim* and somewhat seeming to lack a deeper study. One example is Rule 11.22 on the minimum information which must be provided in the offer document, this was introduced word for word from Article 6 of the Directive and no further requirements were added by the Maltese legislator.

Similarly, the definition of *'acting in concert'* has been transposed word for word as that provided in Article 2 (1) (d) of the Directive. The definition in the Directive creates a number of open-ended questions and a

---

[41] For a number of reasons which are beyond the scope of this chapter.
[42] Directive 2004/25/EC of the European Parliament and of the Council of 21 April 2004 on takeover bids.
[43] Chapter 11 of the MFSA Listing Rules.
[44] Some references are also found in the Malta Financial Services Authority Act (Chapter 330); in the Financial Markets Act (Chapter 345, Laws of Malta); in the Professional Secrecy Act (Chapter 377, Laws of Malta) and in the Prevention of Financial Markets Abuse Act (Chapter 476, Laws of Malta).
[45] Guidance Notes to Chapter 11, Listing Rules.

number of national supervisory authorities have come up with guidelines and presumptions of circumstances which would be tantamount to 'acting in concert'. A similar list by the MFSA would surely be welcome since the Listing Rules simply provide a brief explanation.[46]

On the contrary it is somewhat confusing to note that for other provisions the Maltese legislator seems to have gone a step further than just a word for word implementation. By way of example, Malta has decided to introduce the board neutrality rule on a mandatory basis. No other Member State has chosen to impose this rule where it was not applicable in full before, except for Malta.[47] A number of measures have been included in what seems to be an exercise to provide for extra shareholder protection. One such case is the limitation on the reversibility of a company decision to apply the breakthrough rule, which reversibility could create confusion on the market.[48] Other new protective measures include the squeeze out and sell-out rules; the definition of voluntary bid; prior approval of the offer document; and the duty to inform the shareholders that a decision to launch a bid is made.

One cannot but mention that some optional measures in the Directive were on the contrary not taken up in the Maltese text, like the option offered by Article 5.4 of the Directive to the supervisory authorities to adjust the equitable price according to pre-established criteria. On the contrary in Malta, the parties are free to determine whether the highest offer price is fair based on the criteria established in Rule 11.39. Likewise the application of the proviso to Article 6.2 has been excluded in that no approval is required by the Authority of the offer document. The Authority will be merely informed about the document.

On a more positive note, the author notes that the Listing Rules have been amended almost on an annual basis, the result being that a certain element of fine-tuning creating clarity on the provisions have been achieved. One example is in the case of the launch of the mandatory bid. Article 5 (1) of the Directive stipulates that the bid must be launched at the earliest opportunity. At first this was left *ad verbatim* in the Maltese

---

[46] Rule 11.3 of the Listing Rules: *Subsidiary Undertakings, Controlled Undertakings, Parent Companies or any other Group Company of any person cooperating with the Offeror or the Offeree Company shall be deemed to be Person(s) Acting In Concert with that other person and with each other.*

[47] Brussels, 21.02.2007 SEC(2007) 268 COMMISSION STAFF WORKING DOCUMENT Report on the implementation of the Directive on Takeover Bids.

[48] Introduced also by the UK.

Listing Rules, contrary to a number of Member States who provided guidance by setting a specific time period which qualifies as the "earliest opportunity". However in recent years, the Listing Rules have been amended to provide that an offeror shall inform the Listing Authority of a Bid and shall announce his decision to launch the Bid within seven days of acquiring a Controlling Interest.[49] Furthermore, the offeror shall draw up and make public, not later than twenty one calendar days from announcing his decision to launch a bid.[50]

The implementation of the Takeover Directive in Malta, similar to the implementation of a number of EU Company Law Directives, is somewhat confusing. On the one part we find parts thereof which were practically inserted word for word from the Directive, whilst in other parts we note additional protective measures over and above that which is stated in the Directive as well as optional provisions which were (in some cases) and were not (in other cases) taken up. Does this mean that the implementation exercise was carried out diligently whereby the Directive was truly implemented and pondered upon provision by provision rather than a blanket automatic implementation? Could this thus mean, that any ad verbatim provisions are purposely so?

On the contrary, being that there was minimal (almost inexistent) takeover legislation in Malta prior to the take-over Directive; could this be another case of a missed opportunity? Whereby the Maltese legislator could have gone beyond merely implementing to the minimal standard and going into the maximum amount of details possible to have a sound and robust take over legislation in Malta. By way of example, the supervisory authority (in Malta's case the MFSA) could have been granted extensive powers had the legislator taken up all the measures of the Directive[51] as has been seen in the right to adjust the equitable price of an offer.

6   CONCLUSION

This chapter has examined the implementation process in Malta of the EU Company Law Harmonisation Programme. In many areas the measures provided for in the Directives and/or Regulations were already to be

---

[49] Rule 11.15 of the Listing Rules.
[50] Rule 11.19 of the Listing Rules.
[51] Tanti Karl J. 'The Takeover Bids Directive: A Critical Analysis of its Implementation in Malta and other EU Member States' (LL.D. Thesis, University of Malta 2014).

found in the foundations of the Maltese corporate system prior to Malta's accession to the European Union. Particularly since the 1995 Companies Act was largely based on the EU Company measures existent at the time. Thus, the implementation process in Malta was more of a refinement rather than a complete overhaul.

This chapter has evidenced that in essence Malta is almost entirely complaint with the EU Company law Harmonisation Programme and that the majority of measures have been fully transposed. This was even confirmed by the Commission prior to Malta's accession to the Union. The only major exception seems to be the nullity provisions in the First Company Law Directive.

It is however the author's view that in numerous cases implementation could have been much more than a mere word for word transposition. It would have surely been a more welcoming approach had the legislator steered clear of mere transposition of minimum requirements and ad verbatim transposition lacking attention; and directed towards greater substantive features. The Second Company Law Directive for instance was successfully transposed but its implementation could have been an opportunity of creating clarity where the Directive lacked it. Same goes for the Societas Europea legislative document which was a somewhat missed opportunity to introduce worker board-level representation in Malta. This chapter has highlighted a number of lacunas in the respective transposition documents. It is not clear whether these omissions in the implementation arise due to incorrect drafting or whether these are a result of a conscious decision made by the legislator.

Looking ahead, new modernising measures are constantly being discussed at European level, corporate social responsibility, digitalisation measures, cross border transfers and divisions and corporate governance being just a few of the various propositions. It is expected that these trends will keep shaping Maltese Company law.

CHAPTER 8

The Implementation of the Alternative Investment Fund Managers Directive in Malta

Christopher P. Buttigieg

1 INTRODUCTION

The EU Alternative Investment Funds Managers Directive[1] (AIFMD) together with the EU Undertaking for Collective Investment in Transferable Securities Directive[2] (UCITSD) are the two main pieces of EU legislation, which regulate the field of collectives investment schemes and their service providers in Europe. The UCITSD regulates those schemes (including their service providers) that are considered adequate for retail investors. In contrast, the AIFMD regulates the fund managers of schemes which mainly target professional investors. The very first

---

[1] Directive 2011/61/EU.
[2] Directive 2009/65/EU.

C. P. Buttigieg (✉)
University of Malta, Msida, Malta
e-mail: christopher.p.buttigieg@um.edu.mt

I. Sammut, J. Agranovska (eds.), *The Implementation and Enforcement of European Union Law in Small Member States*, https://doi.org/10.1007/978-3-030-66115-1_8

version of the UCITSD was adopted in 1985, whilst the AIFMD was adopted in 2009. The EU Commission has recently triggered the review of the AIFMD,[3] and it is, therefore, reasonable to consider and examine: (i) the origins of this EU Directive;(ii) several important regulatory requirements which emanate therefrom; and (iii) the manner it was transposed in Malta and developments since then.

This chapter examines the AIFMD from Malta's perspective. It analyses the most significant points made by Malta during the process that led to the adoption of the AIFMD Level I and II text. The chapter also examines the transposition of the AIFMD in Maltese Law and the implementation of the AIFMD in practice from a supervisory perspective. The changes brought about by the AIFMD and the policy decisions made by Maltese authorities during the transposition process and beyond have strengthened the regulatory framework for investor protection and financial integrity in Malta.

Nonetheless, several challenges, such as the absence of a depositary passport and the lack of convergence in the application of the regulation, have resulted from the AIFMD. As will be argued in this paper, the depositary passport remains an issue of contention at the EU level. On the other hand, issues, such as the extent of supervisory convergence have been partly tackled through the implementation of new mechanisms such as the European Securities and Markets Authority (ESMA) Supervisory Coordination Network.[4] Both of these challenges are examined as part of this chapter.

More than a decade has passed since the Commission issued a proposal for an AIFMD, which formed part of the EU policy response to the 2007–2008 financial crisis. The crisis demonstrated that financial regulation was too lax and that the supervision of financial institutions too fragmented. As a response to the crisis, the European Institutions implemented a significant revamp of the European regulatory framework by widening the scope of regulation and the extent of detail of substantive law applicable to securities markets, to ensure a more stable and resilient financial system in Europe. Also, the European Securities and Markets Authority (ESMA) became operative with strong powers to make regulation in the form of technical standards and the tools to force supervisory convergence at a national level. ESMA was also vested with a *de facto* pan-European supervisory role for credit rating agencies and trade repositories and had the function of coordinating colleges of supervisors for central counterparties. Recent amendments to the ESMA Regulation and other EU legislation, such as European Markets Infrastructure Regulation have granted additional supervisory powers to this authority in the field of (i) central counterparties, (ii) European critical benchmarks (currently LIBOR, EURIBOR and EONIA) as well as of the third-country administrators subject to the recognition regime under the Benchmarks Regulation and (iii) data reporting service providers, namely Approved Reporting Mechanisms (ARM), Approved Publication Arrangements (APA), and Consolidated Tape Provider (CTP) under the Markets in Financial Instruments Directive/Regulation.[5]

The ultimate objective of the significant reform to regulation and supervision being that of strengthening investor confidence in the financial system and ensuring that the mistakes of the past which caused the financial crisis are not, as far as possible, repeated in the future. It is therefore not surprising that the new legislative initiates aim at addressing systemic risk issues in addition to investor protection, which was the main objective of securities regulation adopted at the start of this century as a result of the EU's financial services action plan. The benchmarks for regulation and supervision have thus been heightened. In this regard, however, it is relevant to point out that while the alternative investment fund industry was not a major cause of the financial crisis, past failures that could have caused systemic risk, such as the failure of Long Term Capital Management in the US way back in 1998, justified regulatory intervention. The financial crisis gave policymakers the impetus to go ahead with the regulation in this field. The recent fallout from the suspension of the Woodford Equity Income Fund has again raised doubts whether the existing regulation of funds is sufficient to ensure proper systemic stability.[6]

The adoption of the AIFMD, which regulates the activity of all fund managers (AIFM) that manage alternative investment funds (AIF), is part of the European process for the strengthening of the financial system. An AIF is defined as all those funds which are not regulated in terms of the

[5] https://www.esma.europa.eu/press-news/esma-news/esma%E2%80%99s-supervisory-coordination-network-concludes-its-work last accessed on 1 August 2020.
[6] https://www.bankofengland.co.uk/-/media/boe/files/financial-stability-report/2019/december-2019.pdf last accessed on 1 August 2020.

UCITS Directive,[7] which directive regulates retail collective investment schemes. The AIFMD seeks to give management companies access to the internal market based on mutual recognition between the Member States, which is contingent on *quasi*-maximum harmonisation of regulation and regulatory and supervisory convergence. Malta, an EU Member State, is a jurisdiction of choice for international financial services, particularly in the funds' sector with over 600 funds, 70 fund managers, 20 fund administrators and 12 depositaries established in Malta. The scope of the AIFMD is wide and, as a consequence, it captures a significant part of the Malta fund industry.

The following are the central themes of the paper and arguments made therein:

[A] The implementation of the AIFMD has allowed Malta to reconsider the structure of its regulatory framework applicable to collective investment schemes and their service providers. The outcome of this process was the adoption of an MFSA Rulebook, which is more complete and specific in terms of regulation that applies to particular areas of financial business and which addresses the risks that arise from the activities undertaken by licensed entities. The changes to the Rulebook implemented as part of the AIFMD implementation process have strengthened Malta's regulatory framework for investor protection and the integrity of the financial system.

[B] The AIFMD requires the depositary to be established in the Member State of the AIF.[8] The lack of competition from external depositaries may result in inefficiencies and higher charges applied by the local depositary business. The restriction on the free movement of depositaries impacts the development and growth of the funds' industry in the affected Member States. Following the adoption of AIFMD and UCITS V Directive,[9] the extent of harmonisation of the activity of depositaries is sufficient to allow a framework for mutual recognition between the Member States to operate effectively in this field, thereby creating a depositary passport. However, given the alleged importance of the proximity of supervision of the depositary by the financial supervisor of the AIF, the depositary passport has been rejected. The paper argues

---

[7] Directive 2009/65/EU.
[8] Directive 2011/61/EU, article 21.
[9] Directive 2014/91/EU.

that the current level of harmonisation of EU law, regulating entities that provide depositary services to investment funds, is enough to allow a passport to operate effectively based on mutual recognition in this area. The point is made that the obligation for the depositary to be established in the same Member State of the investment fund[10] is a barrier to the cross-border business that cannot be justified on the bases of insufficient regulatory harmonisation but may be partly resulting from the lack of mutual trust between the Member States concerning the supervision of depositaries. Recommendations are made on how this supervisory conundrum could be addressed.

[C] Financial regulation on its own is not enough to ensure investor protection and guarantee the integrity of the financial system. Supervision and enforcement action is equally important. Experience in financial supervision suggests that without supervision and enforcement, the industry may be inclined not to comply with regulation, which in turn may result in the failures of the past being repeated in the future. Ultimately, the financial crisis which created the impetus for the adoption of the AIFMD did not only result from *among other things* a failure to regulate the shadow financial system but also from a failure to carry out effective supervision and to take enforcement action where necessary.

The rest of the chapter is subdivided into two additional sections. Section 2 examines the Malta experience briefly during the AIFMD legislative process and the issues raised by Malta during the different stages of this process. Section 3 analyses the transposition of the AIFMD in Malta. Concluding remarks are made at the end of the paper, including a note on how regulatory issues on the activity of the funds' industry could shape the regulatory landscape in the future. The author was responsible for negotiating, transposing and implementing the AIFMD. The preparation of the chapter has benefited from his experience in this field. The author has already published the points made in certain parts of this paper in the professional journal 'The Accountant' and the Malta Financial Services Authority's Newsletter.[11] This is an updated version of a paper on the same subject which was published in 2015 in *Id-Dritt* Volume XXV.

---

[10] Directive 2009/65/EC, article 23 (1) and Directive 2011/61/EU, recital 35 and article 21 (5).

[11] C Buttigieg, 'Negotiating and Implementing the AIFMD: The Malta Experience' (2014) The Accountant – Spring Issue; C Buttigieg and I Agius, 'Malta – Regulation of AIF

2   AIFMD Legislative Process

This section of the chapter examines the most significant points made by Malta during the negotiation process, which led to the adoption of the AIFMD level I and II text and is divided into two subsections.

Section 2.1 examines Malta's concern regarding Europe's failure to implement a depositary passport, which concern was raised during the debate in Council on the Level I text of the AIFMD. This part of the paper also gives some historical background on the issues surrounding the development of an internal market for depositaries. The debate on the depositary passport and the governance mechanisms that may be applied to make such a passport feasible is further examined in Sect. 3.2.2 of Sect. 3 of the paper.

Section 2.2 analyses the points made by Malta on the letter-box entity requirements, which were debated during the discussions on the Level II text of the AIFMD. The debate on substance and outsourcing continues further to the UK's decision to withdraw from the EU and as part of the European Commission's review of the AIMFD.[12] In this regard, this section of the article will examine the action taken by ESMA to ensure a certain degree of convergence regarding UK entities wanting to establish a presence in the EU 27. The paper argues that these measures should apply to similar situations which go beyond BREXIT.

2.1   AIFMD Level I: The Depositary Passport

The Commission's proposal for the regulation of the alternative investment funds industry was published in April 2009.[13] It immediately became

Managers' (2014) MFSA June Newsletter 5–8; C Buttigieg and C Farrugia, 'Practical Implementation of AIFMD in Malta: The MFSA's Authorisation Process' (2014) MFSA August Newsletter 2–5. All documents are available on Dr Christopher P. Buttigieg's SSRN author   page   http://papers.ssrn.com/sol3/cf_dev/AbsByAuth.cfm?per_id=1823197 accessed on 1 September 2014.

[12] https://www.esma.europa.eu/press-news/esma-news/esma-recommends-priority-topics-in-aifmd-review#:~:text=AIFMD%20has%20provided%20a%20successful,funds%20in%20Europe%20since%202011.&text=ESMA%20has%20also%20learned%20from,to%20apply%20these%20lessons%20learned. Last accessed on 1 August 2020.

[13] Commission, Proposal for a Directive of the European Parliament and of the Council on Alternative Investment Fund Managers and amending Directives 2004/39/EC and 2009/.../EC, COM(2009) 207 final http://goo.gl/up5ubW last accessed 1 September 2014.

the subject of controversy, particularly with the hedge fund industry in London threatening to move outside the EU.[14] The Commission's proposal required greater transparency, restrictions on leverage and a higher degree of capital held by fund managers. This specific regulation was required to fulfil EU policymakers' commitment to apply harmonised EU regulation in fields of finance which were largely unregulated before the financial crisis. However, the Commission's proposal came under scrutiny as having been prepared in haste and without proper consultation.[15] In particular, it tried to apply a one-size-fits-all regime to an industry which is characterised by very different types of players. Member States raised the same points during the meetings of the Council of the European Union and by MEPs at the European Parliament.

Along the way, the various issues of concern raised during the initial stages of the debate were tackled through revisions to the Commission's proposal. However, other concerns were triggered during this process. This was the case of the depositary passport, which was Malta's main issue during the debate on the level I text.

The Commission's proposal required the appointment of the depositary by the AIF having the role of safekeeping the assets of the fund and monitoring the activity of the fund manager.[16] The proposal required the depositary to be a credit institution in the EU, thereby allowing free movement in the field of depositary services.[17] As a result of discussions in Council and at the specific request of several Member States, the text was amended to include a requirement that the depositary had to be established in the same Member State of the AIF.[18] This created an issue for the Member States where the depositary industry was not yet fully developed, as the lack of competition from external depositaries would most likely result in inefficiencies and higher charges applied by the local depositary business. Moreover, it was Malta's view that the restriction on the free

---

[14] Jones S, 'EU rules would see hedge funds go overseas' Financial Times 21.08.09.

[15] 'Pay Back Time', The Economist 19.11.09 http://goo.gl/s9fe7C last accessed 1 September 2014.

[16] Commission *supra* note 360.

[17] Commission *supra* note 360.

[18] The author is the Director of the Securities and Markets Supervision Unit of the Malta Financial Services Authority and participated in the negotiations in Council on the Commission proposal for a Directive regulating alternative investment fund managers.

movement of depositaries would have a serious impact on the development and growth of the funds' industry in the affected Member States.[19]

To better understand the issues surrounding the establishment of an internal market for depositaries, it is relevant at this stage to examine the historical context on the development of a depositary passport. Analysing the history is relevant to understand the present position.

The Commission's first attempt to establish a depositary passport was made as part of the 1993 UCITS Proposal which recommended the creation of an internal market for depositaries of UCITS, thereby overcoming the regulatory limitation to mutual recognition concerning this type of service provider. Further to the introduction of the Second Banking Directive[20] and the Investment Services Directive[21] which created an internal market for credit institutions and investment firms, it was felt that the necessary conditions had been established to allow UCITS the freedom to choose a depositary established in another Member State which had been authorised in terms of these Directives to provide safekeeping and administration services. On this proposed development for the internal market in financial services, the 1993 UCITS Proposal explained:

> When the directive was adopted in 1985, the principles of the EC-passport for credit institutions and investment firms and of home country supervision had not been laid down, and it was, therefore, natural to require an establishment. However, after the adoption of the Second Banking Coordination Directive and the Investment Services Directive, the logical consequences should be that the establishment requirements for EEC-coordinated depositaries should be deleted.[22]

In terms of the 1985 UCITS Directive,[23] credit institutions and investment firms which provided depositary services were specifically not allowed to take advantage of the freedoms to provide services and establishment stipulated in the TFEU Treaty, the Second Banking Directive and the Investment Services Directive. The UCITS Directive was thus creating a

---

[19] *supra* note 365.
[20] Directive 89/646/EEC.
[21] Directive 93/22/EEC.
[22] Commission, 'Proposal amending Directive 85/611/EEC on the Coordination of Laws, Regulations and Administrative Provisions Relating to UCITS', Com(93)37, 09.02.93 http://goo.gl/rRSdJO last accessed on 15 March 2014.
[23] Directive 85/611/EEC.

limitation to mutual recognition in this field. Those Member States where the depositary industry was not developed were as a result put at a disadvantage. Given the lack of competition from external depositaries, this would give rise to inefficiencies within the local depositary business which would generate extra costs for the UCITS established in these Member States. The investor would, in the end, bear such costs.

One may argue that the creation of a depositary passport was and still is necessary to generate competition, which would also guarantee an adequate level of efficiency within the depositary industry. The passport would broaden the choice of depositaries available to AIFs and UCITS, which would be able to pick the best offer suited to their needs and would benefit from a higher degree of competition which generally results in a reduction of fees to the UCITS and overall costs to the investor.

At the time of the 1993 UCITS Proposal, the authorisation procedure for credit institutions and investment firms together with the harmonisation of the ongoing regulatory requirements, which had to be satisfied by these entities respectively in terms of the Second Banking Directive and Investment Services Directive, had created a number of safeguards to guarantee and to ensure an adequate level of protection for investors. Thus, there seemed to be no economic, regulatory or supervisory rationale to impede the application of the mutual recognition principle in the field of depositary and to operate an EEA passport for depositaries.

Notwithstanding the benefits which would have been derived from the depositary passport, the UCITS II Proposal never made it till the end of the legislative process. One of the main bones of contention was the proposals relating to depositaries,[24] concerning which, there was significant disagreement even at the Level of the European Parliament. In this regard, it is worthwhile examining the issues raised by the Rapporteur of the European Committee on Legal and Citizens' Rights of the European Parliament on the UCITS II Proposal.

MEP Perreau De Pinninck suggested two fundamental reasons why depositaries should not be granted a passport in terms of the directive.[25] He argued that the Commission's proposal to grant credit institutions and

---

[24] Clifford Chance, 'Single Market Update Services' (1996) 9 *Journal of International Banking and Financial Law* 457.

[25] European Parliament, 'Report of the Committee on Legal Affairs and Citizen's Rights on the 1993 UCITS Proposal', (A5-0268/1993) 01.10.93 http://goo.gl/rRSdJO last accessed on 15 March 2014.

investment firms the possibility to passport depositary services on the basis that they were already authorised to provide safekeeping of assets and administrative services in terms of the Second Banking Directive and the Investment Services Directive as confusing the function of mere safekeeping of assets with the complex role that a depositary must fulfil concerning collective investment schemes. MEP De Pinninck specifically remarked:

> The depositary of a UCITS does not restrict itself to correct safe keeping of deposited assets (collection of dividends or interest, presenting securities for redemption, acting in cases of capital increases or new issues, etc.); it also does the work of high added value, such as supervising the management company and its investment policies, calculating the cash value of the fund, etc.... Thus, the functions of a depositary of a UCITS are not those described in the directives, and it is extremely simple to describe these tasks as being no more than safekeeping and administration of securities.[26]

Moreover, MEP De Pinninck felt that allowing a depositary passport would create a number of legal issues, such as which legal system should apply in case of default where the depositary may be found negligent and therefore liable to the Scheme, as well as technical complications, in the form of a lesser level of coordination and cooperation between the management company and the depositary, which would, in the end, result in lesser protection afforded to the investor. Based on these two fundamental points, he recommended that the depositary of a UCITS should not be given an internal market passport and should continue to be established in the same Member State as the UCITS.

The position taken by MEP De Pinninck suggests a possible concern shared by policymakers within the European Parliament that mutual recognition concerning depositaries would not be possible. There existed a lack of sufficient harmonisation concerning the requirements which dictate the duties that should be carried out by a depositary for this service provider to properly fulfil its monitoring and safekeeping role in the best interest of the UCITS and the investors. Besides, the EU proposal had not provided for the harmonisation of the criteria which an entity must satisfy before it may be eligible and permitted to act as a depositary of a UCITS.

---

[26] European Parliament, 'Report of the Committee on Legal Affairs and Citizen's Rights on the 1993 UCITS Proposal', (A5-0268/1993)01.10.93 http://goo.gl/rRSdJO accessed last accessed on 15 March 2014.

Neither did the proposal provide for a robust harmonised prudential and conduct of business regulatory framework focusing on depository duties, which in the field of financial regulation is considered as yet another fundamental variable for the proper functioning of mutual recognition between financial supervisors and consequently the proper application of an internal market passport.

Moreover, basing oneself on the remarks by MEP De Pinninck regarding possible legal issues that could arise as a consequence of the liability of depositaries to the Scheme where the depositary is found to have acted negligently, it is logical to conclude that mutual recognition in this field and the application of an internal market passport would have also required a certain degree of harmonisation concerning civil liability. Specifically, in establishing whether a depositary should be subject to an obligation of means or an obligation of result with regards to the performance of its duties, where significant differences existed between the Member States. These were considerably ambitious steps for policymakers at this early stage of the integration of EU financial services. In the end, policymakers considered that the UCITS II Proposal did not contain enough harmonisation of substantive requirements of investor protection type to allow mutual recognition with regards to the depositary business to operate properly.

The AIFMD proposal was an opportunity to revive the debate on the depositary passport. Malta made the point that a depositary passport was necessary to complete the internal market for the funds' industry and that the mechanisms for such a passport to operate had already been established, particularly given the extent of existing harmonisation of the requirements applicable to credit institutions and investment firms in the EU. In Malta's view, the extent of harmonisation of the activity of depositaries should have allowed a framework for mutual recognition between the Member States to operate effectively in this field. However, the majority of Member States in Council was, at that stage, not yet convinced about the desirability of mutual recognition in the field of depositary services, particularly given the alleged importance of the proximity of supervision of the depositary by the financial supervisor of the AIF. Malta further argued that unless a full depositary passport was allowed, Member States should as a minimum be granted the option to permit EEA credit institutions and investment firms to get access to their market and provide depositary services within their territory. This was a pragmatic solution to address the depositary passport challenge during the stage of the AIFMD legislative process.

Ultimately, the requests made by Malta and the other Member States having a similar view resulted in a compromise whereby a transitional provision for four years was included in the AIFMD—until July 2017.[27] This transitional provision gave the Member States the discretion to allow AIFs established on their territory to appoint depositaries in the other Member States. This discretion was however restricted to the appointment of depositaries that are authorised as credit institutions in their home Member State. Furthermore, the text of the directive was amended to include a recital which invites the European Commission to put forward an appropriate horizontal legislative proposal which *inter alia* governs the right of a depositary in one Member State to provide services in the other Member States.[28] The overall intention of these amendments had been that of giving the Member States, where the depositary industry is not yet fully developed, sufficient time to allow their depositary industry to grow, while at the same time giving the European Commission the time to put the depositary passport back on its legislative agenda. This materialised with the publication of the 2012 UCITS VI Consultation,[29] which included a specific section on depositary passport and further work carried out by the European Commission in due course.[30] A proposal for a mechanism which should allow the depositary passport to work is made in Sect. 3.2.2 of this chapter.

2.2   AIFMD Level II: Requirements on Letter Box Entities

At level 2 of the AIFMD legislative process, the major issue of contention emerged from the requirements which regulate the delegation by an

[27] Directive 2011/61/EU, article 61 (5).

[28] Directive 2011/61/EU, recital 37.

[29] European Commission, Undertakings for Collective Investment in Transferable Securities (UCITS): Product Rules, Liquidity Management, Depositary, Money Market Funds, Long-Term Investments: Consultation Document (26 July 2012, Brussels) p. 11, available https://ec.europa.eu/finance/consultations/2012/ucits/docs/ucits_consultation_en.pdf last accessed on 30 January 2020.

[30] For an analysis of the consultations carried out by the European Commission which cover the depositary passport see: C Buttigieg, 'The rationale for a depositary passport', Chapter 20, D Zetzsche "The Alternative Investment Fund Managers Directive" Third Edition Wolters Kluwer. Also see C Buttigieg et al., 'Establishing an EU Internal Market for depositaries' Journal of Financial Regulation and Compliance 2020.

AIFM to a sub-manager, specifically the requirements on letter-box enti-ties. The version of the AIFMD Delegated Regulation issued in March 2012 *inter alia* stipulated a quantitative test whereby, if the totality of the individual tasks delegated by the AIFM substantially exceeded the tasks carried out by itself, the AIFM was to be considered a letter-box entity. This meant that the fund manager would no longer be considered an AIFM for the directive. This provision raised significant concerns within the hedge fund industry, particularly given the accepted market practice for fund managers to make the high-level policy decisions directly while delegating the day-to-day stock picking and risk management of the port-folio to another firm in the EU or a third country. This accepted market practice allowed the realisation of a certain degree of economies of scale.

The proposed rule on letter-box entity meant that the AIFM would have to undertake much of the previously delegated activity directly. This would have made the prevailing delegation model unworkable for an AIFM and would have resulted in a significant amount of restructuring within the industry, with the cost being passed on to investors. This was Malta's most significant concern at this stage of the AIFMD legislative process. Malta, together with the other Member States, argued in favour of a more workable solution concerning the letter-box entity require-ments. Ultimately, the Commission moved away from the quantitative determination of a letter-box entity, by replacing the proposed rule with an approach which requires the assessment of compliance of the delega-tion structure with an established set of qualitative criteria.[31] However, this meant that the mechanism for assessing the delegation arrangements would result in different interpretations of the relevant requirements at the national level and, as a consequence, in a fragmented approach to the supervision of AIFM delegation structures and opportunities for supervi-sory arbitrage.

In an attempt to resolve the risks resulting from an uneven approach to the interpretation of the requirements on letter-box entities, the Commission Delegated Regulation stipulates that ESMA may issue guide-lines to ensure a consistent assessment of delegation structures across the Union. ESMA prioritised work on AIFMD at Level III, particularly: (1) the negotiation of a memorandum of understanding with various Non-EU jurisdictions for the directive; and (2) the establishment of a consistent approach to the application of the reporting by AIFM and the

---

[31] Commission Delegated Regulation (EU) 231/2013.

implementation of the requirements on remuneration. However, it did not immediately initiate work in the field of delegation by AIFM. This was eventually partially addressed through the implementation of the Supervisory Coordination Network (SCN).

The SCN was established in the aftermath of the BREXIT vote and as a result of ESMA's concerns regarding supervisory competition between NCAs to attract UK business that wants to retain a presence in the EU while continuing to operate from London. The SCN, the mandate of which was completed in May 2020, had as its objective the enhancement of mutual understanding of NCAs through information exchange, the sharing of good practices, and the discussion of key issues arising from the relocation of functions or activities from the UK into the EU27. The network, which was coordinated by ESMA, sought to promote consistent decisions by NCAs concerning financial entities establishing a presence in the EU. It ensured that UK firms did not take advantage of inconsistent approaches to supervision, particularly concerning delegation, across the EU, when making their decision where to locate their European business. One may argue that this mechanism was effective in achieving supervisory convergence and the implementation of best practice across the EU. Indeed, the discussion within this Committee encouraged a convergent approach concerning the processing of applications for a licence in the EU 27 from entities established in the UK and the treatment of proposals for the delegation by such entities. Because of the effectiveness of the SCN to achieve convergence, it is reasonable to suggest that such a mechanism should be more frequently adopted for the attainment of this high-level ESMA objective.

3   THE TRANSPOSITION PROCESS

This section of the chapter examines the transposition process of the AIFMD, the legislative changes made for this purpose and the choices made by policymakers during this process which are particular to Malta. In the context of the paper, this section is important as it examines how the implementation of the AIFMD changed the dynamics of Maltese regulation applicable to AIFM and AIFs and makes suggestions on how the directive can be improved to achieve a more effective internal market in the field of investment funds.

This section, which is divided into two subsections, demonstrates how the AIFMD implementation process resulted in the adoption of an MFSA

Rulebook, which is more complete and specific in terms of regulation that applies to particular areas of financial business and that addresses the risks that arise from the activities undertaken by licensed entities.

Section 3.1 examines the changes to Malta's legislative framework. Section 3.2 analyses the areas of regulation which are particular to Malta. In the latter part of this section, a proposal is made for a depositary passport based on (i) mutual recognition of regulation and supervision which is contingent on harmonised regulation and supervisory convergence; and (ii) supervisory processes that are built on the principles of reflexive governance and the implementation of a system of colleges of supervisors established in terms of the ESMA regulation.

3.1 Changes to Malta's Legislative Framework

The transposition of the AIFMD was handled by the MFSA, which is an independent and autonomous public body established by an act of Parliament, the Malta Financial Services Authority Act.[32] The MFSA is Malta's single financial services regulator and supervisor with *inter alia* the responsibility of achieving investor protection and the integrity of the financial system and advising the government on matters relating to policy in the field of financial services. Malta is a jurisdiction of choice for the establishment of international financial services and has a growing funds sector, which mainly targets professional investors.

As the AIFMD has an impact on the majority of fund management companies and collective investment schemes established in Malta, the implementation of the directive became a top priority on the Authority's regulatory agenda. To address the implementation challenges, the Authority set-up an Implementation Working Committee which was *inter alia* responsible for suggesting amendments to the local legislative framework for the AIFMD. The Committee had three main objectives: (i) carrying out the correct transposition and implementation of the AIFMD and subsidiary legislation; (ii) ensuring a smooth transition from the existing regime for the regulation of Non-UCITS fund managers, which was largely based on MiFID, to the AIFMD regime; and (iii) ensuring that certain features of the regime, such as the framework for the regulation of professional investor funds, would be retained.

---

[32] Chapter 330 of the Laws of Malta.

In Malta, the transposition of the AIFMD required amendments to the Investment Services Act, 1994 ('the Act').[33] By way of background, the Act regulates the activity of investment firms, fund managers, collective investment schemes, custodians and fund administrators. The amendments to the Act, which implement the AIFMD, provided for the licensing of an AIFM and alternative investment funds ['AIF']. The first schedule to the Act was also amended to include 'collective portfolio management of assets' as an integral part of the service of management of investments.

The Act is supplemented by the following legal notices adopted by Minister of Finance in terms of the Act:

- Investment Services Act (Alternative Investment Fund Manager) Regulations,[34] which enhance the MFSA's powers *qua* competent Authority for the AIFMD;
- Investment Services Act (Alternative Investment Fund Manager) (Passport) Regulations,[35] which apply to AIFM exercising passporting rights in terms of the AIFMD;
- Investment Services Act (Marketing of Alternative Investment Funds) Regulations,[36] which regulate the cross-border marketing of AIFs; and
- Investment Services Act (Alternative Investment Fund Manager Third Country) Regulations[37] ['Third Country Regulations'], which implement the third country provisions, including the framework applicable to the national private placement regime and the choice of the Member State of reference by third-country AIFMs.

In addition to the Act and the legal notices, changes were also carried out to the MFSA's Investment Services Rules.[38] In terms of the Act, the MFSA has the power to issue Investment Services Rules stipulating requirements and conditions concerning activities of licensed entities, the conduct of their business, their relations with customers, the public and other parties, their responsibilities to the MFSA and any other matters as the Authority may consider appropriate. The MFSA has issued (and/or

---

[33] Chapter 370 of the Law of Malta.
[34] Legal Notice 115 of 2013.
[35] Legal Notice 114 of 2013.
[36] Legal Notice 113 of 2013.
[37] Legal Notice 116 of 2013.
[38] MFSA Investment Services Rules http://goo.gl/GWHN3p accessed 11.09.14.

amended, as the case may be) several Investment Services Rulebooks that generally aim at supplementing the high-level regulatory principles stipulated in the Act and which transpose various pieces of EU financial regulation such as the AIFMD, the Markets in Financial Instruments Directive (MiFID),[39] the UCITS Directive[40] and the Capital Requirements Directive.[41]

The Investment Services Rules for Investment Services Providers ['ISP Rulebook'] which regulate the activity of investor firms, fund managers and custodians ('depositaries'), was amended to implement the governance, compliance, capital, risk management, the conduct of business and transparency requirements applicable to AIFM. In addition, as part of the AIFMD project the Authority decided to restructure the ISP Rulebook, the ongoing obligations of which apply to investment services providers in general, into four parts which apply depending on the specific type of activity undertaken by the licensed entity, these being: (i) MiFID investment firms; (ii) UCITS managers; (iii) AIFM; and (iv) depositaries (Fig. 8.1).

3.2   Fields of Regulation: Particular to Malta

This section examines those areas of regulation which are particular to Malta and strengthen Malta's regulatory framework for investor protection and the integrity of the financial system. Specifically the: (i) licensing framework for *de minimis* fund managers; (ii) implementation of the requirements on remuneration; (iii) transitional depositary passport; and (iv) implementation of rulebooks applicable to AIF.

3.2.1   De minimis Fund Managers

The part of the Investment Services Rulebook that applies to AIFM contains specific regulation applicable to *de minimis* AIFM.[42] Malta decided to regulate *de minimis* AIFM with a stricter regime then what is prescribed in the AIFMD for this type of manager. Policymakers in Malta were of the view that a licensing regime is preferable than mere registration as it is in

---

[39] Directive 2004/39/EC.
[40] Directive 2009/65/EC.
[41] Directive 2013/36/EU.
[42] MFSA Investment Services Rules for Investment Services Providers, Part B III http:// goo.gl/rQNhPL last accessed on 18 August 2014.

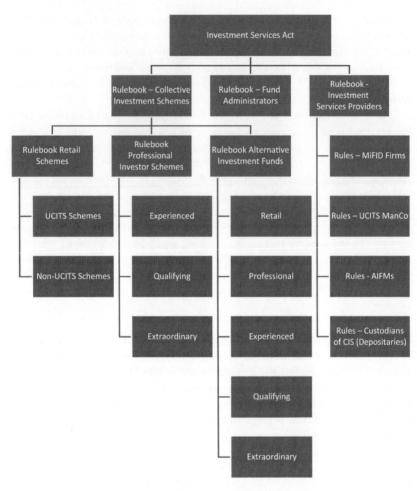

Fig. 8.1 The structure of the MFSA's Investment Services Rulebook after the implementation of the AIFMD

the best interest of investor protection and the integrity of the financial system that all fund managers are subject to a robust but proportionate regulatory framework.[43] Mere registration without regulation and supervision does not give comfort to investors that they are being treated fairly and that their investments are being made in a way which is not in breach of good general principles for market integrity.

The framework applicable to *de minimis* fund managers in Malta prescribes governance, transparency and conduct of business requirements. Still, it does not extend to the specific requirements set in the AIFMD that aim at addressing: (i) systemic stability concerns, such as the requirements applicable to AIFMs that manage leveraged funds; and (ii) the regulatory concerns that result from corporate finance through specific obligations applicable to AIFM that manage funds which acquire control over non-listed companies. Moreover, it was deemed important that fund managers irrespective of the size and complexity of their operations should be subject to Malta's money laundering and financing of terrorism deterrence framework.[44] This is important to ensure that no operator remains unchecked from a money-laundering perspective, which is critical for safeguarding the reputation of Malta's financial centre. Recent AML/CFT scandals in Malta and abroad have strengthened the position that all fields of financial business should be covered by AML/CFT regulation as failing to do so may result in opportunities for the abuse of the system which impacts the overall integrity of the market.

Therefore, *de minimis* AIFMs are subject to regulation and supervision in Malta, the only distinction between AIFM and *de minimis* AIFM being the level of regulation and the intensity of supervision by the MFSA. It is reasonable to suggest that Malta's approach in this regard addresses potential issues of investor protection and confidence, while at the same time ensures that AIFM of small size is not forced into regulatory straightjackets that are designed for large operators and are not, as a consequence, relevant given the size, nature and complexity of their business.

---

[43] MFSA Consultation on the Rulebook applicable to *de minimis* licence holders, 22.03.13 http://goo.gl/MxuObY last accessed on 18 August 2014.
[44] Chapter 373 of the Laws of Malta.

3.2.2   Transitional Depositary Passport

Malta exercised the optional transitional provision that allowed an AIF to engage a depositary in another Member State until 22 July 2017.[45] The implementation of AIFMD was an important step for the strengthening of investor confidence in the alternative investment fund industry.[46] In this regard, the requirement to appoint a depositary to safe-keep the assets of the fund and to monitor the AIFM is an important investor protection requirement. Nonetheless, the requirement that the depositary should be established in the same Member State as the fund[47] goes beyond what is necessary to achieve the investor protection objective of the regulation. The restriction on the place of establishment of the depositary limits the jurisdictional options for promoters of investor funds restricts the choice of depositaries. It lessens the competition within the depositary industry. The restriction goes against the internal market objectives set in the Treaty of the European Union (TFEU) and the directive.

In the EU, harmonisation is not implemented for its sake but to allow the internal market to operate based on single Rulebook (maximum harmonisation) or mutual recognition (minimum or *quasi*-maximum harmonisation). However, while as a result of AIFMD and the UCITS V Directive,[48] there is now significant harmonisation of the conduct of the business of depositary services, a depositary passport has not been implemented. It is submitted that this illogical position is the unfortunate outcome of European processes that are largely driven by national protectionist agenda, which are prevailing over and creating barriers to the operation of the European Internal Market project. It is submitted that the main issue which is preventing the depositary passport to be implemented is more likely to be the desire of certain Member States to retain control over the depositary business which services the funds that are established in their jurisdiction, and possible mutual distrust between the Member States concerning the supervisory capabilities at the national level for the integrity of the depositary business. To address this concern and implement the depositary passport one may venture at proposing a solution based on mutual recognition that is contingent on: (i) harmonisation of regulation

---

[45] Directive 2011/61/EU, article 61(5).

[46] N. Fitzpatrick, 'The Man Behind AIFMD: Executive Interview with Ugo Bassi the European Commission's Head of Asset Management' (2011) Funds Europe 18–19.

[47] Directive 2011/61/EU, article 21(5).

[48] Directive 2014/91/EU.

and supervisory processes that are built on the principles of reflexive governance that leads to convergence of supervisory practices; and (ii) the implementation of a system of colleges for cooperation established in terms of the ESMA regulation.

From a supervision perspective, a system for reflexive governance of financial supervision based on tools for supervisory cooperation, resulting in convergence, would seem to be the optimum solution to allow mutual recognition to work in the field of depositary services. Reflexive governance is a process that promotes learning from diversity. It is characterised by flexibility, participation, power-sharing, de-centralisation, deliberation, experimentation, identification and benchmarking of best practices, knowledge-creation and revisability.[49] The overall focus of the process is a continuous search for better approaches to address the governance problem. The constructive and valuable feature of a process of reflexivity in governance is that the outcome of the learning-process bends back on the participants that have instigated and participated in the said process, and where exchanges between different participants in the process can result in innovation, as each participant will have to reconsider its policies with a view of improving them, in the light of the successes and failures of others.[50] For reflexive governance to work, participants must be equipped to become active in the decision-making process and must be supported through *inter alia* institutional arrangements for cooperation and debate. The ESMA standing committee for investment management[51] could be the ideal forum to kick start this process.

Nonetheless, on the assumption that the global custodians active in Europe[52] are the players that would exercise a passport to provide depositary services across the EU and which would compete on a cross-border level, one could argue that centralised supervision at European Level would, in the first instance, appear to be a more suitable basis for the

---

[49] O DeSchutter and J Lenoble (eds), 'Reflexive Governance: Redefining the public interest in a pluralistic world' (Hart, 2010) and S Deakin, 'Reflexive Governance and European Company Law' (2009) 15(2) European Law Journal 224–245.

[50] DeSchutter and Lenoble *above*.

[51] The Investment Management Standing Committee undertakes ESMA's work on issues relating to collective investment management, covering both harmonised and non-harmonised investment funds. More information on the Standing Committee is available http://goo.gl/nbuAdr last accessed 13 September 2014.

[52] Info available from the Global Custodians Web-site http://goo.gl/WXq6bg last accessed on 18 August 2014.

depositary passport, as shared supervision may be highly inefficient and may not be adequate to ensure stability. However, given the investor protection concerns that could arise from the losses suffered in case of failure of a depositary, national financial supervisors would want to retain supervisory control over the depositary business. Retaining responsibility for supervision and easy access to the depository is, in the end, the main reason why certain Member States have not yet come to terms with the idea of having a depositary passport. Therefore, it is most likely that the supervisors of AIFs, UCITS and the management companies serviced by the depositary, would want to participate in the supervision of the depositary together with the depositary's home financial supervisor.

To resolve the possible supervisory inefficiencies that could result from fragmented supervision involving several supervisors, while addressing the existing desire for national supervision, it is submitted that a measure that should be considered is the setting up of colleges of supervisors coordinated by ESMA.[53] This solution would leave supervision at the level of the home Member State while recognising the need for the other Member States to take a role in the supervisory process. However, it has been suggested that there might be limitations to this type of mechanism for the coordination of supervision of cross-border financial institutions.[54] Non-harmonised mandates and powers of financial supervisors that form part of the college could result in lack of proper leadership in the college and failures in consolidated supervision which would generally undermine the effectiveness of the college of supervisors.[55] On the other hand, a properly coordinated and strongly led college of supervisors would create a forum for discussion, mutual cooperation and learning which would, in turn, enhance a process of reflexivity in financial supervision that would contribute to the overall process of convergence.

3.2.3   MFSA Rulebooks Applicable to AIFs
Malta has a tradition as a product regulation jurisdiction. In general, the Investment Services Act requires collective investment schemes established in Malta to obtain a licence from the MFSA. The Authority's

---

[53] Regulation (EU) No1095/2010, recital 36 and article 21.

[54] D Alford, 'Supervisory Colleges: The global financial crisis and improving international supervisory coordination' (2010) 24(1) Emory International Law Review.

[55] K Alexander, R Dhumale & J Eatwell, 'Global Governance of Financial Systems: The International Regulation of Systemic Risk' (Oxford University Press, 2006).

regulatory framework distinguishes between retail funds[56] and professional funds.[57] Both types of funds are subject to specific governance and transparency requirements. In addition, retail funds are also subject to additional investor protection type rules which seek to ensure diversification through the application of requirements that regulate the structure and/or composition of the portfolio of AIFs. The AIFMD regulates the activity of AIFM and not the AIF. However, Member States may continue to regulate the activity of the AIF at the national level.[58]

During the process that led to the implementation of the AIFMD in Malta, the MFSA decided to adopt the Investment Services Rules for Alternative Investment Funds ['AIF Rulebook'], a rule book for the establishment of funds which are compliant with the AIFMD.[59] While the MFSA opted to retain the existing regulatory framework applicable to professional investor funds, it decided to reinforce the framework for the regulation of the funds' sector by establishing a rulebook that regulates self-managed funds, which in terms of the AIFMD qualify as the AIFM. Third-party managed funds that are targeted for distribution as AIFs across Europe. Apart from stipulating an exhaustive list of service providers which the AIF is required to appoint, the AIF rulebook also sets requirements on the governance and transparency of the fund.

The Authority also published a rulebook which applies to loan funds, being AIFs that specialise in the granting of loans.[60] These rules are meant to regulate the direct origination of loans by the fund or the acquisition by the fund of a portfolio of loans or a direct interest in loans which gives rise to a direct legal relationship between the Scheme as the lender and the borrower. This Rulebook attempts to address the funding gap resulting from the deleveraging of banks by creating an alternative funding channel for the economy. In particular, the funding of long-term projects such as the financing of infrastructure or the purchasing of aircraft or ships. In preparing rules applicable to loan funds, the MFSA attempted to address

[56] MFSA Investment Services Rules for Retail Collective Investment Schemes http://goo.gl/gNjrm2 last accessed on 19 September 2014.

[57] MFSA Investment Services Rules for Professional Investor Funds http://goo.gl/EbHLkN last accessed on 19 September 2014.

[58] Directive 2011/61/EU, recital 10.

[59] MFSA Investment Services Rules for Alternative Investment Funds http://goo.gl/tKbFFb last accessed 13.09.14.

[60] MFSA Standard Licence Conditions applicable to Collective Investments Schemes authorised to invest through loans http://goo.gl/CGj6Z3 accessed 13.09.14.

possible shadow banking concerns by adapting requirements which traditionally apply to credit institutions, such as the requirement to establish and implement a credit risk policy that guides the granting of credit by the fund. In this connection, the MFSA took into account the various studies and policy recommendations on the regulation of shadow banking published by the Financial Stability Board.[61] Without specific product regulation which tackles the risks that emerge from the granting of loans, it would be difficult to ensure that these type of funds operate soundly and do not form a threat to the integrity of the financial system.

In due course, the MFSA investment services rulebook was further amended to introduce another AIF type, specifically the Notified Alternative Investment Funds (NAIFs). For this product, the AIFM is responsible for ensuring that the NAIF is compliant with the applicable requirement. Indeed, by making a notification in respect of an AIF, the AIFM undertakes responsibility for that AIF and the fulfilment of its obligations. An AIFM is required to comply with its ongoing obligations in respect of an AIF, its investors and its regulator under the AIFMD and relevant rules and regulations thereunder.

The implementation of the rulebooks applicable to AIFs demonstrates how the AFIMD implementation process was used as an opportunity to develop further the MFSA's regulatory framework applicable to the funds' industry. Indeed, the outcome of the implementation process was the adoption of an MFSA rulebook which is more complete and specific in terms of regulation that applies to particular areas of financial business and which address the risks that arise from the specific area of activity undertaken by collective investment schemes and service providers. The changes to the Rulebook implemented as part of the AIFMD implementation process, have strengthened Malta's regulatory framework for investor protection and the integrity of the financial system.

3.2.4   Implementation of the Requirements on Remuneration

The MFSA has implemented the ESMA Guidelines on sound remuneration policies under the AIFMD[62] except for paragraph 18 of the

---

[61] Financial Stability Board, 'Strengthening Oversight and Regulation of Shadow Banking: An Overview of Policy Recommendations' August 2013 http://www.financialstability-board.org/wp-content/uploads/r_130829a.pdf?page_moved=1 accessed 13.10.14.

[62] ESMA, Guidelines on sound remuneration policies under AIFMD, ESMA/2013/232 http://goo.gl/Xs0rR1 last accessed on 19 September 2014.

guidelines. This paragraph stipulates that the delegate of an AIFM, who has been delegated investment management activities, must be subject to regulatory remuneration requirements which are equally as effective as those applicable under the Guidelines and those appropriate contractual arrangements must be in place to ensure that there is no circumvention of the remuneration rules. ESMA has therefore extended the remuneration provisions in the directive with the intent that entities to which AIFMs delegate investment management activities are also subject to the guidelines. The recitals of the UCITS V Directive are demanding ESMA to take a similar position concerning delegation structures in the context of UCITS.[63]

The adoption and implementation of requirements on remuneration are fundamental to address the possible detrimental effect of poorly designed remuneration arrangements on the sound management of risks. Perverse remuneration incentives are one factor among many that contributed to the financial crisis.[64] As a result, the regulation of remuneration has been on international policymakers' agenda, amongst others the Financial Stability Board, which has been monitoring the implementation of its principles for sound compensation practices.[65] Therefore, the imposition of remuneration requirements is a mechanism which seeks to control the risk-taking behaviour by AIFM and aligning the interests of identified staff of the AIFM with those of investors in the AIF managed by the AIFM.[66] However, as a result of the uneven approach to the regulation of remuneration between Europe and the rest of the world,[67] the ESMA guideline that is applicable in the event of delegation may cause difficulties in the setting up of delegation structures where the delegate is established outside the EU.

Therefore, the MFSA originally opted not to implement paragraph 18 of the ESMA Guidelines. In this regard, to address the concerns that

---

[63] Directive 2014/91/EU.

[64] Financial Stability Forum, 'FSF Principles for Sound Compensation Practices' 02.04.09 www.financialstabilityboard.org/publications/r_0904b.pdf last accessed on 19 September 2014.

[65] Financial Stability Board, 'Implementing the FSB Principles for Sound Compensation Practices and their Implementation Standards' 04.11.14 http://www.financialstability-board.org/what-we-do/policy-development/building-resilience-of-financial-institutions/compensation/ last accessed on 19 September 2014.

[66] Directive 2011/61/EU, Recital 24.

[67] FSB, *above*, 6–11 & 13.

delegation structures may be applied to circumvent the European requirements on remuneration, while at the same time allowing delegation structures between EU and non-EU fund managers to continue existing
without restrictions, the MFSA applied a supervisory procedure for monitoring the effective implementation of remuneration requirements by
local fund managers. In circumstances where the delegate was not subject
to remuneration requirements which are equivalent to those indicated in
the AIFMD, the MFSA expected the relevant AIFM to coordinate the
implementation of adequate and robust risk management processes and
procedures to be followed by the delegate and also required the relevant
AIFM to carry out more rigorous control and oversight of the delegate's
activity. As part of this process, the MFSA considered these issues in the
context of the directive's overall objectives of avoiding excessive risk-
taking and alignment of interests, and the scope for the delegate to materi-
ally affect the AIF's risk profile. It is reasonable to suggest that this
supervisory procedure achieved the same outcome as paragraph 18 of the
ESMA Guidelines, however without disrupting the existing delegation
structures.

Nonetheless, in due course, and further to pressure exerted by ESMA
which sought to ensure a harmonised implementation of its Remuneration
Guidelines, the MFSA adopted a set of proportionality guidance notes
which included guidance on the implementation of paragraph 18.[68] To
further understand the impact of the application of these guidelines, the
MFSA eventually carried out a thematic review focusing on compliance
with the remuneration provisions in terms of the AIFM Directive.[69] The
review was designed to verify the extent to which the selected licence
holders were adhering with the remuneration requirements in terms of the
AIFM Directive, including how these were being complied with and
applied in practice. Key findings, such as the failure of several AIFMs to
document monitoring procedures and arrangements as well as findings
which are being carried out on the delegate, were identified and disclosed

[68] MFSA, 'Guidance Notes on the Application of the Proportionality Principle in relation
to ESMA Guidelines on Sound Remuneration Policis unde the UCITS Directive and the
AIFMD' 9 May 2017 https://www.mfsa.mt/wp-content/uploads/2019/01/20170509_
GuidanceNotes.pdf accessed last accessed on 18 September 2020.

[69] MFSA, Thematic Review focusing on Compliance with the Remuneration provisions in
terms of the AIFM Directive' 11 November 2016 https://www.mfsa.mt/wp-content/
uploads/2019/08/20161111-Circular-Thematic-Review-Remuneration.pdf accessed last
accessed on 18 September 2020.

to the industry in the form of further guidance to strengthen compliance in this field.[70]

This section examined the regulatory framework, which implements the AIFMD in Malta and demonstrates how the transposition of the directive has resulted in a more robust regulatory framework for the alternative investment fund industry. In the final analysis, it is reasonable to argue that financial regulation on its own is, however, not enough to ensure investor protection and guarantee the integrity of the financial system. Supervision and enforcement action is equally important. Experience in financial supervision suggests that without supervision and enforcement, the industry may be inclined not to comply with regulation, which in turn may result in the failures of the past being repeated in the future. Ultimately, the financial crisis which created the impetus for the adoption of the AIFMD did not only result from *inter alia* a failure to regulate the shadow financial system but also from a failure to carry out effective supervision and to take enforcement action where necessary.

Effective enforcement sets an example whereby other operators become more attentive not to commit regulatory failures. Indeed, "punishment does not take place primarily and per se for the correction and good of the person punished, but for the public good so that others may become terrified and weaned away from the evils they would commit."[71] It is therefore important for enforcement action to be directed not only at the licensed entity but to extend to the individuals responsible for the failures. The US Federal Deposit Insurance Corporation's action against directors of banks that failed during the financial crises is an interesting example of an action that may, in the end, have an enduring effect on the behaviour of others that remain in the industry[72] and is the sort of action which financial supervisors, should take where serious failures are identified.[73]

---

[70] Ibid.

[71] *Directorium Inquisitorum*, edition of 1578, Book 3, pg. 137, column 1.

[72] D Douglas, 'FDIC waging legal battle against hundreds of former bank leaders' Washington Post 23rd August 2013 http://goo.gl/ZFjNjx last accessed on 19 September 2014.

[73] It is worth mentioning that the MFSA is already adopting the approach of taking action against the officials of licensed entities. For example in 2017 it issued a reprimanded against the directors of a collective investment scheme and restricted their activity for a period of two years for failing to effectively monitor the activity of the fund manager. M Vella, 'Former Finance Minister gets MFSA reprimand over Falcon Funds fiasco' MaltaToday 05.10.2017 https://www.maltatoday.com.mt/business/business_news/81029/former_finance_minister_tonio_fenech_gets_mfsa_reprimand_over_falcon_funds_fiasco#.Xzzz9mgzY2w accessed 18.08.2020.

202 C. P. BUTTIGIEG

Consequently, it is submitted that in the absence of robust supervision and effective enforcement action the adoption of financial regulation to safeguard the investors and the financial system would be futile as these objectives would not be realised.

4   Conclusion

This chapter has examined the AIFMD from Malta's perspective and analysed the most significant points made by Malta during the negotiation process, the transposition and implementation of the AIFMD. It is argued that the changes brought about by the AIFMD and the policy decisions made by Maltese authorities during the transposition process have strengthened the regulatory framework for investor protection and financial integrity in Malta. However, the implementation of the AIFMD does not stop here. The development of new regulation to address the risks that emerge from the financial system is an ongoing project, and presently the debate is once again focusing on whether asset managers are systemically relevant.

ESMA continues to undertake projects that will strengthen the comparability and sharing of data on fund management in Europe between financial supervisors. These projects form part of the European effort to pool more data and to strengthen the mechanisms for the monitoring of the financial system to identify possible threats to financial stability. In this connection, the systemic relevance of asset managers and whether large players should be treated as SIFI is a topic, the outcome of which may have a considerable impact on the way we look at the asset management industry and the future regulation and supervision of this field of business. The present debate revolves around the idea that fund investors are subject to panics and destabilising 'runs' that can create 'fire sales' that drive down markets, and spread damage to ther investors and institutions.[74] As

[74] US Office of Financial Regulation, 'Asset Management and Financial Stability' September 2013 http://goo.gl/Y0fbq7; Financial Stability Board (FSB) and International Organisation of Securities Commissioners (IOSCO), 'Consultation – Assessment Methodologies for Identifying Non-Bank Non-Insurer Global Systemically Important Financial Institutions' January 2014 http://goo.gl/ZNI24f; A Haldane, Speech – Bank of England 4th April 2014 http://goo.gl/KpjVgx; S Maijoor, Can asset managers be too big to fail? ESMA 10th June 2014 http://goo.gl/KNl07G; International Monetary Fund, 'The Asset Management Industry and Financial Stability' Chapter 3, Global Financial Stability Report 2015; Financial Stability Board, 'Policy Recommendations to Address Structural Vulnerabilities from Asset

a result, policy action will likely continue being taken to impose on such players additional requirements on capital, recovery and resolution.[75]

Nevertheless, the debate is still ongoing, and clearly, not everyone agrees with such proposals.[76] The issue remains an open question, but it is an important one as any action in this regard will most certainly have an impact on the regulation of asset management and the industry's future development, including Malta's financial centre.

Management Activities' 12 January 2017; European Systemic Risk Board, 'Recommendations on Liquidity and Leverage risks in Investment Funds' 7 December 2017; European Systemic Risk Board, 'Recommendation on Liquidity Risks in Investment Funds' 6th May 2020.

[75] See the macro prudential rules in the Capital Requirements Regulation (Regulation (EU) No 575/2013); the Capital Requirements Directive (Directive 2013/36/EU) and Bank Recovery and Resolution Directive (Directive 2014/59/EU).

[76] US SEC Commissioner Gallagher on the OFR Report, 15 May 2014 http://goo.gl/1XFFW4; Hal S. Scott, Director of the Committee on Capital Markets Regulation and Professor – Harvard Law School http://goo.gl/w7npwX; and P Scott Stevens, 'Preserving the Unique Role of Asset Management' Speech at Fourth Annual Malta Conference 18 September 2014 http://www.ici.org/pressroom/speeches/14_pss_malta all documents were last accessed on 13 October 2014.

CHAPTER 9

Long Term Residency Rules in Malta: An Undefeatable Obstacle Course for Third-Country Nationals?

Ivan Mifsud

1   Introduction

Malta's economic boom has resulted in its attracting foreigners to its shores, mostly for work. This includes third-country nationals who for work purposes require a Single Permit. Single permits are granted for one year and are renewable. After several years they can apply for long term residence, which gives them more rights and a certain amount of flexibility they would not have enjoyed until then, but obtaining this requires satisfying several formalities. These formalities were made more onerous a few years ago when the local legislation was amended, introducing 'integration measures' which resulted in it becoming nearly impossible to apply for long term residence status successfully. It is argued that Malta profiteers from this near impossibility.

I. Mifsud (✉)
University of Malta, Msida, Malta
e-mail: ivan.mifsud@um.edu.mt

I. Sammut, J. Agranovska (eds.), *The Implementation and Enforcement of European Union Law in Small Member States*,
https://doi.org/10.1007/978-3-030-66115-1_9

Malta is a magnet for foreign workers, owing to a strong economy which not only survived the downturn of 2008 but went on to flourish and grow, leading to the current economic boom.[1] The demand for workers in different sectors, including health, construction and catering, is extremely high[2] and is predicted to continue in this respect.[3] Workers flock to Malta from other EU member states, and also from outside the European Union.[4] Third-country nationals, with whom this chapter is concerned, are required to apply for Single Permits, which must be renewed annually. Still, in due course, these third-country nationals may seek Long Term Residency. The procedures followed are based on the relevant EU Directives, as transposed into Maltese legislation.[5] Acquiring a single permit requires the satisfaction of several formalities. Still, such is the demand for foreign labour that the responsible state entity has streamlined the procedure and made it easier to complete successfully. The author of this chapter is concerned with the next step, which is the fact that while in theory, a third-country national can seek long term residence, with all the benefits this brings with it, in practice, the Maltese Government has transposed the long-term residency rules into Maltese law through Subsidiary Legislation 217.05, in such a way that is intentionally aimed at making it extremely difficult if not downright impossible, for third-country nationals to obtain long-term residence status.

2   THE INITIAL STEP: OBTAINING A SINGLE PERMIT

Subsidiary Legislation 217.17 seeks to transpose into Maltese Law, the European Council's Directive 2011/98/EC of 13 December 2011. It lays down the procedure to be followed when applying for a Single Permit for residence and work purposes in Malta. These applications are handled

[1] https://home.kpmg.com/mt/en/home/insights/2017/05/an-analysis-of-the-maltese-economy.html accessed on 18 February 2018.
[2] 30,564 EU workers and 12,407 non-EU (official statistics tabled on the House of Parliament on 26 June 2018).
[3] 'Malta needs foreign workers, Joseph Muscat tells Unions' (The Malta Today, 2 May 2018).
[4] '43,000 foreign workers in Malta. Cabinet backs plan to bring over non-EU workers' (Times of Malta, 27 June 2018). This figure, on Maltese standards, is considerable, given that Malta's population stands at 432,331 (http://www.worldometers.info/world-population/malta-population/ accessed on 9 September 2018). These foreign workers represent ten per cent of the total population.
[5] Subsidiary Legislation 217.17.

by Identity Malta[6] but must be preceded by efforts on the employer's part to recruit a local person or other EU Citizen, before applying for a Single Permit. As part of the vetting process, Identity Malta consults a number of other stakeholders, including Jobsplus.[7] Among other things, Jobsplus verifies that such efforts have been undertaken and that the employment of a third-country national is well and truly a last resort because the Labour Market Test[8] has not yielded any suitable candidates. The process for obtaining the Single Permit, in practice, requires patience and perseverance, because of all the formalities which have to be satisfied, in terms of copies of documentation required and other formalities such as giving feedback after advertising vacancies, and confirmation of the integrity of letters of recommendation. It is, however, doable, and Identity Malta is as flexible as the rules permit, because the government is under pressure from prospective employers, who need permits for their workers.

3 AFTER FIVE YEARS: APPLYING FOR LONG-TERM RESIDENCE

After a minimum of five years residing in Malta on a Single Permit, or rather five Single Permits at €280.50 each,[9] a third-country national might wish to apply for Long Term Residency. The relevant legislation[10] states as its purpose that of implementing the provisions of Council Directive 2003/109/EC and 2011/51/EU concerning the status of third-country nationals who are long-term residents.[11] If the individual succeeds in

---

[6] https://identitymalta.com/?lang=mt last accessed on 18 February 2018.

[7] The government authority responsible for employment-related issues.

[8] As it is referred to. This involves advertising the vacancy on Jobsplus' vacancy for at least two weeks, giving feedback to Jobsplus on the manner in which any interested applicants were treated and stating why none were chosen for the job, taking out two paid advertisements in the local press and then giving further feedback to Jobsplus on how the process went. Only after all this may somebody apply for a Single Permit. A number of positions listed in the 'Malta Vacancy Exemption List', are exempt from the 'Labour Market Test'. Furthermore vacancies related to the i-gaming and blockchain industry are not only exempt from the Labour Market Test but in fact applications for single permits are expedited, to the extent that single permit applications are processed within a week.

[9] The fee levied by Identity Malta for each application, including renewals. An exception is made for homebased personal carers for the elderly, the fee of which is €27.50.

[10] S.L.217.05

[11] Except where stated otherwise, these Council Directives shall be referred to as 'the Directive'.

obtaining long term residence, they obtain several rights which they did not previously enjoy.[12] Here however lies the crux: they must first reach that stage. Once long term residence status is obtained, Third Country Nationals are no longer merely tolerated[13] on a year-by-year basis, but enjoy several rights and freedoms.

However, as already stated, one has first to get there, and obtaining Long-Term Residence requires:

- continuous legal residence in Malta for five years before the application for long-term residence;[14]
- proof of stable and regular resources having subsisted for a continuous period of two years before applying for long-term residence;
- proof of appropriate accommodation comparable with that of a Maltese family;
- a valid travel document;
- sickness insurance.[15]

The above list is not exhaustive: 'integration conditions' to be satisfied are listed in regulation 5(3)(a) and (c):

---

[12] These include automatic renewal of such status every five years and access to self-employed activity (regulations 8 & 11, S.L.217.05). The granting of long term residence status has been viewed as a positive development (Theodora Kostakopoulou, *Invisible Citizens? Long Term Resident Third Country Nationals in the EU and their Struggle for Recognition* in Richard Bellamy and Alex Werleigh (eds) *Citizenship and Governance in the European Union* (2001) (Continuum Studies in Citizenship) 180.

[13] The country's interest is clearly to import labour to sustain economic growth. That is its only interest in the matter. It thus tolerates these third country nationals, because it needs them. The author intentionally uses the term 'tolerates' in the civil law sense where tolerance justifies enjoyment of a thing until the conceding party clearly indicates that they are withdrawing the concession (*Philip Agius v. Emanuel Agius*, Court of Appeal, 30 May 2014 p. 14). The author intends that while the relationship is regulated by law thus granting the individual an amount of legal certainty (e.g. all other things being equal, one knows that they are in Malta for a year once the permit is granted) the government makes no commitment with the individual third country national beyond the one year period and enjoys discretion granting, not renewing, or under particular circumstances even withdrawing the permit (for example if an illegality is committed the single permit is withdrawn; similarly if the worker loses their job the permit is also terminated).

[14] Ibid., reg. 4.

[15] Ibid., reg 5(2).

- attendance of a course of at least one hundred hours' duration, on the social, economic, cultural and democratic history and environment of Malta in the last twelve months' before applying for long term residence, and achieving at least seventy-five per cent pass mark in an examination on these topics;
- providing evidence that the necessary fees charged concerning the courses, etc., have been paid.

The first requirement, achieving a seventy-five per cent pass mark in a written examination on Maltese history and the environment is steep. By comparison, the pass mark when reading for a degree at the University of Malta is forty-five per cent.[16] The author of this chapter draws parallels with *Commission/Netherlands*,[17] which concerned a fee of 800 Euro to be paid for a long term residence. While the Court recognised the Member State's discretion when levying fees, such fees should not limit the *effet utile* of the Directive. The Court also ruled that procedural rules such as fees could not restrict the acquisition of the status and that the fee was disproportionately high, being seven times higher than the fee for a national identity card. The author queries whether a 75 per cent pass mark limits the *effet utile* of the Directive and that it is disproportionally high when compared with pass marks such as those required at the state-owned University to successfully read for a degree including an LL.B. (Hons.), and M.A. (Advocacy). Furthermore, persons of a very low level of education are excluded from ever getting long term residence, because they will be unable to follow a course and sit for an exam.

The requirement regarding payment of fees attracts apprehension on the author's part, mostly because of the way the requirement is worded.[18] While immigrant integration is a national competence,[19] it is submitted that listing payment of fees as an 'integration condition' is highly

---

[16] https://www.um.edu.mt/__data/assets/pdf_file/0003/258753/GradingSheet.pdf accessed on 30 September 2018.

[17] C-508/10, judgment of 26 April 2012.

[18] '5(3)(a) In order to be eligible to apply for long-term resident status, a third country national shall provide evidence that he has complied with the following integration conditions.... (c) provides evidence that the necessary fees charged in relation to the courses, examinations and certificates referred to above have been paid' (Reg 5(3)(c)).

[19] https://ec.europa.eu/migrant-integration/the-eu-and-integration/framework accessed on 13 December 2018.

questionable. 'Integration' is officially described as 'inclusion'.[20] One understands that dues have to be settled, but to label such dues as 'integration conditions' is legislatively wrong: fees are nothing other than means how to raise money. They have nothing to do with inclusion or integration. Secondly, the specific wording where fees are concerned also leaves the door open for an evil administrator to impose prohibitively expensive fees despite the earlier cited *Netherlands* case. If these are made prohibitively expensive, then they will serve as a barrier to prospective long term residents. There is reason to be concerned with the wording of the law, especially when one compares with other local legislation where fees are concerned, but the government has different priorities. In development planning for example, with the construction industry regarded as a pillar of the Maltese economy and a developers' association which makes no secret of its relationship with the major political parties,[21] fees are imposed. Their payment is mandatory, but the lawmaker not only made an effort to keep these on the low side[22] but even catered for extending credit to developers.[23] One may also make comparison with Article 9 of the Freedom of Information Act,[24] where the lawmaker specifically guarded against abuses when levying fees and ensured that fees are not a barrier to the right of access to information.[25] Nothing of the sort exists to protect prospective long term residents; on the contrary, these are labelled as 'integration conditions' when they are anything but conducive to such inclusion.

---

[20] 'Communication from the Commission to the European Parliament, the Council, the European Economic and Social Committee and the Committee of the Regions', Brussels, 7.6.2016 p. 2. It considers pre-departure and arrival measures, education, employment and vocational training, access to basic services, active participation and social inclusion.

[21] 'For business, political parties are like two big shops says Chetcuti' (Malta Today, 10th November 2015) and 'Both Labour and the Nationalist party leaders have courted Sandro Chetcuti, the president of the Malta Developers Association, to attract the might of the construction lobby to their electoral chances' Malta Today, 12th April 2017.

[22] 'Developers' Association welcome reduction in MEPA tariffs' (Malta Today, 12 April 2013).

[23] Reg. 5, S.L.552.12.

[24] Laws of Malta, chapter 496.

[25] '9.(1) Subject to subarticle (2) and to any regulations issued under this Act, a public authority may charge a fee to an applicant for access to a document in accordance with this Act.

(2) Any fee set by a public authority shall not exceed the cost of making a document vailable to the applicant, whereas if regulations issued as aforesaid prescribe a range of standard fees,

such fees shall not exceed the average cost of making documents available to applicants.

The situation gets worse. While prospective long-term residents may save up or borrow money to pay the fees, and perhaps depending on their level of education, find the time to attend the stated courses and pass the exam in Maltese history and the environment with flying colours, it is a different matter concerning the following integration requirement stipulated in regulation 5(3)(b):

> Regulation '5 (3) (*b*) has obtained a pass mark of at least sixty-five per cent after being assessed by the competent authorities to have achieved the equivalent of Malta Qualifications Framework Level 2 in Maltese;'

In 2006 when S.L.217.05 was originally enacted, there was no mention of 'integration conditions', and regulation 5 of 217.05 used to read as follows:

> 5. (1) A third-country national wishing to obtain long-term resident status shall apply in writing to the Director.
>
> (2) When applying for long-term resident status in accordance with sub-regulation (1), the third-country national shall provide evidence that he has
>
> (a) stable and regular resources which are sufficient to maintain himself and the members of his family without recourse to the social assistance system in Malta and which would be equivalent to, at least, the amount of the national minimum wage in Malta with an addition of another twenty per cent income or resources for each member of the family;
>
> (b) accommodation regarded as normal for a comparable family in Malta and which meets the general health and safety standards in force in Malta;
>
> (c) a valid travel document;
>
> (d) sickness insurance in respect of all risks normally covered for Maltese nationals for himself and the members of his family;
>
> (e) met the conditions set out in regulation 4.

> (3) Regulations issued as aforesaid may provide for the payment of a fee specifically for the processing of a request for access to documents, and for the payment of such a fee on presentation of the request.
>
> (4) Where a public authority decides to charge an applicant a fee, it shall advise him accordingly and inform him that he has the right to complain to the Commissioner under article 23 if he feels that the fee is excessive:
>
> (----)
>
> (5) A public authority may waive any fees payable in respect of a particular application if, in the opinion of the authority -
>
> (a) the fee payable is so small as to be not worth collecting; or
>
> (b) payment of the fee would cause financial hardship to the applicant, bearing in mind the applicant's means and circumstances...'

No exams were required; no courses had to be attended. The pendulum began to swing the other way, from 'doable' to the other extreme, with the 2010 amendment,[26] when the 'integration conditions' were introduced, including the language exam at seventy-five per cent pass mark. What follows is the exact wording of the 2010 addition[27] to regulation 5 of S.L.217.05:

> (3) To be eligible to apply for long-term resident status, a third-country national shall provide evidence that he has complied with the following integration conditions, namely:
>
> (----)
>
> (b) has obtained a pass mark of at least seventy-five per cent after being assessed by the competent authorities to have achieved the equivalent of Malta Qualifications Framework Level 2 in either Maltese or English; and
>
> (c) provides evidence that the necessary fees charged concerning the courses, examinations and certificates referred to above have been paid.

The inclusion of 'integration conditions' is permissible, according to Council Directive 2003/109/EC of 25 November 2003.[28] At first glance, one finds no objection to attempts to integrate these people with Maltese society, or to making them learn some Maltese economics, history, etc. As regards passing an examination in either English or Maltese, it is also acceptable to require long term residents to be able to communicate in either of Malta's official languages and to assess them in one way or another. Considering what long-term residence implies, including that a person moves from being tolerated in Malta practically solely on the basis that their labour is needed, to a right to remain here which in due course can even lead to full Maltese and EU Citizenship, should not come without effort on the third-country national's part. If it involves taking lessons and studying, one may argue that the third-country national should do what it

---

[26] L.N. 370 of 2010.

[27] As it originally stood, prior to the 2014 amendment discussed below.

[28] Artice 5(2) of which reads as follows: '2. Member States may require third-country nationals to comply with integration conditions, in accordance with national law.' Also article 14(3): 'Member States may require third-country nationals to comply with integration measures, in accordance with national law. This condition shall not apply where the third-country nationals concerned have been required to comply with integration conditions in order to be granted long-term resident status, in accordance with the provisions of Article 5(2). Without prejudice to the second subparagraph, the persons concerned may be required to attend language courses.'

takes if they truly want to become a long term resident within the European Union. Dora Kostakopoulou writes that 'citizenship allegedly must be earned'.[29] Yet she warns that this approach is 'anachronistic', while Triadifilopoulos regards such an approach as a 'new brand of old-style xenophobia'.[30]

One must bear in mind that the EU Directive specifically requires as follows:

> *(10) Għandu jiġi preskritt sett ta' regoli li jirregolaw il-proċeduri għall-eżami tal-applikazzjoni għall-istatus ta' residenti ta' perjodu twil ta' żmien. Dawk il-proċeduri għandhom ikunu effettivi u maniġġabbli, u jagħtu kont ta' l-ammont normali tax-xogħol tal-amministrazzjonijiet tal-Istati Membri, kif ukoll ikunu trasparenti u ġusti, sabiex joffru ċ-ċertezza legali adattata lil dawk konċernati. Dawn ma għandhomx jikkostitwixxu mezz biex ifixklu l-eżerċizzju tad-dritt tar-residenza.*

The author intentionally cited the Directive in the Maltese tongue, to give the reader a taste of the Maltese language and its complexities, with words derived from English superimposed on a Semitic foundation, and with special spelling and letters such as the 'ħ' with a slash as opposed to the 'h' without one and the 'ż' with a dot as opposed to the 'z' without one. In English, the cited provision reads:

> (10) A set of rules governing the procedures for the examination of the application for long-term resident status should be laid down. Those procedures should be effective and manageable, taking account of the normal workload of the Member States' administrations, as well as being transparent and fair, to offer reasonable legal certainty to those concerned. They should not constitute a means of hindering the exercise of the right of residence.[31]

The cited provision lays down two important principles, the first being that the member state authorities have the right to regulate procedures and examine requests for long-term residence. Still, while doing so, the same authorities must be fair and also they must not abuse their authority

---

[29] 'The Anatomy of Civic Integration' *The Modern Law Review* (2010) 73(6) 935.

[30] Triad Triadafilopoulos (2011) Illiberal Means to Liberal Ends? Understanding Recent Immigrant Integration *Policies in Europe, Journal of Ethnic and Migration Studies*, 37:6, 861–880.

[31] Emphasis added by the author.

to create hurdles on the course of those seeking long-term residence. It is also noteworthy that the Directive speaks about the 'right of residence'. Long-term residence is depicted as a right, not a concession gracefully bequeathed by the ruling bureaucracy on the common man. The bottom line is that those who satisfy reasonable requirements are to be granted long-term residence in the member state. The same Member State may even impose less stringent requirements, but not more:

> 17. 'The possibility of applying more favourable national provisions is not excluded by the Treaty...' Regrettably, the same Directive allows for the imposition of integration measures: '5(2) Member States may require third-country nationals to comply with integration conditions, in accordance with national law'.

Here lies the undoing of the Directive, with integration being cited as a guise for restrictions.[32] As already stated, as a result of the 2010 amendments, obtaining long term residence became much more difficult. However, things took a turn for the worse in 2014[33] with regulation 6(c) being amended: '(c) in paragraph (b) of regulation 5(3) thereof the words "in either Maltese or English" shall be substituted by the words "in Maltese".'

In 2015[34] another amendment was passed: '2. Regulation 5 of the principal regulations shall be amended as follows: (----) (b) in paragraph (b) of sub-regulation (3) thereof, for the words "at least seventy-five per cent" there shall be substituted the words "at least sixty-five per cent".'

The bottom line is that one of the 'integration measures' is that the third-country national seeking long-term residence must sit for an exam in written Maltese, and must obtain a mark of at least 65%. As stated above, Maltese is no easy language to master, the more so where writing it is concerned.

---

[32] S K Goodman does not mince her words, explaining how the imposition of such integration conditions could be a 'significant impediment' to the goal of integration and referring to the 'alternative motivation' behind immigration rules. The policy makers are using 'integration measures' to impose restrictions. (Sara Wallace Goodman (2011) Controlling Immigration through Language and Country Knowledge Requirements, West European Politics, 34:2, 235–255).
[33] L.N. 197 of 2014.
[34] L.N. 366 of 2015.

4   SEEKING TO ADDRESS THE SITUATION

The resulting situation is as the present that the third-country national must sit for a written exam in the Maltese language and obtain a minimum mark of sixty-five per cent, down from the seventy-five per cent required imposed in 2014. The author of this chapter had long objected to this requirement and also sought to convince the authorities that the clock should be turned back to pre-2014 when a prospective long-term resident had to pass an exam in either English or Maltese. In this regard, a complaint was lodged with the European Commission on 23rd July 2016.[35] It was submitted that while the language of Malta is Maltese, according to article 5 of Malta's Constitution both English and Maltese are our official languages, and a knowledge of English suffices to live and work in Malta, and for integration purposes. The author also submitted an online search, which indicates that at least in 2016 when the complaint was lodged, the Maltese Government has raised its bar much higher than others within the same European Union (Table 9.1):

It was further submitted to the EU Commission, that:

> From http://www.bbc.co.uk/languages/european_languages/countries/index.shtml it emerges that those of the above EU Member States which impose a language requirement, only require knowledge concerning their official language. Malta seems to be an exception, with the government has raised the bar for third-country nationals, by imposing a high pass mark in one of its two official languages, which happens to be far from easy to learn and also under the circumstances not conducive towards further integration; in the sense that the Maltese people know English so well that nobody will be excluded from society by not knowing how to read and write in the Maltese language!

Finally, it was submitted that this requirement fails the Proportionality criteria, being neither suitable nor necessary for achieving the aim, whether this aim is 'integration' (for the reasons given earlier, namely that knowledge of Maltese language is not required for integration in Malta), or the aims intended to be reached by Council Directive 2003/109/EC.

The EU Commission acknowledged receipt of this complaint by email dated 12th October 2016 and sent a 'Pre-Closure' letter on 10th January

[35] Ref: Chap (2016) 1968.

Table 9.1 Language requirements for residence permits

Italy	No language requirement listed	http://www.poliziadistato.it/articolo/10723-EC_residence_permit_for_long_term_residents/
France	"Evidence that you have a good knowledge of the French language."	http://www.expatica.com/fr/visas-and-permits/Moving-to-France-Guide-to-French-visas-and-permits_101096.html
Germany	"possess adequate German language skills."	http://www.expatica.com/de/visas-and-permits/A-guide-to-German-citizenship-and-permanent-visas_108795.html
Netherlands	"You have to prove that you are integrated into Dutch society, and can speak, read and write Dutch by taking a civic integration exam."	http://www.expatica.com/nl/visas-and-permits/Dutch-permanent-residence-in-the-Netherlands_108418.html#NonEUPermanent
Belgium	The requirement to prove that you can speak one of the three languages is linked with citizenship, not residence.	http://www.expatica.com/be/visas-and-permits/How-to-apply-for-Belgian-citizenship_100133.html
Cyprus	Certificate of knowledge of the Greek language (level A2) for foreigners (if necessary)	http://www.moi.gov.cy/moi/CRMD/crmd.nsf/All/D0B62F3A3B68AFA8C2257D2C0037B99D?OpenDocument
Austria	Proof of basic language proficiency in German	http://www.austria.org/residence-permit/
Luxembourg	Any document proving the applicant's integration into Luxembourg society (e.g. certificate of language courses, club member card, testimonial evidence)	http://www.guichet.public.lu/entreprises/en/ressources-humaines/recrutement/ressortissant-pays-tiers/resident-longue-duree/
Sweden	No mention of the language requirement	http://www.migrationsverket.se/English/Private-individuals/EU-citizens-and-long-term-residents/Long-term-residents/Long-term-resident-in-Sweden.html

Bulgaria	No mention of the language requirement	http://www.investbg.government.bg/en/pages/starting-a-business-residence-permits-certificates-cards-121.html https://www.angloinfo.com/bulgaria/how-to/page/bulgaria-moving-residency-residence-permits
Spain	No mention of the language requirement	http://www.expatica.com/es/visas-and-permits/How-to-get-Spanish-citizenship_107634.html
Sweden	No mention of the language requirement	http://www.migrationsverket.se/English/Private-individuals/EU-citizens-and-long-term-residents/Long-term-residents/Long-term-resident-in-Sweden.html

2017. The EU Commission made some interesting observations, namely that:

- in Case C-579/13, the Court of Justice of the EU observed that the acquisition of knowledge of the language of the host country facilitates communication, encourages interaction and the development of social relations. It also makes it less difficult for third-country nationals to access the labour market and vocational training;
- since Maltese is one of the two official languages of Malta, which is considered the 'mother tongue' by the almost totality of the Maltese population, to impose the knowledge of Maltese as a precondition for long term residence status should be considered as falling within the discretion left to the Member States by Article 5(2) of the Long-term Residence Directive (LTR) Directive;
- Regarding the compliance of integration conditions with the principles of proportionality and effectiveness, in the same Case C-579/13 the Court held that 'since the obligation to pass an examination... ensures that the third-country nationals concerned acquire knowledge which is undeniably useful for establishing connections with the host Member State, it must be held that such an obligation does not, by itself, jeopardise the achievement of the objective pursued by Directive 2003/109, but may on the contrary contribute to their achievement"; and that "the means of implementing that obligation also must not be liable to jeopardise those objectives, having regard, in particular, to the level of knowledge required to pass the civic integration examination, to the accessibility of the courses and material necessary to prepare for that examination, to the amount of fees applicable to third county nationals as registration fees to sit that examination, to the consideration of specific individual circumstances, such as age, illiteracy or level of education".

The EU Commission concluded that, based on the information provided, it was not able to assess whether the means of implementing the Maltese language test for the acquisition of the LTR status are liable to jeopardise the objectives of the LTR directives. The author was invited to provide further information which might demonstrate the existence of an infringement or a continued infringement of EU law.

In reply to the above, through an email dated 2nd February 2017, the EU Commission was informed as follows:

The means of implementing do indeed jeopardise the objective sought to be achieved, for the following reasons:

i.   venue. The courses in the Maltese language are held at Hal Far, which is way outside the urban zone and very difficult to access by public transport.
ii. time of courses. These are held at around 16.00. This means that to attend the course in the highly inaccessible area of Hal Far, the third-country national will have to catch a bus at about 14.00. Which employer is willing to let his staff leave work so early, to attend a course in Maltese, that will not benefit the employer at all, but only the employee?
iii. how regularly the courses are held. The organisation of these courses is supposed to be 'demand-driven'. Members report to the Malta Serb Community that they have asked to attend a course leading to Maltese exam and were told that no such courses were available for the time being. This situation is so bad that some NGOs in Malta are trying to secure funding to hold the courses themselves at more user-friendly times, in more accessible locations and more frequently; it is hereby respectfully submitted that the fact that NGOs are considering this option indicates the extent to which the government is failing in its obligation;
iv. level of education. Please keep in mind that the bulk of third-country nationals who come to Malta, come for work purposes. They are labourers, who therefore have a low level of education. This makes it even harder for them to attend the courses and obtain the required level and marks in their eventual exam.

By means of a letter dated 14 December 2017, the Directorate General, Migration and Home Affairs informed the author of this chapter that following initial analysis of the issues raised, it concluded that further information is required from the national authority concerned before it could respond fully to the letter of complaint. The complaint was transferred to the EU Pilot application under reference EUP(2016)8993. The Commission undertook to assess whether there are grounds to launch a formal infringement procedure. On 19 February 2019, the same Directorate General informed that 'based on the information provided by the Maltese authorities' it concluded that Malta was acting within the discretion which the LTR Directive allows. Because no details were given as to what information the Maltese authorities provided, and on what the Commission based its conclusions, the author of this paper wrote back to the same Directorate that 'the reply... should be reasoned and backed by the statistics and information which led your Unit to conclude that the

Maltese Government's position is proportionate and, importantly, that the Maltese Government is not abusing the discretion which the LTR directive tolerates...'.

5   FINAL OBSERVATIONS

Moritz Jetz refers to the balance between achieving integration of foreigners on the one hand, without undermining the effectiveness, objective and purpose of the relevant directives. Integration measures are perceived as being legitimate objectives, at least in principle, but must not serve to filter people.[36] This is indeed the concern of the author of this chapter: Malta needs foreign workers, and for this reason, the Maltese Government has worked continuously to streamline the process of applying for and processing of applications for Single Permits. This, however, is as far as it seems to go: long term residencies do not suite the Maltese government. One must keep in mind that the Maltese authorities are benefitting from this situation: the country benefits from the income generated from fees linked with the annual renewal of residence permits; the government is also benefitting from third-country nationals enjoying fewer rights[37] and from a situation where people come to work and then pack up and leave when things get too tough because they have no ties with Malta and no right except to reside for work in Malta. It is indeed of concern that the Maltese Government benefits from tightening the rules; it is also of concern to read statements such as:

> It was a timely reminder to the Maltese that they owe a large part of their present prosperity to foreign workers and should be wary of killing the goose laying the golden eggs. "Like every country which becomes wealthy, we need to attract people who do certain kinds of work, and these people are themselves creating wealth—they are paying National Insurance, and since many will leave within six or seven years, they will not even receive any pension."[38]

---

[36] 'Integration measures, integration exams, and immigration control: *P and S* and *K and A*' (53: 1065–1088, 2016).

[37] Which implies less obligations on the Country.

[38] These are the reported words of the Maltese Prime Minister https://www.maltatoday.com.mt/news/national/85584/analysis_malta_foreign_workers_pensions_population#.W5mDTugzaM8 accessed on 12 September 2018.

The Maltese Prime Minister, as cited above was undoubtedly depicting the reality as it is, this being that foreign workers move on before they can reap the reward of having lived in Malta and paid national insurance. The question, however, remains, whether they would be so ready to move if long-term residence and the rights which come with it were not next to impossible to obtain? Easing long term residence requirements by amending or removing the 'integration measures' would be less convenient and less profitable for Malta and therefore, to the minds of some, the Maltese language exam must remain, together with the other exams and the extremely high pass marks. It would also help Malta's coffers that the fees attached to applications for single permits remain, no matter how affordable or unaffordable they may be.

CHAPTER 10

Industrial and Intellectual Property Rights and Malta's EU Accession

Jeanine Rizzo

1 Introduction: Pre-accession

Malta's intellectual property regime is one which mirrors the nation's more recent political history. It is a reflection, through and through, of Malta as a nation: influenced by English law during the time as a British colony, moving on to standing alone in the country's interest once Malta achieved independence and became a republic, shaped by international alliances and more recently by European Union membership. According to information released by the Maltese Industrial Property Registrations Directorate (hereinafter the "IPRD"), the vesting of rights to intellectual property owners has been possible in Malta since 1911 in respect of copyright and since 1899 for inventions, trademarks and designs.

The Industrial Property (Protection) Ordinance (1900) and the Copyright Act (1911) which were in force in Malta were forward-looking pieces of legislation since they were based on UK intellectual property laws. In 1899 Malta had laws for the protection of patents, designs and

J. Rizzo (✉)
University of Malta, Msida, Malta

© The Author(s), under exclusive license to Springer Nature Switzerland AG 2021
I. Sammut, J. Agranovska (eds.), *The Implementation and Enforcement of European Union Law in Small Member States*,
https://doi.org/10.1007/978-3-030-66115-1_10

trademark. Medicines could be granted patents, for instance. This was avant-garde at the time.

Once Malta achieved independence in 1964, things started to change with a push for Malta to become, in its own right, a member of various intellectual property (hereinafter "IP") international agreements. Malta worked to ratify the Berne Convention for the Protection of Literary and Artistic Works in 1964 and the Paris Convention for the Protection of Industrial Property in 1967. These were followed shortly by Malta's ratification of the Universal Copyright Convention in 1969. Malta kept moving forward in the IP realm, and shortly thereafter, in 1977, joined the World Intellectual Property Organisation ("WIPO"). Some years later, Malta positioned itself as a founder member of the World Trade Organisation ("WTO") in 1994. WTO membership required ratification of the Agreement on Trade-Related Aspects of Intellectual Property Rights ("TRIPS Agreement"). The TRIPS Agreement bound Malta as of the year 2000.

Updating Malta's laws in view of a possible accession to the EU had also begun in the 1990s, which meant that Malta's laws were being revised to incorporate the EU's *acquis*. In 1996, Malta's application to become an EU Member State was frozen, interrupting pre-accession works which were already ongoing. However, this did not stop the legal work that was going on in the background. Especially concerning IP, Malta did not only have the EU *acquis* to prepare for, but there were also international obligations that had to be tended to.

The year 2000 was a pivotal year for Malta's IP laws. By that time, Malta's application to join the EU had been revived. Laws had to be reviewed and updated not only because Malta was gearing up for membership of the European Union, but also because Malta was under an obligation to update its laws due to the WTO TRIPS Agreement responsibilities. Malta had negotiated a five-year transition period for implementation of the TRIPS Agreement provisions. This ran in parallel with the EU pre-accession project which entailed re-examining and reworking Malta's laws across the spectrum, naturally also encompassing Malta's IP laws as part of such a project.

2   NEGOTIATING MALTA'S IP LAWS

As Malta worked towards EU membership, the EU in its own right was implementing legislation that encompassed basic rules and requirements which were enshrined in various international agreements—which have been run through above. The resulting situation was that Malta, in its own steam, was gearing up for implementation and ratification of those international agreements, while at the same time balancing other rules which were introduced by the EU's *acquis*. This led to a delicate exercise by the Maltese negotiators and law drafters, the focus of which was always to keep Malta's best interests as the focal point and as a guiding light during EU accession negotiations.

It is for this reason that negotiators and law-makers were looking at the instances in existing Maltese legislation which gave Malta a competitive edge and worked towards preserving them or extending them (through a derogation) for as long as permissible. One shining example of this is the derogation for generic medicines which was negotiated pre-accession. Maltese patent law provided a rule whereby persons were allowed to carry out certain limited actions which would normally constitute an infringement of a third party's registered patent—in the world of generic pharmaceuticals, and this would, for example, include, testing the product and packaging the product, processes which would usually take years to complete. This is commonly referred to as the Roche-Bolar exemption, named after the US case which paved the way. Malta was, and still is, a host nation to producers of generic pharmaceutical products. However, this was incompatible with EU rules. Therefore a derogation was successfully negotiated and agreed to in order not to disrupt one of Malta's industries.

3   THE EFFECT OF ACCESSION ON IP LAWS

In the lead-up to Malta's accession, IP laws, as already mentioned, were the Industrial Property (Protection) Ordinance (1900) (the "Ordinance") which dealt with trademarks, patents and designs, and was last amended in 1998 before being replaced; and the Copyright Act, which dealt with copyright and was enacted in January 1970 with the last amendment carried out in 1995 before being repealed and replaced. As work progressed on the implementation of the *acquis*, the Ordinance was reworked, and its focus split so that some of the intellectual property rights were given their own separate legislative Act. That is why in the year 2000, the publication of Acts dealt with more specific types of IP rights: a new Copyright Act, Chapter 415 of the Laws of Malta; the Trademarks Act, Chapter 416 of the Laws of Malta; and the Patents and Designs Act, Chapter 417 of the Laws of Malta—the latter dealing with both patents and designs.[1]

It was not just these Acts which were promulgated in the field of IP. Malta Customs, for instance, also had to undergo a pre-accession revision of Customs laws related to IP. The overlap between Customs and IP found its fulcrum in the 2000 Intellectual Property (Cross-Border Measures) Act (Chapter 414 of the Laws of Malta), which is a piece of legislation which combines *ex officio* Customs action, with private action, mirroring and implementing EU legislation in this regard. Thanks to Chapter 414, applications may be filed by IP rights-holders who wish to alert Customs of their IP in a bid to fight counterfeiting. This Act has been a successful tool in Maltese Custom's arsenal, with the Maltese office gathering numerous accolades for the sterling work done. It has been reported that Malta Customs ranks third overall in the EU[2] for the number of seized counterfeit goods, with a total of 2.4 million counterfeit articles confiscated in 2018.[3]

The European Union legislation had a widespread effect on the laws which deal, in a large or a small way, with IP rights. So much so that there are too many EU laws with an IP element to list here. Suffice it to say that it was not just the main Acts dealing with the individual IP rights and Customs laws that were affected. Still, the spillover was far greater: laws dealing with food, geographical indications of origin, product labelling, wine, eco-labels, medicines, spirit drinks, domain names, genetically modified organisms, consumer protection, comparative advertising and food labelling were all affected in some way or other. This is either due to there being a legislative act directly dedicated to the IP subject, or of the treatment of IP, or IP repercussions forming part of a wider piece of EU legislation. Whether a Regulation or Directive, these laws were all reflected into Maltese law and are applicable in Malta.

For the sake of brevity, this chapter shall only reflect on the laws dedicated to the individual IP rights: the Copyright Act; the Trademarks Act;

---

[1] https://legislation.mt/ last accessed on 1 July 2020.

[2] https://timesofmalta.com/articles/view/malta-ranks-third-in-eu-for-number-of-fake-goods-intercepted-by.736394 last accessed on 1 July 2020.

[3] https://ec.europa.eu/taxation_customs/sites/taxation/files/2019-ipr-report.pdf Report on the EU customs enforcement of intellectual property rights: Results at the EU border, 2018, last accessed on 1 July 2020.

the Patents and Designs Act; together with ancillary and subsidiary legislation such as the Enforcement of Intellectual Property Rights (Regulation) Act or the Artists Resale Rights Regulations under the Copyright Act.

4 COPYRIGHT

As already mentioned, Malta's Copyright Act has mixed roots which reflect the country's past as a colony. While some countries and authors look at the EU's involvement in copyright legislation as *dirigisme*, the ultimate aim is the harmonisation of rules across all EU Member States, since there remain large swathes of differences among the Member States and their transposition of EU Copyright Directives. More recently, the EU's specific aim has been to enable copyright protected goods and services to move freely within the internal market—this can be seen from the Regulations and Directive passed in 2017 and 2019. Malta played an important role in the first half of 2017 since the listed EU copyright laws were discussed and negotiated under the Maltese presidency of the Union.

Currently, the EU's copyright regulatory framework is comprised of a set of thirteen Directives and two Regulations:

1. Directive on rental right and lending right and on certain rights related to copyright in the field of intellectual property ("Rental and Lending Directive"), 19 November 1992 and codified on the 12 December 2006;
2. Directive on the coordination of certain rules concerning copyright and rights related to copyright applicable to satellite broadcasting and cable retransmission ("Satellite and Cable Directive"), 27 September 1993;
3. Directive on the legal protection of databases ("Database Directive"), 11 March 1996
4. Directive on the harmonisation of certain aspects of copyright and related rights in the information society ("InfoSoc Directive"), 22 May 2001;
5. Directive on the resale right for the benefit of the author of an original work of art ("Resale Right Directive"), 27 September 2001;
6. Directive on the enforcement of intellectual property right ("IPRED"), 29 April 2004;
7. Directive on the legal protection of computer programs ("Software Directive"), 23 April 2009;

8. Directive on the term of protection of copyright and certain related rights amending the previous 2006 Directive ("Term Directive"), 27 September 2011;

9. Directive on certain permitted uses of orphan works ("Orphan Works Directive"), 25 October 2012;

10. Directive on collective management of copyright and related rights and multi-territorial licensing of rights in musical works for online use in the internal market ("CRM Directive"), 26 February 2014;

11. Regulation on cross-border portability of online content services in the Internal Market ("Portability Regulation"), 14 June 2017;

12. Directive on certain permitted uses of certain works and other subject-matter protected by copyright and related rights for the benefit of persons who are blind, visually impaired or otherwise print-disabled (Directive implementing the Marrakech Treaty in the EU), 13 September 2017;

13. Regulation on the cross-border exchange between the Union and third countries of accessible format copies of certain works and other subject-matter protected by copyright and related rights for the benefit of persons who are blind, visually impaired or otherwise print-disabled (Regulation implementing the Marrakech Treaty in the EU), 13 September 2017;

14. Directive laying down rules on the exercise of copyright and related rights applicable to certain online transmissions of broadcasting organisations and retransmissions of television and radio programmes (amending the Satellite and Cable Directive), 17 April 2019;

15. Directive on copyright and related rights in the Digital Single Market ("DSM Directive"), 17 April 2019;

Apart from the above, additional instruments harmonise the legal protection of topographies of semiconductor products. At the same time, other legislative acts such as the E-commerce Directive and the Conditional Access Directive contain provisions relevant to the exercise and enforcement of copyright.

Internationally, the EU legislative acts reflect Member States' obligations under the Berne Convention, the Rome Convention, the 'TRIPS' Agreement and the 1996 WIPO Copyright Treaty and the WIPO Performances and Phonograms Treaty. More recently, the EU signed two other WIPO Treaties: the Beijing Treaty on the Protection of Audiovisual

Performances and the Marrakesh Treaty to Facilitate Access to Published Works for Persons who are Blind, Visually Impaired or otherwise Print Disabled. As one can easily discern, the EU's approach to copyright matters has been piecemeal—especially when this is compared to the treatment of other IP rights. It started in 1992, with the horizontal approach adopted concerning rental and lending rights and certain related rights. This Directive focused on certain matters within the copyright ecosystem, namely neighbouring rights (i.e. those rights afforded to performers, producers and broadcasters), and the rental and lending right. The 1996 Database Directive introduced a *sui generis* IP right—a new IP right dedicated to the protection of databases per se. This new right targeted a lacuna in the space left by technological developments and the ever-increasing use of databases in commerce.

The amendments brought about in Maltese copyright law in the year 2000 included the above developments—we see the Copyright Act introducing the rental and lending right as one of the acts which are exclusively within the control of the copyright owner, together with reproduction and broadcasting; the *sui generis* database right was given its own space within the Copyright Act, which is separate to the protection of databases under copyright; the term of copyright was extended from 25 years *post mortis autoris* to 70 years *post mortis autoris*, thanks to the Term Directive.

Fundamental changes were later brought about by the InfoSoc Directive in 2001—introducing the "making available" right to deal with new ways of data exchange on the Internet, most notably file sharing; the introduction of legislative protection for digital rights management (DRM) systems, and the creation of many different limitations to copyright, i.e. exceptions to copyright infringement. In terms of the latter, the EU enacted a list of permitted acts, which marked a change in Maltese law from our previous list of permitted acts which included the umbrella term "fair dealing". This umbrella term was removed, marking a shift from the Common Law "fair use" exception, in favour of the European system whereby each type of permitted use is specifically listed—the EU left the implementation of these limitations voluntary on all Member States, apart from one limitation which protected users from claims of copyright infringement due to transitory and incidental copies being made by hardware without any intervention by the user, such as those which are done automatically when software is running. This latter limitation was mandatory on all Member States, including Malta, and has been transposed into the Copyright Act as we know it today. As for the other listed limitations,

Malta transposed them all, introducing all the exempted scenarios to Maltese copyright law.

Malta's membership with the World Intellectual Property Organisation also meant that in 2009, Malta acceded to the WIPO Copyright Treaty and the WIPO Performances and Phonograms Treaty. The EU had also implemented these treaties into its laws—with the result that Malta's transpositions of the Treaties were not simply done to fulfil Malta's obligations as a party to these Treaties, but also as an EU Member State. This makes the transposition process doubly delicate: having to balance national interests with obligations arising due to EU membership.

It is not just the Copyright Act which has been shaped by the EU's harmonisation efforts. Subsidiary legislation under the Copyright Act also reflects the EU's influence on Maltese laws: the creation of the artist resale right and the rule that artists of visual and plastic works of art are to receive part of the sale price on the second or subsequent sale of their art via an art market professional; the legislation for orphan works; the reworking of legislation regarding the establishment and functioning of collective rights-management organisations; and the extension of the term of copyright for neighbouring rights from 50 years to 70 years from the date on which the work has been produced or communicated to the public. These are all separate acts of subsidiary legislation which transpose separate EU legislative acts dealing with each particular subject.

The more recent amendments regard the implementation of the Marrakech Treaty on access by the visually impaired. We also await the transposition into Maltese law of the controversial DSM Directive which includes new limitations to copyright infringement, including the infamous Article 13 (now Article 17 of the Directive).

While trying to be as brief as possible, it can be seen that Maltese copyright laws have been greatly influenced not only by the international conventions to which Malta is a party but also by the EU copyright *acquis* and harmonisation efforts by the EU in this sector.

5   TRADEMARKS

From occupying one part of the Ordinance, the subject of trademarks soon migrated to having its own dedicated legal Act. The 2000 Trademarks Act transposed EU legislation on the subject—most notably the Trademarks Directive. Maltese law, therefore, introduced the definition of a trademark as harmonised by the EU, while putting in place provisions dedicated to defining trademarks, listing the absolute and relative ground of refusal of a trademark application, laying down the parameters of trademark infringement and outlining the corresponding trademark limitations.

Looking through the EU trademark *acquis*, one can see that the first steps taken to approximate the laws between the Member States started in 1988.

1. European Union trademark delegated regulation (repealing Delegated Regulation (EU) 2017/1430), 2018
2. European Union trademark implementing regulation (repealing Implementing Regulation (EU) 2017/1431), 2018
3. European Union trademark regulation, 2017
4. Directive to approximate the laws of the Members States relating to trademarks, 16 December 2015
5. Regulation amending Council Regulation (EC) No 207/2009 on the Community trade mark and Commission Regulation No 2868/95 implementing Council Regulation (EC) No 40/94 on the Community trademark, and repealing Commission Regulation (EC) No 2869/95 on the fees payable to the Office for Harmonisation in the Internal Market (Trade Marks and Designs), 16 December 2015
6. Council Regulation on the Community trade mark, 26 February 2009
7. Directive of the European Parliament and the Council to approximate the laws of the Member States relating to trademarks, 22 October 2008
8. Council Regulation on the Community trade mark, 20 December 1993
9. First Council Directive to approximate the laws of the Member States relating to trademarks, 21 December 1988

The European Union had also, very importantly, set up its own Community Trade Mark. This trademark registration process grants the owner a right that is valid across all EU Member States, present and future. This has, in recent years, been reformulated and developed by the EU, and is now called the European Union Trade Mark ("EUTM") and it is administered by the EU Intellectual Property Office ("EUIPO") which is based in Alicante, Spain. Trademarks are registered rights, meaning that the EU in creating the EUTM has created a registration system for trademarks comprising not only of a legal foundation but also an administrative office which runs a registration process, as well as presiding over litigation (including mediation) regarding trademark conflicts. This is no small feat and is set up by the Trademarks Regulation.

Running in parallel are the legal acts, the Directives, which approximate the laws of the different Member States which have their own national, or in the case of the Benelux regional, trademark registers and registration processes. In this way, the gaps existing between trademark laws of the different Member States are slowly closing.

This effectively had an impact on Malta in two ways: (1) the Maltese national system suddenly had to coexist with the European trademark system, and (2) national laws had to be upgraded to fit into the harmonisation efforts of the Union.

On the registration front, having a European system coexist alongside a national system meant that two registrations had to exist in parallel: the national trademark and the EUTM. The EU Regulations, therefore, created the rule that a EUTM, as an object of property, shall be dealt with in its entirety, and for the whole area of the Union as a national trademark registered in the Member State. A EUTM application which has been accorded a date of filing shall be equivalent to a regular national filing. This has led to the creation of further rules where national courts are appointed as Union courts when deciding on matters (such as infringement) related to EUTMs. This happened recently in Malta where the First Hall of the Civil Court, had to exercise its role as a Union court since the trademark being invoked in the proceedings was a EUTM.

Coming to the harmonisation of Maltese trademark law with EU law, changes took place when the law on trademarks migrated from the Ordinance to the Trademarks Act, Chapter 416 of the Laws of Malta, and therefore in line with EU trademark Directives. The definition of a trademark and the absolute and relative grounds for refusal of a trademark application was introduced in the 2000 Act. These were stark changes to the rules as provided for in the Ordinance. The Ordinance contained more procedural rules than substantive rules, with Chapter 416 introducing more substantive rules, such as the grounds for refusal of a mark, as referred to above. However, the basis for trademark law had similar roots throughout. Another main change that stands out is that under the Ordinance a trademark had a lifespan of fourteen years, while under the Act a trademark had a term of 10 years. Until a few years ago, trademark attorneys in Malta were renewing trademarks for clients which were valid for 14 years from the date of application if that application was filed before January 2001—which is the date when Chapter 416 came into force.

Quite apart from the substantive and procedural changes to Maltese law that were brought on by Malta's accession to the EU, membership meant that Malta had a seat at the table when it comes to the IPRD. The IPRD represents Malta on the EUIPO Administrative Board and Budget Committee and also participates in liaison meetings on trademarks, designs and technical cooperation. In addition, the Maltese office participates in and implements several projects under the Cooperation Fund administered by EUIPO, which seeks to create and provide tools and projects for the benefit of the national IP offices and users of the trademark and design systems in the EU. One project the IPRD has successfully implemented with the assistance of the EUIPO has been the creation of an online portal for all IP registration and filing needs, moving us from a paper-based system to an online filing system. The EUIPO, based in Alicante, also outsources work to the IPRD concerning checking the morality of word marks applied for as EUTMs—this is because a mark which infringes public morality is denied registration according to EU law.

More recently, we have seen the EU's reworking of trademark law with the enacting of a new Regulation as well as a new Directive. 2019 has seen some further developments in the area of trademarks in Malta—recent EU changes to the trademark canon meant that significant changes had to be carried out to the Trademarks Act, so much so that the Act was reformulated—Malta waved goodbye to Chapter 416 of the Laws of Malta and welcomed Chapter 597 of the Laws of Malta. This did bring some significant changes, not only to substantive provisions but also to procedural trademark matters in Malta.

Chief of all substantive changes was the major overhaul of the definition of a trademark—it is a definition that has evolved from existing in a world where all marks are registered in a book-type register, therefore paper-based, with all of its limitations, to a reality of digital registers, which are searchable at the click of a button. Key issues which in the past would have stopped a trademark from being registered (according to the famous Sieckmann criteria that a trademark needed to be clear, precise, self-contained, easily accessible, intelligible, durable and objective) were being transformed with the advent of new technologies and rendered non-issues (in some cases). We, therefore, see the most controversial change to the definition of a trademark, that migrated from the trademark needing to be "graphically represented" to being "capable of being represented on the register". In the past, a sound recording could not be graphically represented unless it was reduced to musical notes; however, in this digital age, we can play and hear a sound file with the click of a button.

The EU's Trademark Directive, which is the legislative Act dedicated to harmonising national laws, repeated this evolved definition from the Regulation. However, it also brought with it an important procedural change for trademarks in Malta: it re-introduced an opposition process for trademark applications at the national level. Briefly, what this means is that once a trademark application is submitted, before the trademark is registered, third parties are given the right to put forward their objection to the mark being registered due to their having a pre-existing, and conflicting, right. The EUTM system contains an opposition process, so Maltese practitioners and rights-holders were already exposed to this procedure.

Maltese practitioners were exposed to an opposition process earlier than this—this is because the trademark filing and registration system under the Ordinance also included an opposition procedure. The transposition of the new trademark Directive has meant a return to the opposition process. This brings with it renewed responsibilities on the IPRD in Malta, and in turn, has meant that the IPRD's relative grounds searches have greatly diminished to an examination of identical or similar marks registered only in Malta. This has shifted much of the onus off of the IPRD and onto third parties, who would need to file an opposition application should they wish to see the application stopped. Until 2019, the IPRD would carry out relative grounds searches for all trademark filings based on searches in the national and EU registers. This is now becoming very limited, and the IPRD will take on a new role with oppositions—which includes the publication of an official gazette for all trademark filings.

6   PATENTS AND DESIGN RIGHTS

The two remaining IP rights are being dealt with together since Maltese law has placed them within the same Act. However, they are not dealt with equally by the EU—while design rights form the subject of Union law and harmonisation along similar lines as trademark law, the road to a unitary patent has been fraught with obstacles.

6.1 Designs

Designs were dealt with under the Ordinance in Malta, with a part dedicated to "Designs and Models of Manufacture". However, the Ordinance provided that if a new design of a model of manufacture is registered, the proprietor will obtain the copyright, and not a standalone design right as we know it today, in the design or model. This registration would last for a five-year term, which could be renewed for a second and then the third term of 5 years. This all changed in 2003 to reflect the EU's Design Right.

The EU first started discussions on introducing the Design Right in the late 1950s. However, concrete legislation on the subject only materialised in 1998—by way of comparison, the Community Trademark was introduced in 1996. The 1998 Directive was a harmonising tool between the Member States, cementing the role of designs in the business world.

In 2001, the EU enacted the Designs Regulation, which went on to create two new Union-wide rights: the Registered Community Design and the Unregistered Community Design Right. The EUIPO, or OHIM as it was known then, started accepting applications for registered designs in 2003—right around the time Malta's laws were updated to cater for designs. The Unregistered Design Right, on the other hand, requires no registration as the name itself suggests. Similarly to copyright, the unregistered design subsists automatically. The reason why the EU introduced both a registered and unregistered design is to cater to the needs of all industries.

Chapter 417, the Maltese Patents Act, was updated in 2003 to become the Patents and Designs Act. The expanded title meant that a new part was added to the Act which dealt solely with designs. This was done via an Act that amended various legislation, including the Trademarks Act to introduce terms such as "European Union" and "Member States" in preparation for EU accession, while also transposing the EU's Designs Directive into Maltese law.

Malta, therefore, had a new system dedicated to designs—one that recognised the design as a standalone right, no longer linked to copyright. The requirements of novelty and individual character were introduced for the successful registration of a design right. And once Malta became a member of the EU in 2004, just like with trademarks, the national design right started to coexist with EU-registered design rights as well as the Unregistered Design Right.

6.2   Patents

The EU has a turbulent past with enacting legislation to create a single, unitary patent that would cover the EU as one territory with one application and one registration. Efforts had started in the 1970s and have failed along the way due to the lack of unanimous consensus. Once EU rules changed due to the larger membership of the Union, the enhanced cooperation procedure allowed a majority of Member States to come together, and this procedure was used to create a Unitary Patent package.

The motivation behind this is the streamlining of the patent application process for the benefit of EU applicants, especially small and medium-sized enterprises. The applications, translations, costs and numerous different time frames for patent applications has been a deterrent to many applicants. The EU has therefore undertaken to ease this burden by creating a unitary patent system in collaboration with the already-existing European Patent Office (EPO)—the EPO is not an EU institution, but an independent pan-European office established by the European Patent Convention (EPC). Malta acceded to the EPC in 2007.

Much can be said about the unitary patent and the long and winding road that has brought the EU to the adoption of the unitary patent and how we are all still waiting for its fruits to come into force. Twists and turns have cropped up at every opportunity—such as Constitutional issues, the establishment of patent courts and tribunals, and Brexit. Briefly, the EU's unitary patent trajectory was born in a Commission proposal in December 2010, which culminated on 17 December 2012, when the European Council and the European Parliament reached a formal agreement on two EU Regulations for the creation of the enhanced cooperation for the Unitary Patent—these deal with the creation of a patent with unitary effect, and with a language regime applicable to the unitary patent respectively. Spain and Italy challenged these Regulations, but the CJEU later rejected their actions. Alongside the regulation stands the Agreement on a Unified Patent Court (UPCA) which is an intergovernmental treaty between participating states outside the framework of the EU, published by the Council of the European Union on the 11 January 2013. The UPCA is open for accession to all EU member states and was first signed on the 19 February 2013 by 24 EU Member States, including all the states participating in the enhanced cooperation, and subsequently signed by Italy and Bulgaria, leaving only Poland, Spain and Croatia. The rule in force is that following ratification by at least 13 states, which must include

Germany, France and the UK, the provisions for the Unitary Patent and the language regime will enter into force. Therefore, the 'patent package' is a legislative initiative consisting of two regulations and an international agreement that lay the foundation for the creation of unitary patent protection in the EU, with the ratification of the UPCA still ongoing.

It must be said, however, that the unitary patent has played a decisive role in influencing Maltese laws because the Patents and Designs Act has been amended to transpose into Maltese law provisions required for Malta's adherence to the patent package.

The unitary patent is planned to coexist in parallel with national patents, and the pre-existing structure for European Patents ("EP") as administered by the EPO. Lest we forget, the EPO (similarly to the Patent Cooperation Treaty "PCT") does not grant a European Union-wide (or international) patent; on the other hand, it is an application simplification process, whereby an application may be submitted to one central office, and after a centralised examination of the application, the application is transmitted to the territories listed by the applicant at the time the application was submitted. This effectively means that the EPC and the PCT route would, at a second stage, communicate the application to the national (or regional in some cases) offices indicated by the applicant and live therein as a national patent.

The unitary patent is the EU's attempt to replicate the ease and cost-efficiency of the EUTM and EU Registered Design for patents. However, the lack of unanimity, the language issues, and the court system created have all proved to be spokes in the wheels in the achievement of this vision. For if the unitary patent is ever achieved, many small and medium-sized enterprises, including many Maltese businesses, would benefit from a system which would rid the applicant of multiple patents coexisting in various European jurisdictions, the various technical translations required of the patent document, and therefore the corresponding costs (costs which would be application costs and maintenance costs, and translation fees). The unitary patent would rid an applicant of multiple proceedings within the EU (or within a majority of EU member states), with the EU-block being dealt with as one territory. In contrast, other extra-EU territories can be dealt with one at a time. At present, it is simply too much of an administrative and financial burden on all applicants.

The unitary patent system is accompanied by legislation regarding language and translations, and the creation of a Unitary Patent Court (the "UPC"). The central section of the UPC will be located in Paris, with sections scheduled for Munich, and originally for London. Furthermore, the UPC will consist of national and regional courts—for Malta, and the decision was taken to have a national court since participation in a regional court would only place further financial burdens on Maltese parties who would have to travel outside of Malta to attend regional UPC hearings.

A minimum of thirteen Member States is needed to ratify the UPCA. Out of those thirteen, there is a small group of countries who must ratify the Agreement for it to come into force. Malta has ratified the UPCA, and Chapter 417 was amended to introduce the Patent Tribunal for this reason. However, with Brexit and the UK listed as one of the mandatory jurisdictions, questions arise concerning the future of the UPCA and the unitary patent.

Over and above all that has been discussed so far, the subsidiary legislation under Chapter 417 has focused on supplementary protection certificates for pharmaceutical products, and the protection of plants. In 2007, Malta became a member of the Patent Cooperation Treaty and of the European Patent Convention—two international instruments which strive to achieve a more streamlined patent application process. The IPRD represents Malta in both fora, furthering Malta's best interests in this technical subject. Chapter 417 was therefore amended to transpose into Maltese law not only the provisions related to the unitary patent and the UPC but also the EPC and PCT.

7   EXHAUSTION OF RIGHTS

One of the main elements the EU introduced was the Single Market within the Union. This is, in turn, founded on the pillars of fundamental freedoms—one of which is the fundamental freedom of movement of goods and services within the internal market. European Union law strives to find a balance between the rights and obligations created throughout the *acquis*. One such balance is that which must exist between the exclusive rights granted by intellectual property rights, which are very much like monopoly rights, and free competition and the fundamental freedoms operating within the Single Market.

One way in which the EU has managed to strike this balance is by introducing the doctrine of exhaustion. The doctrine posits that when a right-holder introduces a product bearing an IP right, say a trademark, on the internal market, the right-holder loses any control they may have had on that particular product bearing that IP right. Not all rights arising under the IP rights are extinguished after the first introduction on the market, but a large majority are. Taking the example of trademarks, once a product bearing the mark is placed by the right-holder, or with his consent, on the market, the right holder's right to use the trademark to limit the subsequent movement of that particular product is extinguished. That means that once the product is legitimately placed on the market, it can move around freely. This was done to curb the partitioning of the market based on different trademark registrations or any such limitations. In the realm of trademarks, we would see producers use different names and therefore registered trademarks in different parts of Europe, for example. It is important to note that when referring to "product" here, it is not the product generally, but a particular item with a unique serial number.

For this reason, parallel importation became a legitimate endeavour, as long as the product which is being parallel imported, also referred to as the "grey good", was first placed on the market by the right-holder or with their consent. This led to a spate of cases in which the limits of the doctrine of exhaustion were tested. These can form the subject of their own dedicated examination, and we shall not dive into such details here, but suffice it to say that the Court of Justice of the European Union ("CJEU") has been regularly called upon to determine how far parallel importers could go. This was due to several developments, testing the limit of what could be bought from one Member State to be sold in another. What started to happen was that importers were removing the trademark applied in Member State A and replacing it with the trademark used in Member State B. This was made possible because the right-holder was using various trademarks in different jurisdictions. The problem being faced here is that the removal of a trademark amounts to an act of trademark infringement—and it is also a criminal offence in Malta. Other issues featured, for example, the removal of the product from the packaging it was purchased in and the repackaging in a format that the consumers in the Member State were accustomed to.

This led to instances of stickers being placed on packaging to replace the new branding with the known one, or even full repackaging of the product itself by the parallel importer. The over-stickering and the repackaging were too much for some right-holders who sued to safeguard their intellectual property rights. As a result, a list of "dos" and "don'ts" handed down by the CJEU in this regard, so that the rights of the right-holders are balanced with the free movement of the product.[4] The CJEU held that a trademark owner might legitimately oppose the further commercialisation of a pharmaceutical product imported from another Member State unless:

- Use of the trademark to oppose the marketing of the imported products would amount to the artificial partitioning of the markets between member states.
- The repackaging cannot affect the original condition of the product inside.
- The new packaging identified who has repackaged the product and who the manufacturer is.
- The presentation of the repackaged product is not such as to be liable to damage the reputation of the trademark and its owner.
- The importer gives notice to the rights-holder before the product is put on sale, and, on-demand, supplies the rights-holder with a specimen of the repackaged product

This is a unique example of the Courts further complementing substantive law by laying down several requirements that must be adhered to avoid trademark infringement. It has also influenced Maltese law, in the Parallel Importation of Medicinal Products Regulations subsidiary legislation 458.40 enacted under the Medicines Act.

8   ENFORCEMENT

Civil remedies are the subject of the Enforcement Directive enacted by the EU—in a bid to harmonise the remedies offered to EU nationals across the Member States.

This was transposed in Malta by the Enforcement of Intellectual Property Rights (Regulation) Act, Chapter 488 of the Laws of Malta, which introduced separate processes dedicated solely to IP rights and their infringement. There has been widespread cautiousness concerning these rules across the EU, no less in Malta. However, what this legal Act has done, was to shine a spotlight on how IP rights infringement requires their proceedings to preserve evidence and quantify damages.

---

[4] *Bristol-Myers Squibb v Paranova AS*, joined cases C-427/93, C-429/93 and C-436/93.

The Enforcement Directive (2004/48/EC) covers civil remedies on the enforcement of IP rights with rules on evidence, interlocutory measures, seizure of infringing goods, injunctions, and costs. Its main aim was to be an excellent tool in the fight against piracy and counterfeiting by introducing harmonised measures which can be invoked in defence on all types of IP rights. Remedies available to rights holders include the destruction or recall of products from the market, award of damages, and injunctions while safeguarding the rights of the innocent bystander.

The transposition into Maltese law meant that some of the new IP enforcement measures, such as injunctions preserving evidence under Chapter 488 are very similar to the civil warrants, such as the warrant of seizure or the warrant of a prohibitory injunction provided under the Code of Organisation and Civil Procedure (the "COCP"), Chapter 12 of the Laws of Malta. This creates a legal reality whereby owners of IP rights have a choice: either make use of the precautionary measures under the COCP or those under Chapter 488. IP owners are not limited to choose either or, and many times a successful enforcement strategy will include a mix of both Civil acts under the COCP and IP-specific acts under Chapter 488. Maltese courts were, in the past and not any longer, a little rusty as to what time frame should be applied to the Chapter 488 measures—a precautionary warrant filed under the COCP is seen to within hours if not one day. In contrast, the new measures under Chapter 488 were a new animal for the Maltese courts. With experience, the judiciary has become familiar with the measures under Chapter 488 and deal with them as quickly as a Civil warrant. However, the Maltese courts have shown, in the text of their judgments, that they are sometimes uncomfortable with granting the full extent of the measures provided for in Chapter 488. Some measures, such as those on the sharing of information, are seen as being doorways to fishing expeditions and have therefore been used with extreme caution and with limitations imposed by the Maltese courts. This is a common criticism levelled at the Directive itself in the other Member States.

9 COPYRIGHT IN THE DIGITAL SINGLE MARKET

The latest Directive dealing with copyright is the controversial Directive (EU) 2019/790 of the European Parliament and of the Council of 17 April 2019 on copyright and related rights in the Digital Single Market and amending Directives 96/9/EC and 2001/29/EC—otherwise referred to as the DSM Directive.[5]

The objective of the DSM Directive is to modernise EU rules, *inter alia* the key exceptions and limitations in the areas of teaching, research and preservation of cultural heritage or use by heritage institutions and archives, treatment of data mining, and a focus, in particular, on digital and cross-border uses. The Directive seeks to achieve a fair balance between the rights and interests of authors and other right holders, on the one hand, and of users on the other.

The Directive came into force on the 17 April 2019, and the Member States should complete its transposition by the 7 June 2021. At the time of writing this chapter, Malta is working on the transposition of the Directive with consultations being carried out by the entities involved.

10   CONCLUSION

The EU's *acquis* has had a strong influence in shaping Maltese IP laws, as can be seen not only in the legal acts discussed above but in other laws such as those regulating Customs action—including the procedures for combating counterfeits—as well as in other Maltese laws such as consumer legislation and food labelling legislation which include a reference to IP rights and which, in their turn, transpose EU law in Malta. This only highlights the work being done behind the scenes, the lobbying to preserve Malta's interests as a Member State, and the legislative toll this takes on Malta's laws generally. That said, there is still much to do: the more persons and businesses utilise Malta's IP laws, the more will we test the laws currently on our books, and will highlight any areas for future development.

---

[5] Directive (EU) 2019/790 of the European Parliament and of the Council of 17 April 2019 on copyright and related rights in the Digital Single Market and amending Directives 96/9/EC and 2001/29/EC (Text with EEA relevance.) PE/51/2019/REV/1 *OJ L 130, 17.5.2019, p. 92–125.*

CHAPTER 11

The Implementation of EU Criminal Law in the Maltese Legal Order

Stefano Filletti

1 INTRODUCTION

The creation of an Area of Freedom Security and Justice (AFSJ) and developments in EU criminal law have, in a broad way, brought about a positive development in the local legal order.[1] The main contributions to local criminal law can be registered in both substantive and procedural laws. From a substantive law point of view, amendments were registered mostly in areas of financial crime and money laundering. From a procedural aspect, there were both institutional reforms as well as the implementation of specialised instruments of mutual recognition. These instruments have been implemented and applied with success. This, however, does not mean that their application is free from difficulty.

---

[1] Presentation and research derived from doctoral research project undertaken at the Faculty of Laws, University of Malta.

S. Filletti (✉)
University of Malta, Msida, Malta
e-mail: stefano.filletti@um.edu.mt

© The Author(s), under exclusive license to Springer Nature   243
Switzerland AG 2021
I. Sammut, J. Agranovska (eds.), *The Implementation and Enforcement of European Union Law in Small Member States,*
https://doi.org/10.1007/978-3-030-66115-1_11

Generally, it ought to be said that balance between these increased powers of investigation granted or allowed under mutual recognition on the one hand, and the protection of the citizen's right to privacy and data protection, on the other, is indeed a difficult balancing act to achieve and maintain.

2   SUBSTANTIVE AMENDMENTS TO CRIMINAL LAW WITHIN THE REALM OF FINANCIAL CRIME

The greatest impact which EU criminal law has had in Maltese substantive law is in the field of financial crime. This is attributable in part to the fact that at the EU level, there have been numerous legal developments in the field of protection of the financial interests of the EU.

In this field, amendments in criminal law have occurred in Malta through sporadic legislative amendments and administrative interventions. When dealing with substantive crimes relating to the protection of the financial interests of the European Union, the Maltese Criminal Code already contains relative provisions referring to various instances of fraud[2] which now adequately cover the offences within the PIF Directive. One can identify, *inter alia*, the offence of misappropriation,[3] obtaining money by false pretences[4] and the catch-all 'other fraudulent gain'.[5] The offence is aggravated if the perpetrator is a public officer or a person vested with some form of entrustment as well as aggravated by amount.

Malta also has established a solid anti-corruption legal framework[6] providing for bribery[7] (active and passive bribery of domestic public officials) and trading in influence.[8] The sanction in respect of bribery of public officials is imprisonment for a period of six months to eight years.[9] In the case of a magistrate or judge, the term of imprisonment can range from 18 months to 10 years, and in the case of a member of parliament, the

---

[2] Section 293 *et seq*, Cap. 9, Laws of Malta.
[3] Section 293, Cap. 9, Laws of Malta.
[4] Section 308, Cap. 9, Laws of Malta.
[5] Section 309, Cap. 9, Laws of Malta.
[6] Council of Europe, Group of States against corruption (2009) *Third Evaluation Round: Evaluation Report on Malta, op.cit.*, pp. 18–19, paragraphs 94–95.
[7] Chapter 9, Laws of Malta.
[8] Arts. 115, 120 and 121A of the Criminal Code.
[9] Ibid., Art. 115.

sanction is imprisonment for a term from one year to eight years.[10] In addition to imprisonment, a person convicted of bribery may also be punished with temporary or perpetual interdiction, i.e., disqualification from holding a public office or employment with the public sector.[11] The punishment for trading in influence is imprisonment for a term of three years.

The Criminal Code contains provisions regarding prescription[12] (statute of limitation rules). The length of prescription varies according to the gravity of the offence, which is generally reflected by the punishment. For example, active/passive bribery of public officials with a maximum punishment of eight years imprisonment[13] has a prescription period of 10 years, and active/passive bribery of judges with a maximum punishment of 10 years imprisonment[14] has a prescription period of 15 years. The Criminal Code provisions on active and passive bribery also apply to corruption in the private sector.[15] Corporate liability for corruption offences is also specifically dealt with in the Criminal Code,[16] which states that where the person found guilty of a bribery offence is the director, manager, secretary or other principal officers of a body corporate or has the power to represent, take decisions or bind the body corporate. The offence was committed for the benefit of that body corporate. Such a person is deemed to be vested with the legal representation of the body corporate, which shall be liable to a fine. The Code also criminalizes the conspiracy to commit an offence,[17] the attempt[18] and complicity in an attempt[19] of a criminal offence.

As can be seen, the reforms, although limited to the field of financial crime, have been of note. This is a positive implementation of EU criminal legal norms within a local domestic context.

---

[10] Ibid., Arts. 116–118.
[11] Ibid., Art. 119.
[12] Chapter 9, Laws of Malta. *See* Arts. 687–694.
[13] Art. 115(c) of the Criminal Code.
[14] Ibid., Art. 116(a).
[15] Ibid., Art. 121(3).
[16] Ibid., Art. 121D.
[17] Section 48A, Cap. 9, Laws of Malta.
[18] Section 41, Cap. 9, Laws of Malta.
[19] Section 42, Cap. 9, Laws of Malta.

3   INSTITUTIONAL REFORM

When dealing with financial crime and, in particular, the protection of the EU's financial interests, local institutions have been beefed up, and their powers increased to meet the legal expectations prevalent within the AFSJ.

The Attorney General (AG)[20] is the designated competent authority within the European Justice Network (EJN) and Eurojust, which is empowered to facilitate cooperation with other supranational agencies in Malta. The AG is not only formally represented in Eurojust[21] and actively participates in matters of coordination and facilitation of criminal activity of mutual concern, but is also the national contact point within the EJN. Within the AG's office, it is the Criminal Matters Unit, more specifically the International Cooperation Office, which is responsible for coordinating activities with the respective contact points within the network.

The Economic Crimes Unit is a specialized unit within the Maltese Police Force,[22] and it is the special branch or Unit which liaises mostly with Europol. The Economic Crime Unit handles all investigations relating *inter alia* to offences against property, corruption, embezzlement, theft, all forms of fraud, money laundering and white-collar crime. The Economic Crime Unit, therefore, is authorized to act as the official interlocutor with Europol. It is empowered to forward and request sensitive and relative data in the course of investigations as well as to request or provide assistance within Europol channels in the course of an investigation. To complement this Unit in 2019, and Asset Recovery Bureau was set up.

The Internal Audit and Financial Investigations Unit[23] is the official interlocutor of DG OLAF in Malta. The Financial Investigations and European Anti-Fraud Office Related Matters Unit within the Internal Audit Investigative Department (IAID) have the remit to conduct financial investigations in government departments and in any other public or private entities which are in any way beneficiaries, debtors or managers of public funds, including EU funds, to protect such funds against irregularities and fraud or otherwise to assess public or private entities' liability to contribute to such funds.

---

[20] Established in virtue of the Attorney General Ordinance, Cap. 90 Laws of Malta.

[21] http://eurojust.europa.eu/about/structure/college/Pages/national-members.aspx.

[22] Established in virtue of the Police Act, Cap. 164, Laws of Malta.

[23] Established in virtue of the Internal Audit and Financial Investigation Act, Cap. 461 of the Laws of Malta.

Since the IAID is the designated interlocutor of DG OLAF in Malta and is the Anti-Fraud Co-Coordinating Service (AFCOS) for Malta, the IAID Unit can conduct joint investigations with OLAF, the European Anti-Fraud Office, concerning EU funds availed of by Malta.[24] The Unit reports irregularities to DG OLAF on a quarterly basis with respect to pre-accession funds, transition facility funds, structural funds, cohesion fund and agricultural funds. The Unit also provides substantial contributions, including feedback, to various sub-units within OLAF all in charge of protecting the EU's financial interests under different facets.

As can be seen, once more, an effort was made to reform local authorities and key players to be able to interact with both EU agencies and other competent authorities of various Member States, in the proper fulfilment of Malta's obligations prevalent under EU criminal law. This, too, therefore, is another positive development in the process of implementation of EU criminal norms within a local domestic context.

4   PROCEDURAL LAW AMENDMENTS

Great reforms were registered in Maltese procedural law mostly to cater to the implementation of instruments of mutual recognition created and EU level.

4.1   European Arrest Warrants

Without a shadow of a doubt, the European Arrest Warrant (EAW) has been successfully applied in many cases. The EAW has been successful when Malta requested the surrender or return of a foreign national[25] or the surrender of persons resident in Malta to a foreign jurisdiction. There is likewise, no doubt, that the EAW, even from Malta's perspective,

---

[24] In fact Art. 2 of Cap. 461 of the Laws of Malta defines public funds as including: "funds that Government receives, pays, including funds to local councils, or is required to manage under Malta's international obligations, or under any other public funds arising under any other law".

[25] In the case *Police vs Fabio Zulian*, (decided 3 January 2015, Court of Magistrates, a request was made for the return of the accused from Torino, Italy; in the case of *Police vs Dimitrios Drossos* (decided 5 September 2012, Court of Magistrates,) a request was made for the return of a Greek national from Greece; in the case of *Police vs Stephen John Smith* (decided 28 December 2012 Court of Magistrates) a request was made for the return of an English national from London, United Kingdom.

constitutes an important investigative and judicial tool in combating crime. It has aided and facilitated prosecuting officers, to a large extent, in bringing offenders to justice. With the application of the principles of mutual assistance and recognition, the EAW is a streamlined, more efficient and less cumbersome version of the traditional extradition process.

Notwithstanding the overall success, even at the local level, of the application of the EAW, this does not mean that the process is free from hurdles or legal difficulty. Indeed one encounters some serious issues executing EAWs from an EU and local perspective.

4.1.1   Lack of Proportionality: No Stay of Execution Even If the Accused Is Willing to Cooperate

Malta has registered situations in which persons wanted in Malta would be forcibly surrendered to Malta from foreign jurisdictions even where the person wanted effectively rectifies his wrong, or where a person firmly believes that he is unjustly prosecuted. A case in point is that of *Police vs George Clayton*.[26] In this case, the accused was wanted in Malta for having, on 8 May 2009 in Malta, committed the offence of obtaining money by false pretences[27] to the detriment of several Maltese retail outlets. The offence was aggravated by amount.[28] Shortly after having committed these offences, Clayton returned to the UK. An EAW was issued against him. Pending procedures, Clayton had reimbursed the amount misappropriated. In court, he pleaded that upon adducing evidence of payment, this removed any element of criminal responsibility. The matter he argued was a civil issue. This argument was rejected by the UK Courts who ordered his return to Malta in virtue of the EAW which had been issued.

Clayton declared that he was willing to return and also admit to the charges. In addition, the original complainants in Malta declared that they were fully paid and that they had no interest whatsoever in any further criminal prosecution. The Maltese authorities were aware of the fact that the offender had paid back all items defrauded and therefore, in line with various decisions pronounced by the Court of Criminal Appeal, this fact in itself reduced liability of punishment to a great degree. Given his clean record, it was evident that Clayton was, at most, facing a non-custodial punishment and these judicial proceedings were becoming more of an

---

[26] Decided 9 December 2011, Court of Magistrates (Malta).
[27] Section 308, Cap. 9, Laws of Malta.
[28] Section 310, Cap. 9, Laws of Malta.

academic exercise. Notwithstanding all these facts, Malta kept refusing to withdraw its request for an EAW and therefore Clayton had to be forcibly remitted under arrest to Malta. Clayton was arraigned and charged with aggravated fraud. It remains unclear why Malta kept insisting on the forcible return by EAW of the accused, given the basis for the initial request had been extinguished and that, in the circumstances, the cost and expense incurred in the movement of this person accused were not justified.

Effectively, this judgment shows that insistence for the return of a person can also occur where a person rectifies his wrong to the extent that the person to be surrendered will not face a punishment of imprisonment. This highlights a potential issue of proportionality, especially when one compares the seriousness of the offence and the punishment on one side, with the pain and suffering forceable surrender on EU citizens can bring with it. Furthermore, there is no mechanism in local law to ask for a review of the decision for the issuance of an EAW or the insistence for the forceable return or surrender of an EU citizen.

4.1.2   General Comments: Proportionality

In much the same vein, it may be the case that the EAW involves pre-trial detention.[29] Some detention will be experienced given that in executing an EAW, unless there is voluntary submission, the accused under arrest will be forcibly surrendered to the executive police in Malta who will have forty-eight hours to arraign the individual, and in most cases do so under arrest. However, it may also be the case that the foreign court, when appointing and hearing the surrender case arrests the person concerned. There is no rule stipulating the exact period of pre-trial detention or its limitations in the various Member States. Therefore a citizen may experience different pre-trial detention periods depending on the legislation and efficacy of the sending State. Given the complexity of the EAW and in particular that it is seldom possible for a person concerned to challenge the merits of the request (the offence for which a person is requested) the proportionality aspect of the request or for that matter the motivation for the request in the sending State (a matter then to be taken upon the merits of the case in the requesting State), it is crucial to establish clear rules for pre-trial detention in the executing of any part of the EAW. The procedure must, at least from a temporal aspect, be standardized so that fixed time-limits would be applied across the Union. The matter, after all, is a serious

---

[29] EAW surrender proceedings can be held while the person concerned is kept under arrest.

one, involving the restriction of personal liberty of individuals still presumed innocent of any crime. One possible solution to this issue would be the introduction of trials *in absentia*. Another interesting proposition could be the introduction of deferred surrender.

4.2   Attachment and Freezing Orders

Another instrument which generates considerable interest at EU level is the cross-border enforcement of orders for the freezing of assets. Freezing orders are an essential investigative tool aimed at freezing assets in the hands of third parties, allowing for more time to conduct investigations and, more importantly, to secure the confiscation of assets upon conviction. Without such precautionary orders, assets would be dissipated even before a conviction can be secured. This tool has certain draconian effects and can be prejudicial to persons subject to similar orders. Pursuant to the application of the principle of mutual recognition and assistance, a freezing order may be issued upon a request made by a foreign competent authority,[30] according to section 435C of the Criminal Code and Article 10(1) of the Prevention of Money Laundering Act.[31] The effect is similar to a civil garnishee order and applies to all offences. This order is governed by Article 4(6) of the Prevention of Money Laundering Act.[32]

From a Maltese perspective, the freezing of assets may be the result of one of two types of orders issued by the courts. First of all, if there are criminal proceedings presently pending before the courts, then the nature

[30] The Framework Decision on the execution in the European Union of orders freezing property or evidence (2003/577/JHA) was transposed and implemented by means of Subsidiary Legislation number 9.13, Freezing Orders (Execution in the European Union) Regulations made under the Criminal Code, published in Legal Notice 397/07 and subsequently amended by Legal Notice 354/09.

[31] Prevention of Money Laundering Act, Cap. 373 of the Laws of Malta.

[32] Section 4(6) of the Prevention of Money Laundering Act: "Together with or separately from an application for an investigation order, the Attorney General may, in the circumstances mentioned in sub-article (1), apply to the Criminal Court for an order (hereinafter referred to as 'attachment order'): (a) attaching in the hands of such persons (hereinafter referred to as 'the garnishees') as are mentioned in the application all moneys and other movable property due or pertaining or belonging to the suspect; (b) requiring the garnishee to declare in writing to the Attorney General, not later than twenty-four hours from the time of service of the order, the nature and source of all money and other movable property so attached; and (c) prohibiting the suspect from transferring or otherwise disposing of any movable or immovable property."

of the order is that of a freezing order. Alternatively, in the case where no official charge has been made, and hence there are no pending criminal proceedings, then the type of order which has been issued amounts to an attachment order. In such a case it is linked with the investigation of an offence, where one is merely a suspect.

4.2.1 Lack of Proportionality: No Mechanism to Challenge Freezing Orders

It is appropriate to note that this type of order can create legal difficulties. Indeed whereas it is possible for a person to attack the issuance of a freezing order within three days for any reason, including, for instance, the lack of a valid justifiable reason for the issuance of the order or the revocation in part of the order, this would not technically be possible when the order is issued pursuant to a request from a foreign competent authority. In that case, it would not be possible to challenge in a Maltese Court the reasonableness of the request and that, if at all, would have to be done in the court of the country of issue. The three-day time-limit imposed is also too short to adequately prepare any form of application for the revocation of an order when this is done pursuant to a foreign request. It stands to reason that obtaining the relevant information from the foreign jurisdiction can take time. In fact, it has been the case that freezing orders requested by issuing States were successfully challenged in the other Member States but retained in Malta, as it would not be possible to attack the reasonableness of the request if the issuing State gives a specific counter order for the removal of the freezing order.

This system is not desirable because it can very well be the case that any foreign request could theoretically be malicious in nature. The prejudice suffered by any individual served with a freezing order is potentially great. Yet, notwithstanding this gross interference in the enjoyment of one's property, there is no discretion afforded to any presiding judge in revoking or limiting the effects of the freezing order. The judge is bound to accept blindly any request accepted as valid by the AG for the issuance of a freezing order. The only grounds of refusal are the mandatory and optional grounds in the Framework Decision ("FD"). However, no discretion or residual powers are afforded to the judicial authority in reviewing or limiting the freezing order. It can be suggested, in point of fact, that on a matter so evidently delicate, and with order so prejudicial to the interests of any person (physical or legal), one should expect that a remedy is afforded to any party feeling aggrieved with the issuance of a freezing order. One must remember that, as a result of a freezing order, all transactions are frozen, all assets are registered and frozen, and no financial institution (banks, stock exchange and other institutions) would allow movement, transfer of funds or any transactions. Furthermore, it is not possible to operate commercially or civilly in Malta since the order will be formally gazetted meaning that all assets (movables and immovables) are frozen and cannot be touched or disposed of.

The effect of a freezing order is to demand on any person to be denied some form of remedy in certain select cases. Even if one could argue that the Maltese example is one of the best expressions of mutual recognition and assistance, yet it should, by the same token, be true that a balancing act between the effects of these orders and remedies to be afforded to the persons affected has to be achieved. Therefore there is a strong case to argue that possibly this procedure ought to be reviewed in the sense that the application of mutual recognition and cooperation be scaled back slightly to afford an albeit limited right to appeal to challenge the issuance of these orders at any time for select reasons as pinpointed earlier on.

4.2.2   Quantum Subject to the Freezing Order

The problem, however, with freezing orders is wider and can create anomalous situations in their execution. The first and most evident issue relates to the quantum which is actually frozen on the issuance of a freezing order. As soon as an order is issued, all property and monies held in the name of the person concerned are frozen. The totality of assets is frozen, subject always to the right of the person concerned to withdraw monies for his or her maintenance. In other words, the effect of the issuance of a freezing order under Maltese law would entail the freezing of all assets. The effect of such orders is general and draconian. This is not an EU law requirement but will have that effect where a request is made to Malta to issue a freezing order in Malta. No distinction is made on legitimate or illegitimate gains. There is no concept of "ordinary business transactions". Above all, there is no mechanism provided for in criminal law to ask for a review of the issuance of the order or the *quantum* which is effectively frozen.

The matter amounts to a serious problem in that the freezing order, as applied in Malta, does not conform to any rule or principle of proportionality.[33] Moreover, the problem similarly arises in the execution of foreign requests for the freezing of assets. If and when the Criminal Court issues a freezing order pursuant to a foreign request, all assets of the person or company concerned are frozen indiscriminately, leading very often to various difficulties. A freezing order, pursuant to the taking of criminal action and which in other words is precautionary in nature, has a devastating and deeply prejudicial effect on the person concerned. A person affected by a freezing order cannot operate any business whatsoever and can hardly conduct an ordinary life, with access simply to a small sum of money provided for one's maintenance. Such dire consequences arising from freezing orders of this kind are untenable.

4.3   Confiscation Orders

Confiscation orders allow the Member States, subject to certain conditions, to seize and confiscate assets of subject persons in another Member State. This is an important tool to combat trans-boundary crime and to ensure the recovery of assets. That having been said, the confiscation of assets is not a matter free from legal difficulty. The FD on confiscation orders (2006/783/JHA) (as amended by FD 2009/299/JHA), the FD on Confiscation of Crime-Related Proceeds, Instrumentalities and Property (2005/212/JHA), together with the Council Directive on return of cultural objects unlawfully removed from the territory of a Member State (Directive 93/7/EEC) were all implemented into Maltese law, by virtue of SL 9.15, Confiscation Orders (Execution in the European Union) Regulations made under the Criminal Code, published in Legal Notice 464/10 and amended by Legal Notice 426/12. The implementation of these instruments means that local courts can order the confiscation of assets in Malta upon a request by a foreign authority in the execution of a foreign court order to that effect.

In principle, the implementation of the FD on confiscation orders was rather smooth. It is noted that it is the civil court which will ultimately be used to confiscate the property. Issues which arise in the execution of these orders will be discussed in the following chapter. At this stage, however, it is appropriate to mention that even though it is possible to forfeit certain

---

[33] Helenius, D., *Mutual Recognition in Criminal Matters and the Principle of Proportionality – Effective Proportionality or Proportionate Effectiveness?* NJECL 2014/3, Intersentia, 2014.

assets via the civil process in Malta, it is at present not possible to extend this to the recovery of proceeds of crime.

The brief on confiscation orders was developed further. On the 12 March 2012, a Directive proposal[34] was launched, and this identified two main legislative efforts in the field of confiscation, namely,

1. the non-conviction-based confiscation of assets and
2. third party confiscation of assets,

two areas which were found absent in the EU legal framework.[35]

In this spirit, the Commission came up with a Proposal for a Directive on the Freezing and Confiscation of Proceeds of Crime in the European Union.[36] The effect of this proposal would be to attack proceeds of crime which have been transferred to third parties who have not been convicted of any criminal offence. This is a powerful tool with which to combat organized crime, the profits generated from this illegal activity and financing of organized crime. It constitutes the next legal step in freezing and confiscation. It is based on Article 83(1) TFEU. It is apt to note that in August 2020, the minister responsible for justice in Malta announced that steps were being taken to draft local legislation to implement non-conviction-based confiscation.

4.3.1   Difficulties in Executing Confiscation Orders

Confiscation orders would be relatively simple in cases of movables or monies. These are items which can be easily identifiable, easily seized and consequently forfeited. Yet issues could arise where, for instance, a freezing order or confiscation order has been served or executed in the middle of a transaction. In a particular case, the buyer had paid for the acquisition

---

[34] Brussels, 12.3.2012, COM(2012) 85 final, 2012/0036 (COD).

[35] In fact the current legal framework on freezing and confiscation envisages the following instruments: Framework Decision 2001/500/JHA13, obliging States to enable confiscation, to allow value confiscation where the direct proceeds of crime cannot be seized and to ensure that requests from other Member States are treated with the same priority as domestic proceedings; Framework Decision 2005/212/JHA15, which harmonizes confiscation laws; Framework Decision 2003/577/JHA17, which provides for mutual recognition of freezing orders; Framework Decision 2006/783/JHA18, which provides for the mutual recognition of confiscation orders; and Council Decision 2007/845/JHA19 on the exchange of information and cooperation between national Asset Recovery Offices.

[36] 12.3.2012, COM(2012) 85 final.

of a craft in cash, not being a highly expensive one. The documents for transfer had not yet been compiled or registered. A confiscation order issued at that stage against the buyer confiscated both the craft (still registered with the vendor) and the cash actually received from the buyer in furtherance of the sale. There is actually little one can do to prevent similar situations. The problem is compounded by the fact that cash transactions do not easily leave an accurate money trail, which would ordinarily assist a court in determining the origin and motivation for the money transfer.

Even more complex and difficult situations would arise in the confiscation of immovable assets, such as property. Ironically, property might be less difficult actually to identify, although possibly somewhat more complicated to confiscate. Where the property is solely owned by the accused, without any registered privileges or hypothecs, then confiscation would be relatively simple. The confiscation would occur in favour of the Government of Malta.[37] The property would then be transferred to the Lands Authority being the authority responsible for the administration of Government property. Matters complicate themselves further where there are third party rights on the property. Typical examples could be a property which is co-owned,[38] or where there are third party creditors possessing privileges or hypothecs[39] on the property. In cases of co-ownership, it would be reasonable to assume that only the accused's portion would be confiscated. This then can either be retained or disposed of by the Government. Where third party rights are involved, the matter is no less complex. If the right is one arising out of the law, such as lease, emphyteusis, servitudes or privileges, these rights would have to be respected. In cases of registered hypothecs, such as special hypothecs, the law is silent.

4.4   Joint Investigative Teams

Joint Investigative Teams[40] (JITs) are of interest because they offer the possibility for national investigative teams to work together on crimes committed in a number of jurisdictions. This is a matter which is of

---

[37] *Il-Pulizija vs Raymond Mifsud*, Court of Magistrates decided 1st March 2012. In this case a farmhouse was confiscated following a conviction of having run an illegal brothel from this property.
[38] As defined in section 489 *et seq* of the Civil Code, Cap. 16, Laws of Malta.
[39] As defined in sections 1994 *et seq* of the Civil Code, Cap. 16, Laws of Malta.
[40] The FD was implemented in local law in virtue of the Joint Investigation Teams (EU Member States) Regulations.

relevance to the central thesis hypothesis, especially when one considers that the rules of investigation and collection of evidence vary from one jurisdiction to another. There remains a thorny issue as to the probative value of illegally obtained evidence in jurisdictions where such evidence is admissible. JITs were originally envisaged in Article 13 of the 2000 MLA Convention. Given the slow ratification of the Convention, the Commission adopted an FD on JITs.[41] It was originally envisaged that JITs would be useful to bring together the various law enforcement agencies and forces of the various Member States. However, there was great reluctance by the Member States actually to establish and create JITs. The Hague Programme also called upon States to put forward national experts and also to promote the use of JITs.

5   CONCLUSION

EU criminal law has contributed substantially to reforming local criminal law. The reform has not only given effect to Malta's commitment to implement EU criminal law rules. Still, it has enhanced its substantive and procedural laws to allow for better in-depth investigations and prosecutions of transboundary crimes of an economic or financial nature. EU criminal law has deeply impacted local law-defying the traditional insular approach taken in combatting financial crime.

Pursuant to these Regulations, the Attorney General is empowered to request the setting up of a JIT with the forces of other Member States. The terms of reference would have to be subject to a specific agreement to that effect. The overall aim would be to request for assistance in any investigation which would need to be carried out in another Member State.

[41] 2002/465/JHA which had to be implemented by 1 January 2003.

CHAPTER 12

The Implementation of European Privacy Law in Malta

Mireille M. Caruana and Joseph A. Cannataci

1 INTRODUCTION: HISTORICAL BACKGROUND

The status of privacy law in Malta, like that of all EU Member States, is complicated by the fact that it is a matter which is subject to two complementary systems of international law of which Malta is a member. Malta is a full member of the EU and as such subject to EU law such as the General Data Protection Regulation ('GDPR')[1] and Directive 2016/680 ('the Police Directive')[2] but there are important dimensions of privacy which are outside the remit of the GDPR or the Police Directive, yet which are

[1] Regulation (EU) 2016/679 of the European Parliament and of the Council of 27 April 2016 on the protection of natural persons with regard to the processing of personal data and on the free movement of such data, and repealing Directive 95/46/EC (General Data Protection Regulation), OJ 2016 L 119/1.

[2] Directive (EU) 2016/680 on the protection of natural persons with regard to the processing of personal data by competent authorities for the purposes of the prevention, inves-

M. M. Caruana (✉) • J. A. Cannataci
University of Malta, Msida, Malta
e-mail: mireille.caruana@um.edu.mt; jcannataci@sec.research.um.edu.mt

257

regulated by wider European law. The classic example here would be infringements of privacy by national security or other intelligence agencies. National security is a reserved matter in terms of Article 4 (2) of the Treaty on European Union[3] and attempts to discuss these at EU Council level, as, e.g. happened after the Snowden revelations of 2013, were consistently stymied by those Member States who chose to claim that the EU has no competence in such matters. Yet Malta is also a party to the European Convention on the Protection of Human Rights and Fundamental Freedoms of 1950 (European Convention on Human Rights, 'ECHR')[4] and the Council of Europe's 1981 Data Protection Convention (Convention 108)[5] both of which create obligations regarding the protection of privacy even in cases of national security. In those cases, Malta is obliged to provide safeguards and remedies through domestic law and, in the case of exhaustion of domestic remedies, then recourse would be possible on such matters to the European Court of Human Rights in Strasbourg.

The GDPR and the Police Directive did not set out to provide privacy safeguards and remedies in the context of national security since they would have been "ultra vires" had they tried to do so. On the other hand, many European states have, before or since the Snowden revelations, beefed up their domestic legislation and/or witnessed landmark decisions by their own national constitutional courts on privacy-related matters both within and outside the remit of the GDPR and the Police Directive. There are therefore emerging European benchmarks against which the status of privacy law in Malta may be measured, and some of these will be applied in this paper/chapter.

Prior to the GDPR, Malta enacted the Data Protection Act[6] on 14 December 2001, which implemented the EU Data Protection Directive 95/46/EC[7] and came fully into force on 15 July 2003. The passing of this

tigation, detection or prosecution of criminal offences or the execution of criminal penalties, and on the free movement of such data, OJ 2016 L 119/89.

[3] Treaty on European Union 2012/C 326/01.

[4] European Convention for the Protection of Human Rights and Fundamental Freedoms, Sept. 3, 1953, ETS 5, 213 UNTS 221.

[5] Convention for the Protection of Individuals with regard to Automatic Processing of Personal Data, ETS No.108, Strasbourg, 28/01/1981.

[6] Chapter 440 of the Laws of Malta, now repealed.

[7] Directive 95/46/EC of the European Parliament and of the Council of 24 October 1995 on the protection of individuals with regard to the processing of personal data and on the free movement of such data, OJ 1995 L 281/31.

law was motivated by Malta's adoption of the EU *acquis communautaire* in view of her bid to become a member of the European Union; following a referendum on membership held on 8 March 2003, Malta acceded to the EU on 1 May 2004. The Data Protection Act of 2001 was repealed and replaced by the Data Protection Act of 2018,[8] along with its subsidiary legislation, which came into force on 28 May 2018 to implement and further specify the relevant provisions of the GDPR.

2   THE NEW DATA PROTECTION ACT 2018

The main national legal instrument introduced to implement the GDPR in Malta is the Data Protection Act 2018 ('DPA'). The following subsidiary legislation has also been passed under the main Act:

- S.L. 586.01 Processing of Personal Data (Electronic Communications Sector) Regulations (to implement the provisions of Directive 2002/58/EC concerning the processing of personal data and the protection of privacy in the electronic communications sector, as amended by Directive 2009/136/EC. These regulations also implement, and are to be read in conjunction with, the requirements of Regulation (EU) 611/2013 on the measures applicable to the notification of personal data breaches under Directive 2002/58/EC on privacy and electronic communications.)
- S.L. 586.04 Processing of Personal Data (Protection of Minors) Regulations
- S.L. 586.06 Processing of Personal Data for the purposes of the General Elections Act and the Local Councils Act Regulations
- S.L. 586.07 Processing of Personal Data (Education Sector) Regulations
- S.L. 586.08 Data Protection (Processing of Personal Data by Competent Authorities for the Purposes of the ʹPrevention, Investigation, Detection or Prosecution of Criminal Offences or the Execution of Criminal Penalties) Regulations (These regulations transpose Directive (EU) 2016/680 on the protection of natural persons with regard to the processing of personal data by competent authorities for the purposes of the prevention, investigation, detec-

---

[8] Chapter 586, Laws of Malta.

tion or prosecution of criminal offences or the execution of criminal penalties, and on the free movement of such data.)

- S.L. 586.09 Restriction of the Data Protection (Obligations and Rights) Regulations
- S.L. 586.10 Processing of Data concerning Health for Insurance Purposes Regulations
- S.L. 586.11 Processing of Child's Personal Data concerning the Offer of Information Society Services Regulations

This chapter will comment specifically on salient aspects of the implementation of European privacy and data protection law in Malta. This will look at Malta's obligations both in terms of EU law as well as wider European law, especially the ECHR and Convention 108. It is beyond the scope of this paper to engage directly in a critical analysis of specific provisions of the GDPR itself, which as an EU Regulation is directly applicable in Malta. However, prior to engaging directly with the implementation of the GDPR in Malta, it is appropriate to consider the manner in which the fundamental human rights to privacy and data protection are protected within the national legal order. This is followed by a discussion of the reception of substantive GDPR provisions in the national legal order.

3   FUNDAMENTAL HUMAN RIGHTS TO PRIVACY AND DATA PROTECTION IN MALTA

Unlike the Charter of Fundamental Rights of the European Union (CFREU or the 'Charter'),[9] Maltese law does not distinguish between the right to respect for private life and the right to data protection.[10]

---

[9] Charter of Fundamental Rights of the European Union, OJ 2010 C 83/389.

[10] Nor does it need to. It can be easily argued that this does not detract from the level of protection in Maltese law since Article 8 CFREU does not create any new rights which were not already recognised and executable under European law prior to its introduction. The principles of data protection law in Europe are all derived from Convention 108 which in turn credits Article 8 of ECHR, i.e. private and family life, as the human right which it serves to protect. Article 7 CFREU basically replicates Article 8 ECHR and conceptually would have served equally well as a basis to found any action in law relating to data protection. For a fuller description of why and how Article 8 CFREU came into being as a compromise clause see Cannataci Joseph A. and Mifsud Bonnici Jeanne P. Data Protection Comes of Age:

Article 32[11] of the Constitution of Malta provides as follows:

> Whereas every person in Malta is entitled to the fundamental rights and freedoms of the individual, that is to say, the right, whatever his race, place of origin, political opinions, colour, creed, sex, sexual orientation or gender identity, but subject to respect for the rights and freedoms of others and for the public interest, to each and all of the following, namely -(a) life, liberty, security of the person, the enjoyment of property and the protection of the law; (b) freedom of conscience, of expression and of peaceful assembly and association; and (c) *respect for his private and family life*, the subsequent provisions of this Chapter shall have effect for the purpose of affording protection to the aforesaid rights and freedoms, subject to such limitations of that protection as are contained in those provisions being limitations designed to ensure that the enjoyment of the said rights and freedoms by any individual does not prejudice the rights and freedoms of others or the public interest.[12]

This preambular set of limitations is reflected in specific provisions legitimising derogation in the case of each right (except for protection from inhuman or degrading treatment), such as by a provision of law which is 'reasonably required in the interest of public safety, public order, public morality or decency, public health or the protection of the rights and freedoms of others'. Several provisions speak both of 'reasonably required' and 'reasonably justifiable in a democratic society'. The standard is substantially similar to that of the ECHR. This constitutional provision is extremely problematic since, as in September 2020, privacy is the only human right which, strictly speaking, is not actionable in terms of Chapter IV of the Maltese Constitution. The architecture of Chapter IV of the Constitution pivots around Article 46, which provides that:

> (1) Subject to the provisions of sub-articles (6) and (7) of this article, any person who alleges that any of the provisions of articles 33 to 45 (inclusive) of this Constitution has been, is being or is likely to be contravened in relation to him, or such other person as the Civil Court, First Hall, in Malta may appoint at the instance of any person who so alleges, may, without prejudice

---

The Data Protection Clauses in the European Constitutional Treaty, *Information & Communications Technology Law*, Vol. 14, No. 1, 2005, pp. 9–10.

[11] Which, while entrenched, is non-justiciable in terms of Article 46, unlike Articles 33–45 of the provisions in Chapter IV of the Constitution, which are declared to be justiciable.

[12] Emphasis added.

to any other action with respect to the same matter that is lawfully available, apply to the Civil Court, First Hall, for redress.

The way that Chapter IV was designed is that Art 32 (the previous Article 33) was preambular in nature, mentioning each or most of the rights then fleshed out in greater detail in Articles 33–45. Yet private and family life was one of the rights that was not taken up in articles 33–45. When the Constitution was first written, there were other rights which found themselves to be in the same position, i.e. not enforceable in terms of Constitutional Court procedures. The situation was remedied for the right to freedom of discrimination on the grounds of sex in 1991, but that opportunity to remedy matters for privacy was inexplicably lost.

There was, more recently, some debate about the matter following the publication of a White Paper on the introduction of Digital Rights in the Constitution of Malta. Whereas the then Government appeared to be driving for change to Chapter II of the Constitution, it was submitted that what was much more important in the digital age was the treatment of privacy at par with other fundamental rights. A concrete proposal was made[13] to entrench privacy through amendment of Article 41 (protection of freedom of expression) in a manner which would also reflect Malta's status as an EU member state subject to the Charter of Fundamental Rights. This amendment sought to update the Maltese Constitution for each of the four distinct interests[14] protected by Article 8 ECHR with a defined emphasis on fleshing out various aspects, including those of family life, in line with the jurisprudence of the European Court of Human Rights ('ECtHR').

3.1   Proposed Amendments to Article 41 of the Constitution of Malta

Delete existing Art. 41 and instead insert new Art. 41

Art 41—Protection of right to free development of personality and associated rights

---

[13] By the co-author of this paper, J.A. Cannataci.

[14] See also European Court of Human Rights. Guide on Article 8 of the European Convention on Human Rights, updated to 30th April 2020, https://www.echr.coe.int/documents/guide_art_8_eng.pdf last accessed on 12 October 2020.

(1) Every citizen and every natural person resident in Malta is entitled to respect of the supreme values of human dignity, the unhindered development of human personality, justice and political pluralism which shall also be assured by:

a) *the right to private and family life which includes:*

1. *within the meaning of private life, the right to develop and maintain relationships with other people and the outside world. A person's sexual life is part of his private life, of which it constitutes an important aspect. Private life thus guarantees a sphere within which a person can establish relations of different kinds, including sexual ones and thus the choice of affirming and assuming one's sexual identity;*

2. *within the meaning of family life, those relationships which arise out of marriage or co-habitation or a parent and his/her child or such other ties in substance indistinguishable from those created by the traditional family irrespective of the existence of blood ties;*

3. *informational self-determination that is the right of any natural person to choose to communicate or not to communicate information about himself or herself except where the requirement for such information is reasonably provided for by law*

4. *the right of every natural person and the obligation of all data controllers, (including all public bodies, legal and natural persons) to ensure that personal data is only collected, processed and retained in a secure manner for a public, legitimate and specified purpose for a justifiable length of time. The natural person shall also have the right to be notified of the collection and existence of such personal data and to access, demand correction and, where appropriate, deletion of all such personal data. The law shall provide appropriate safeguards for the protection of such rights in a manner where personal data is construed as being any information which can be linked to an identified or identifiable individual.*

5. *the right of any natural person to freedom from surveillance in both physical and virtual space except where such surveillance is carried out by the competent authorities when either an individual is under suspicion of having carried out or being about to carry out a specified criminal offence or for the detection and prevention of crime in*

a physical and public space provided that such surveillance is not excessive and disproportionate in a free and democratic society.

6. *the right of any natural person to freedom from interference with private communication of any form or purpose whether such communication be in writing, spoken, electronic or any other form*

7. *the right of any natural person to freely dispose of himself/herself unless by this he infringes on the rights and freedoms of other or public order.*

b) *the right to freedom of expression which includes:*

1. *Freedom of expression of thoughts, opinions, or beliefs, and freedom of any creation, by words, in writing, in pictures, by sounds or other means of communication in public spaces and in private, irrespective of whether such expression or receipt of ideas occurs in a physical or virtual space.*

2. *the prohibition of any censorship of any form of publication*

3. *freedom from interference with the citizen's access to and receipt or transmission of data using electronic means [whether wired or wireless] irrespective of whether such interference is attempted by the state or by any natural or legal person and irrespective of whether such interference is physical or electronic or economic*

4. *the free setting up of publications using any medium.*

5. *the prohibition of suppression of any publication*

6. *the obligation upon the mass media to make public their financing source which obligation shall be provided for by law.*

7. *provision by law that freedom of expression shall not be prejudicial to the right of personality including the dignity, honour, privacy of a person and to the right to one's own image.*

8. *provision by law that any instigation to national, racial, class or religious hatred, any incitement to discrimination, or public violence, as well as any obscene conduct contrary to morality shall be prohibited.*

9. *provision by law that freedom of expression shall not be prejudicial to intellectual property rights the regulation of which shall also be provided for by law;*

c) *the right to free access to public information which implies that*

1. *a person's right of access to any information of public interest held by a public body shall not be restricted.*

2. *all public bodies shall be bound to provide timely and correct information to citizens in public affairs and matters of personal interest.*
3. *public and private media shall be bound to provide correct information when producing all news and current affairs services and generally all works of non-fiction.*
4. *public radio and television services shall be autonomous. They must guarantee any social and political group the exercise of the right to an equitable portion of broadcasting time. The organization of these services and the parliamentary control over their activity shall be provided for by law.*

2) Nothing contained in or done under the authority of any law shall be held to be inconsistent with or in contravention of sub-article (1) of this article to the extent that the law in question makes provision that is reasonably required in the interests of national security, public safety, public order, public morality or decency, or public health except so far as that provision or, as the case may be, the thing done under the authority thereof is shown not to be reasonably justifiable in a democratic society.

3) Where the police or other competent authorities seize any electronic or other equipment utilized for publication and/or any output intended for publication on reasonable suspicion of it being the means whereby a criminal offence has been committed they shall within twenty-four hours of the seizure bring the seizure to the notice of the competent court and if the court is not satisfied that there is a prima facie case of such offence, that equipment or output shall be returned to the person from whom it was seized within forty-eight hours of it having been seized.

The above 2013 proposals were also intended to introduce into the Maltese Constitution explicit mention of the over-arching right to unhindered development of the personality, the conceptualisation of which was eventually recognised by the UN Human Rights Council in 2017. In this particular vision, three information-related fundamental rights: private and family life, freedom of expression and freedom of access to information were articulated in unprecedented detail, deliberately and explicitly recognising a number of associated rights including gender identity, same-sex marriage, and others, some of which were later incorporated into Maltese law at the status of ordinary legislation.

The debate on this and other matters died down with the change of Government and only enjoyed a slight reprise in the autumn of 2013. Since then constitutional change in Malta has largely been in hiatus.

For the sake of strict accuracy, it is important to note that although privacy is not an enforceable right in terms of Malta's Constitutional provisions on human rights, in actual fact, it is currently possible to sue in the Maltese courts on the grounds of "private and family life" but this is only possible in terms of the European Convention on the Protection of Human Rights and Fundamental Freedoms of 1950 ('ECHR')[15] as incorporated into Maltese law by virtue of the European Convention Act (Act XIV of 1987),[16] which extended the same right of action to the new rights derived therefrom,[17] and not in terms of Article 32 (c) of the Constitution itself. Very unusually for a piece of ordinary legislation, Act XIV of 1987 is enforceable through the Constitutional courts. It can, however, be repealed through a simple majority vote in parliament. The protection afforded by Act XIV 1987 is not considered to be at the same level as the provisions in Articles 33–45 of Chapter IV of the Constitution which is entrenched by Article 66 of the Constitution and require a two-thirds majority in Parliament to be amended. Indeed, although also covered by Act XIV of 1987, other parts of the Constitution's Article 32, specifically the protection from discrimination on the grounds of sex, have since 1987—in 1991 to be exact—been made constitutionally enforceable through a detailed provision in Article 45 of Chapter IV of the Constitution. In contrast, Article 32(c) dealing with private and family life has not received such attention. This lies at the basis of the media debate in 2013 about priorities in Constitutional reform. One of the points of that debate is that an opportunity was missed in 1991 when parts of Article 32 dealing with discrimination of grounds of sex were made enforceable in terms of Article 45 whereas no similar attention was then paid to making Article 32 (c) enforceable. Once again, privacy was then forced to take a back seat to other priorities.

It is respectfully submitted that a priority of the next round of constitutional reform should be to make the right to private and family life enforceable as a constitutional right at par with other constitutional rights and while doing so, parliament should take the opportunity to also elevate to enforceable constitutional status a number of important information-related rights which are important and relevant in the digital age. The

---

[15] European Convention for the Protection of Human Rights and Fundamental Freedoms, Sept. 3, 1953, ETS 5, 213 UNTS 221.

[16] Laws of Malta chapter 319 'European Convention Act', Act XIV of 1987.

[17] European Convention Act, Art.3.

"rights"—or better principles proposed in the White Paper of 2012 went in the right direction. Still, there are other priorities which need to be attended to in constitutional reform before "digital rights" can find their proper context. When priorities like unhindered development of personality, digital on-line privacy and informational self-determination are introduced into Chapter IV, Parliament will have an opportunity of doing that which was impossible in 1964. It is now possible to take advantage of and learn from 60 years of jurisprudence on private and family life within the European Court of Human Rights[18] and distil these into a provision with an enforceable status somewhere between Articles 33–45.

While this would be of great relevance to privacy and the flow of information in the digital age, it should be pointed out that the discussion would then necessarily go beyond "digital rights" since "private and family life" also encompasses notions like sexual preferences and the right to a family life even for couples which are not heterosexual. These are matters on which the European Court of Human Rights has ruled at length and in detail but which the Maltese Parliament came to slightly unprepared for a full and frank, unprejudiced discussion on such matters. "Digital Rights" are motherhood and apple pie when compared to hot topics in the right to family life such as "Do gay couples have an inalienable right to get married in the same way as heterosexual couples do"? Malta has, since 2013, proved that it is capable of "going from zero to hero" when it comes to the right to family life interest protected by Article 8 ECHR. It now needs to do the same when it comes to information-related fundamental rights such as those identified in the proposed draft amendment of Article 41 to the Constitution as reproduced above.

Article 38 of the Constitution of Malta is also in dire need of modernisation, as it refers in a very limited fashion to the fundamental right of bodily and spatial privacy ('no person shall be subjected to the search of his person or his property or the entry by others on his premises') without any trace of a reference to modern concerns regarding, for example, on-line and communications privacy. This may possibly be partially remedied at least by the proposed changes to Article 41 reproduced above. There is no tangible evidence regarding the precise manner in which, if at all, the EU Charter right to data protection (i.e. Art 8) may have influenced the interpretation of national law.

[18] Ibid.

Nevertheless, Article 8 EU Charter was quoted in the judgment of *Dr Jeffrey Pullicino Orlando v the Information and Data Protection Commissioner*.[19] This case concerned the sharing on the blog '*Running Commentary: Daphne Caruana Galizia's Notebook*', of articles including pictures of the claimant, a public figure (formerly a member of the national Parliament, later the Chairman on the Malta Council for Science and Technology 'MCST'), in public but not while exercising his official functions, and disclosing elements of his private life, e.g. at a restaurant or the airport with his partner. The right to privacy, as well as the right to data protection, and the rights relating to freedom of expression and journalistic freedoms, were all mentioned in this judgment—, the judge in the case, was not concerned with distinguishing the right to privacy from the right to data protection. Still, he did note that in terms of Article 2 of the DPA 2001 ' "personal data" means any information relating to an identified or identifiable natural person....'; this is a wide definition and therefore, also includes information regarding the geographical position of a person at a particular time. The judge explicitly considered the collection of this data and its uploading to and sharing on Daphne Caruana Galizia's blog to be an instance of 'processing' of this personal data, referring to the *Lindquist case* (C-101/2001, 6 November 2003). The fact that that information concerning matters that happened in public does not change the fact that processing of personal data had occurred. While quoting Article 8 EU Charter,[20] the judge proceeded to consider the appropriate balancing of the fundamental rights to privacy and freedom of expression. In seeking this balance, case-law of the ECtHR was referred to and quoted.[21] In the instant case, the judge, overturning an earlier decision of the Information and Data Protection Commissioner ('IDPC'), ruled that although the claimant was in public spaces, nevertheless the publication of that information on-line amounted to processing of personal data, and concluded that the claimant's rights had in fact been breached as public interest in sharing that private data had not been made out.

---

[19] Court of Appeal (Civil, Inferior), 30/04/2019.

[20] Ibid, at para. 14.

[21] In particular, *Satakunnan Markkinaporssi Oy and Satamedia Oy v. Finland*, ECtHR 27 June 2017.

4 THE RECEPTION OF SUBSTANTIVE GDPR PROVISIONS IN THE NATIONAL LEGAL ORDER

This section provides some highlights regarding the reception of substantive GDPR provisions in the national legal order of Malta and a review of the limited number of known instances of interpretation of selected substantive provisions of the GDPR by controllers, the national supervisory authority and/or the judiciary of Malta.

4.1 The Principles of 'Fair' Processing, Purpose Limitation and 'Data Minimisation'

In *Maltapost p.l.c. vs Information and Data Protection Commissioner*[22] the Maltese Court of Appeal (Inferior Competence) annulled a decision of the Information and Data Protection Appeals Tribunal.[23] It confirmed the original decision of IDPC. Referring to the 'European Document Retention Guide 2013',[24] as well as to the 2010 Guidelines published by the Office of the EDPS,[25] the Court ruled that the IDPC was right to establish that CCTV footage should, as a general rule, be deleted after a maximum period of seven (7) days.[26] It also agreed that the IDPC was correct to establish a maximum retention period of twenty (20) days for a high-risk area in view of the special circumstances and the nature of work carried out in that area. The judgement interprets the former national Data Protection Act,[27] which transposed Directive 95/46 and has now been repealed and replaced by the GDPR and the Data Protection Act 2018. Nevertheless, the judgment may still be considered authoritative in view of the fact that the core data protection principles remain unchanged or are strengthened compared to the previous regime.

---

[22] Court of Appeal (Inferior competence), Appeal numer 26/2017, 5 October 2018.

[23] Set up under the Data Protection Act 2018, Art.24.

[24] https://www.project-consult.de/files/Iron%20Mountain%20Guide%202013%20European%20Retention%20Periods.pdf accessed on 3 May 2019.

[25] The EDPS Video-Surveillance Guidelines, Brussels, 17 March 2010. https://edps.europa.eu/sites/edp/files/publication/10-03-17_video-surveillance_guidelines_en.pdf accessed on 3 May 2019.

[26] The scientific basis for establishing 7 days as the time limit is still not entirely clear. In some countries (e.g. France) a much longer 28 days is the norm for retention prior to deletion for CCTV footage.

[27] Data Protection Act, Laws of Malta, chapter 440.

4.2   Personal Data as 'Counter-Performance' for the Provision of Digital Content

To the best of the present authors' knowledge, there is to date no evidence of any debate or decision at the national level regarding the validity of personal data as 'counter-performance' for the provision of digital content. However, these authors submit that personal data could be considered as a 'lawful consideration' in terms of Article 966(d) of the Maltese Civil Code. Thus the validity of the contract would be upheld by a court of law.[28]

4.3   The Right Not to be Subject to Automated Decision-Making, Including Profiling

Malta has not yet introduced legislative measures to ensure that the right not to be subject to automated decision-making, including profiling, does not apply in certain situations, pursuant to Article 22(2)(b) GDPR.

4.4   The Right to Erasure

In Malta, there has been considerable debate and controversy surrounding the decision to allow requests for erasure of certain on-line (criminal) court judgments from the public record.[29] Requests are made to the court registrar, who is the Courts' data controller. The Malta IT Law Association ('MITLA') expressed concern, stating that: 'The application of the right to be forgotten with respect to public records needs transparent, justifiable rules.'[30]

---

[28] Civil Code s.987: 'An obligation without a consideration, or founded on a false or an unlawful consideration, shall have no effect'; Civil Code s.988. 'The agreement shall, nevertheless, be valid, if it is made to appear that such agreement was founded on sufficient consideration, even though such consideration was not stated.'

[29] See for example Times of Malta, Court judgment can now 'be forgotten'—former minister expresses disbelief at the decision, 9 March 2018, https://www.timesofmalta.com/articles/view/20180309/local/law-students-request-to-be-removed-from-database-accepted.672714?utm_source=tom&utm_campaign=top5&utm_medium=widget accessed on 2 May 2019; And Times of Malta, 22 judgments removed from the court's online database, 12 April 2018, https://www.timesofmalta.com/articles/view/20180412/local/22-judgments-removed-from-courts-online-database.676092 accessed on 2 May 2019.

[30] Statement by the Malta Information Technology Law Association (www.mitla.org.mt), 16 March 2018, https://www.mitla.org.mt/wp-content/uploads/2018/03/MITLA-Statement-16032018-MITLA-Right-to-be-Forgotten.pdf accessed on 24 May 2019.

On 17 May 2019, it was reported in the local press that the Justice Minister had told Parliament that a total of 176 requests for court judgements to be removed from the public domain had been filed; out of those, 112 judgements were made or are being made anonymous, meaning that the personal details of individuals were or are being removed. A total of 41 requests were rejected while one request was invalid, and another 22 requests were still being considered. In 2014 there was one request. In 2017 there were 21 requests. In 2018 there were 121 requests, and in 2019 there were 33 requests.[31]

It is to be noted that, to date, in Malta, the decisions of the Office of the IDPC are not made publicly available for consultation.

4.5 Reconciling the Right to Data Protection with Freedom of Expression and Information

Article 9(1) DPA provides that 'personal data processed for the purpose of exercising the right to freedom of expression and information, including processing for journalistic purposes or for the purposes of academic, artistic or literary expression, shall be exempt from compliance with the provisions of the GDPR specified in sub-article (2) where, having regard to the importance of the right of freedom of expression and information in a democratic society, compliance with any of the provisions as specified in sub-article (2) would be incompatible with such processing purposes: Provided that when reconciling the right to the protection of personal data with the right to freedom of expression and information, the controller shall ensure that the processing is proportionate, necessary and justified for reasons of substantial public interest.'

Article 9(2) is an implementation of article 85(2) GDPR. This includes exemptions from Chapters II (principles relating to processing) (but no exemption from Article 9 GDPR, processing of special categories of personal data), III (rights of the data subject), IV (controller and processor) and VII (co-operation and consistency). Specific articles of the GDPR are cited in the national law, omitting those articles or sub-articles where exemptions would be unwarranted or inapplicable to the data processing

---

[31] The Malta Independent, Court judgments removed from internet: Right to be forgotten must be respected—Bonnici, 17 May 2019, http://www.independent.com.mt/articles/2019-05-17/local-news/Court-judgments-removed-from-internet-Right-to-be-forgotten-must-be-respected-Bonnici-6736208252 accessed on 24 May 2019.

envisaged; e.g. it is not unreasonable to exclude the right to rectification provided for in Article 16 GDPR from the list of articles compliance with which may be exempted in the situations envisaged by Article 85 GDPR/ Article 9 DPA. The national legislation of Malta does not provide for exemptions from GDPR Chapters V (transfers of personal data to third countries or international organisations), VI (independent supervisory authorities) and IX (specific data-processing situations). This assessment of the exemptions 'necessary to reconcile the right to the protection of personal data with the freedom of expression and information' (Article 85(2) GDPR) does not appear to be problematic.

Article 9(2) DPA excludes Article 9 GDPR from the list of articles from which exemption is granted where personal data are processed 'for the purpose of exercising the right to freedom of expression and information, including processing for journalistic purposes or for the purposes of academic, artistic or literary expression' where compliance with any of the said provisions (specified in sub-article (2)) would be incompatible with such processing purposes. While this derogation would appear to be striking a blow in favour of another fundamental right, that of freedom of expression, the fact that it (understandably) does not include Article 9 of the GDPR could be potentially problematic if the correct legal basis is not accurately established. There are instances where sensitive data protected by Article 9, e.g. data relating to the health or sexual orientation of an individual may be of public interest. What is the legal basis in Maltese law for a journalist to publish certain facts, e.g. the terminal condition of a candidate for or a holder of high office who would normally have revealed such a condition to the electorate? Or reporting that a politician who campaigns for the criminalisation of homosexuality is actually promiscuously gay? In theory, these exceptions to the rules on sensitive data could be provided by the GDPR itself in terms of Art 9 (2) (g) which reads

(g) processing is necessary for reasons of substantial public interest, on the basis of Union or Member State law which shall be proportionate to the aim pursued, respect the essence of the right to data protection and provide for suitable and specific measures to safeguard the fundamental rights and the interests of the data subject;

In the case of Malta, "the Member State law" in question could potentially be the Media and Defamation Act 2018[32] which however does not, at the time of writing, have an explicit derogation to Article 9 GDPR on the grounds of "substantial public interest" and therefore needs to be revisited to plug the existing lacuna.

Malta has not introduced a law pursuant to Article 85(2) GDPR beyond that described, i.e. DPA 2018, Article 9.

4.6   Restrictions

Article 5 DPA provides that the Minister responsible for data protection may, after consultation with the IDPC[33] and with the concurrence of the Minister responsible for justice, by regulations provide for a restriction to the obligations to which the data controller or processor is subject pursuant to Article 23 GDPR.

4.7   Processing for Archiving Purposes in the Public Interest, Scientific or Historical Research Purposes or Statistical Purposes

Article 9 GDPR provides that processing of defined 'special categories of personal data' is allowed if such processing 'is necessary for archiving purposes in the public interest, scientific or historical research purposes or statistical purposes in accordance with Article 89(1) based on Union or Member State law which shall be proportionate to the aim pursued, respect the essence of the right to data protection and provide for suitable and specific measures to safeguard the fundamental rights and the interests of the data subject.'[34] The DPA provides that the controller must consult with, and obtain prior authorisation from, the IDPC 'where the controller intends to process in the public interest: (a) genetic data, biometric data or data concerning health for statistical or research purposes; or (b) special categories of data in relation to the management of social care services and systems, including for the purposes of quality control, management information and the general national supervision and monitoring of such services and systems: Provided that, where genetic data, biometric data or data concerning health are required to be processed for research purposes,

---

[32] Media and Defamation Act 2018, chapter 579, Laws of Malta.
[33] Appointed under article 11 DPA.
[34] GDPR, Art.9(2)(j).

the Commissioner shall consult a research ethics committee or of an institution recognised by the Commissioner for the purposes of this article.'[35]
The research ethics committee consulted by the IDPC is the University
Research Ethics Committee's sub-committee on data protection ('UREC-
DP').[36] It is doubtful that this national law fully satisfies the description
provided by the GDPR (that the law must 'be proportionate to the aim
pursued, respect the essence of the right to data protection and provide for
suitable and specific measures to safeguard the fundamental rights and the
interests of the data subject'). In other words, the requirement of the law
is replaced by a legal requirement of prior authorisation; and supposedly it
is envisaged that the Commissioner, having consulted UREC-DP, would
ensure that there is proportionality, respect of the essence of the right to
data protection etc. before granting authorisation.

Article 6 DPA provides that (subject to appropriate safeguards for the
rights and freedoms of the data subject) controllers and processors may
derogate from the provisions of the GDPR relating to the right of access,[37]
the right to rectification,[38] the right to restriction of processing[39] and the
right to object[40] to the processing of personal data for scientific or historical research purposes or official statistics.[41] Controllers and processors may
also derogate from the aforementioned provisions and additionally from
the GDPR provisions relating to the notification obligation regarding the
rectification or erasure of personal data or restriction of processing,[42] and
the right to data portability[43] for the processing of personal data for
archiving purposes in the public interest. In both instances such derogations are allowed 'in so far as the exercise of the rights set out in those
Articles: (a) is likely to render impossible or seriously impair the achievement of those purposes, and (b) the data controller reasonably believes

[35] Art.7 DPA.
[36] Webpage https://www.um.edu.mt/urec.
[37] GDPR, article 15.
[38] GDPR, article 16.
[39] GDPR, article 18.
[40] GDPR, article 21.
[41] 'Official statistics' is a term defined in the legislation as 'information collected, analysed
and produced for the benefit of the society to characterize collective phenomena in a considered population and produced by the National Statistics Office as provided for by law, or by
other national authorities as designated by Eurostat following recommendation by the
National Statistics Office.'
[42] GDPR, article 19.
[43] GDPR, article 20.

that such derogations are necessary for the fulfilment of those purposes.' Where such data processing serves at the same time another purpose, the derogations apply only to processing for the purposes referred to in the said Article. This national provision is an implementation of the exemptions allowed in article 89(2) and (3) GDPR, transposed in terms which closely follow those of the said GDPR.

4.8 Processing of the National Identification Number

Article 8 DPA provides that an identity document[44] may only be processed when such processing is 'clearly justified having regard to the purpose of the processing and—(a) the importance of a secure identification; or (b) any other valid reason as may be provided by law: Provided that the national identity number or any other identifier of general application shall be used only under appropriate safeguards for the rights and freedoms of the data subject pursuant to the Regulation.' This is clearly an implementing provision of article 87 GDPR. The terminology of the GDPR is closely followed, and the local implementation does not add anything of substance thereto. In practice in Malta, it is not uncommon for national identity numbers to be collected and processed, and such is often done without regard to strict necessity requirements.[45]

4.9 Transborder Data Transfers

Article 10 DPA provides that in the absence of an adequacy decision pursuant to Article 45(3) GDPR, the Minister responsible for data protection may, following consultation with the IDPC, or an international organisation for important reasons of public interest. This appears to be an implementation of article 49(5) GDPR. Rather than actually implement the option, the DPA allows for such possible future implementation by subsidiary legislation.

---

[44]'Identity document' is defined as a legally valid identity document as provided in the Identity Card and Other Identity Documents Act (chapter 258, Laws of Malta).

[45]This practice is generally uncontroversial in Malta and as a result documentary evidence to support this claim is not available.

4.10   The Information and Data Protection Commissioner

The office of the Information and Data Protection Commissioner is set up under article 11 DPA. In the implementation of Article 58(1)(f) GDPR, the national law provides that in the exercise of the investigative powers pursuant to Article 58 GDPR, or any other law, the Commissioner may request the assistance of the executive police to enter and search any premises.[46] The national law further provides that in the event of joint operations with supervisory authorities of one or more other the Member States, the IDPC may, where appropriate, confer powers, including investigative powers, on the seconding supervisory authority's members or staff: Provided that such powers are exercised under the guidance and in the presence of the IDPC.[47] This provision appears to be implementing article 62(3) GDPR.

5   DOMESTIC ENFORCEMENT OF DATA PROTECTION LAW

5.1   The Office of the Information and Data Protection Commissioner

The relevant public authority is the Office of the IDPC.[48]

The IDPC is appointed by the Prime Minister after consultation with the Leader of the Opposition, to perform the duties of the supervisory authority for the purposes of Chapter VI of the GDPR.[49] The IDPC is responsible for monitoring and enforcing the application of the provisions of the DPA 2018 and the GDPR, in order to protect the fundamental rights and freedoms of natural persons concerning the processing of personal data and to facilitate the free flow of personal data between Malta and any other Member State.[50] The DPA 2018 also provides a list of disqualifications to hold office as Commissioner, e.g. if s/he is a Minister or a Member of the House of Representatives, or a judge or magistrate of the

---

[46] Data Protection Act, Art.16(1).

[47] Data Protection Act, Art.16(2). Under national law, 'Commissioner' means the Information and Data Protection Commissioner appointed under Art.11 and includes any officer or employee of the Commissioner authorised by him in that behalf.

[48] Website portal https://idpc.org.mt/en/Pages/Home.aspx.

[49] DPA, Article 11(1).

[50] DPA, Article 11(2).

courts of justice.[51] The IDPC must have the qualifications, experience and skills, in particular in the area of the protection of personal data, required to perform his or her duties and exercise his or her powers in accordance with GDPR Article 53(2).[52]

In the exercise of his tasks and powers, the Commissioner acts with complete independence and is free from external influence, whether direct or indirect and must neither seek nor take instructions or direction from any person or entity.[53] Any officers or employees of the Commissioner are chosen by the Commissioner and are subject to his exclusive direction.[54]

The IDPC has a separate and distinct legal personality and is capable of entering into contracts, of acquiring, holding and disposing of any kind of property for his tasks and powers, of suing and being sued, and of doing all such things and entering into all such transactions as are incidental or conducive to the effective performance of his tasks and exercise of his powers.[55]

The tenure of office of the IDPC is of five years, and he is eligible for reappointment on the expiration of his term of office.[56] The Commissioner may not be removed from his office except by the Prime Minister upon an address of the House of Representatives supported by the votes of not less than two-thirds of all the members thereof and praying for such removal on the ground of proved inability to perform the duties of his office (whether arising from infirmity of body or mind or any other cause) or proved misbehaviour.[57]

The Commissioner performs the duties assigned to him under the DPA 2018 and the GDPR and the functions assigned to him under the Freedom of Information Act[58] and any other law.[59] S/he has the power to institute civil judicial proceedings in cases where the provisions of the DPA 2018 or the GDPR have been or are about to be violated.[60] The IDPC may seek

---

[51] DPA, Article 11(3).
[52] DPA, Article 11(4).
[53] DPA, Article 12(1).
[54] DPA, Article 12(3).
[55] DPA, Article 13(1).
[56] DPA, Article 14(1).
[57] DPA, Article 14(2).
[58] Laws of Malta, Chapter 496.
[59] DPA, Article 15(1).
[60] DPA, Article 15(2).

the advice of and may consult with, any other competent authority in the exercise of his/her functions under the DPA and the GDPR.[61]

It has been reported that for the period 25 May 2018 to 28 January 2019, in Malta, over one hundred (100) personal data breaches were notified to the IDPC, with seventeen (17) GDPR fines being imposed by the same. Per capita, the Maltese figures are significant.[62]

5.2   Complaint Handling by the IDPC

The Office of the IDPC informed the author that all complaints received by the Office are investigated and that the degree of investigation may depend on the nature of the case; no 'selective to be effective' approach is taken.[63]

5.3   Sanctioning Data Protection Infringements

On 18 February 2019, the IDPC issued his decision to the Lands Authority after concluding an investigation of a data breach, that was brought to his attention by the Times of Malta on 23 November 2018.[64] The findings of the investigation established that the online application platform available on the Authority's web portal lacked the necessary technical and organisational measures to ensure the security of processing. The Lands Authority was found to have infringed the provisions of GDPR Article 32 and, in terms of the DPA 2018 Article 21, was served with an administrative fine of €5000. The level of the fine was stated to have been reached after the Commissioner took into account the circumstances set out under GDPR Article 83(2). The temporary ban imposed on the Authority's web portal was lifted. It was stated that the Lands Authority offered their full and unrestricted collaboration to the IDPC during the course of the entire investigation.[65]

---

[61] DPA, Article 15(3).

[62] DLA Piper GDPR data breach survey, https://www.dlapiper.com/en/uk/insights/publications/2019/01/gdpr-data-breach-survey/ accessed on 4 May 2019.

[63] Meeting at the Office of the IDPC held on 23 May 2019.

[64] https://www.timesofmalta.com/articles/view/20181123/local/massive-lands-authority-security-flaw-dumps-personal-data-online.694982 accessed on 4 May 2019.

[65] Press release https://idpc.org.mt/en/Press/Pages/Lands-Authority-Personal-Data-Breach.aspx accessed on 4 May 2019.

Article 21 of the DPA implements GDPR Article 83(7) and provides that the IDPC may impose an administrative fine on a public authority or body of up to €25,000 for each violation and additionally €25 for each day during which such violation persists, which fine shall be determined and imposed by the IDPC in accordance with the procedure stipulated in Article 26 of the DPA, for infringement under Article 83(4) of the GDPR. The fine that the IDPC may impose on a public authority or body for infringement of GDPR Article 83(5) or (6) (in accordance with the same procedure under Article 26 of the DPA) must not exceed €50,000 for each violation and additionally €50 for each day during which such violation persists. Administrative fines on a public authority or body are to be imposed by the IDPC after giving due regard to the circumstances of the case pursuant to GDPR Article 83(2).

Further to the GDPR, Article 22 of the DPA provides that (without prejudice to the provisions of DPA Article 21 and GDPR Article 83) any person who—(a) knowingly provides false information to the IDPC when so requested by the IDPC pursuant to his investigative powers under GDPR Article 58, or any other law; or (b) does not comply with any lawful request pursuant to an investigation by the IDPC—shall be guilty of an offence against this article and shall, upon conviction, be liable to a fine (*multa*) of not less than one thousand, two hundred and fifty euro (€1250) and not more than fifty thousand euro (€50,000), or to imprisonment for six months, or to both such fine (*multa*) and imprisonment: Provided that no proceedings shall be instituted in respect of any offence under this article except where the IDPC provides information to any officer of the Executive Police.

5.4 Damages for Intangible Harm and Their Quantification

Malta's legal system awards damages for intangible harm in some areas, most notably in cases dealing with human rights, defamation and intellectual property law. Save for a recently introduced exception,[66] the right of the plaintiff in an ordinary tort action to recover damages for intangible harm is not acknowledged by statute in Malta. It seems that when awarding damages for intangible harm (termed 'moral damages' in the Maltese legal system), and in the absence of concrete evidence to calculate

---

[66] See Act XXXII of 2018, Art.15 (discussed below).

damnum emergens[67] and/or *lucrum cessans*,[68] the Maltese courts tend to use their discretion *arbitrio boni viri*[69] in establishing the amount of compensation to be awarded.

5.4.1   Civil Damages

In Malta, the courts have traditionally affirmed that moral damages are not awarded in an ordinary action for civil damages under the law of tort or quasi-tort, but admitted this possibility under human rights law.[70] However, this traditional position has been contested and challenged as this means that moral damages may be awarded against the State in a case brought before the Civil Court, First Hall (in its Constitutional jurisdiction),[71] and potentially appealed before the Constitutional Court, but not in a case brought against a private individual (or the State[72]) before the (ordinary) Civil Courts (First Hall, and potentially appealed before the Court of Appeal.) While the argument has been made for the horizontal effects of fundamental human rights (understood not as 'holding individuals responsible for human rights violations' but as 'keeping human rights principles in mind when judicially interpreting private law'),[73] this is not uncontroversial.[74]

In *Busuttil v Muscat*,[75] the Civil Court (First Hall) held that the aesthetic facial injury suffered by the applicant due to medical negligence

---

[67] Actual damages sustained.

[68] Ceased/lost profits; losses of future earnings arising from any permanent incapacity, total or partial.

[69] 'According to the judgment of a fair man.'

[70] For a fuller account see D. E. Zammit, 'How human rights have influenced Maltese civil liability jurisprudence', in R. Magion (Ed.), *The UN Declaration of Human Rights: 70 years on*, Malta, Fondazzjoni Celebrazzjonijiet Nazzjonali, 2018, p.34; referencing C. Micallef Grimaud, 'Article 1045 of the Maltese Civil Code: Is Compensation for Moral Damage Compatible Therewith?', *Journal of Civil Law Studies*, Vol. 4, No. 2, 2011, pp. 481–513. Cf. also Wadge, Alison (2018) *Moral Damages in Public Law with particular reference to remedies arising from Human Rights Action*, Unpublished LLD dissertation, University of Malta.

[71] Under Article 46 of the Constitution of Malta.

[72] Cf. Article 46(2) proviso, Constitution of Malta.

[73] Zammit (n 73) 36.

[74] See Bonello, Giovanni (2018). *Misunderstanding the Constitution—2: Can individuals be sued for human rights violation?* Sunday Times of Malta, 14 January 2018, https://timesofmalta.com/articles/view/Misunderstanding-the-Constitution-2-Can-individuals-be-sued-for-human.667891 accessed on 12 July 2019.

[75] Linda *Busuttil illum Cordina et. v. Dr Josie Muscat et.* Civil Court (First Hall), 30 November 2010.

violated the Constitution of Malta protected the value of psycho-physical integrity which is held, the European Convention of Human Rights and Article 3 of the EU Charter of Fundamental Rights, which states that: 'Everyone has the right to respect for his or her physical and mental integrity.' Holding that the ordinary law must be interpreted in a manner that is 'constitutionally compliant', the Civil Court interpreted the Civil Code (chapter 16 of the Laws of Malta) in this light. In particular, the Court focused on Articles 1033 and 1045 of the Civil Code:

> Any person who, with or without intent to injure, voluntarily or through negligence, imprudence, or want of attention, is guilty of any act or omission constituting a breach of the duty imposed by law, shall be liable for *any damage* resulting therefrom.[76] (authors' emphasis)

> The damage which is to be made good (....) shall consist in the *actual loss* which the act shall have directly caused to the injured party, in the expenses which the latter may have been compelled to incur in consequence of the damage, in the loss of actual wages or other earnings, and in the loss of future earnings arising from any permanent incapacity, total or partial, which the act may have caused.[77] (authors' emphasis)

The Court held that the words 'any damage' and 'actual loss' were broad enough to encompass damage to psycho-physical integrity as a justification for a compensatory damages award to the victim. It then proceeded, *arbitrio boni viri*, to compensate plaintiff by awarding €5000 in damages, which were stated by the court to be non-patrimonial (that is to say, 'moral') in character.

However, the Court of Appeal in Fenech & Others v Malta Drydocks[78] and subsequent cases[79] did not follow the same approach to human rights envisaged in Busuttil v Muscat, which itself was revoked on appeal.[80] In the latter judgment, the Court of Appeal reiterated the orthodox position, simultaneously affirming the non-compensability of moral damage in the

---

[76] Civil Code, Article 1033.

[77] Civil Code, Article 1045.

[78] Court of Appeal, 3 December 2010, Writ Number 1427/1997.

[79] See for e.g. *John Mary Abela et. v. Policy Manager tal-Malta Shipyards fi hdan il-Ministeru ghall-Infrastruttua, Trasport u Komunikazzjoni noe. et.* Constitutional Court, 11 April 2011, Writ Number 25/2009/1.

[80] *Linda Busuttil et. v. Dr Josie Muscat u Tania Spiteri*, delivered by the Court of Appeal on 27 June 2014, Writ Number 2429/1998/1.

context of ordinary civil liability litigation and the adequacy and sufficiency of the compensation thus granted, even understood as an ordinary remedy for a human rights violation.

Harm to the patrimony (civil damages) in Malta is quantified, where *lucrum cessans* damages are concerned, by means of the orthodox multiplier/multiplicand formula.[81] In the previous judgments, it appeared to be the settled position of the Maltese courts that moral damages, provided they were expressed in terms of the categories of compensable patrimonial damages, were rendered *indirectly* compensable. This usually required the individual judge to interpret the applicable heads of damage flexibly enough, to incorporate or exclude particular forms of non-patrimonial damage according to his or her sense of what was required to achieve a *restitutio in integrum*[82] in the case at hand and by relying on the court's discretion to adapt its damages awards to the particular circumstances of the case before it under Article 1045(2):

> The sum to be awarded in respect of such incapacity shall be assessed by the court, having regard to the circumstances of the case, and, particularly, to the nature and degree of incapacity caused, and to the condition of the injured party.

The developing *status quo* was dramatically impacted by *Brincat and others v Malta*,[83] a case which concerned ship-yard repair workers who were exposed to asbestos for a number of decades beginning in the 1950s to the early 2000s which led to them suffering from asbestos-related conditions. The ECtHR held that the non-compensability of moral damage in the context of ordinary civil liability litigation (for damages arising out of tort or contractual liability) meant that access to a human rights remedy could no longer be denied whenever an alleged victim of a human rights violation sued the Government for compensation of moral damages. The

---

[81] Cf. *Grech Trevor vs Agius Lawrence*, Civil Court, First Hall, 17 October 2018, Reference 1030/2013 (currently under appeal). See also Bugeja Carlos (2019) The court's calculator, Times of Malta 11 February 2019, https://timesofmalta.com/articles/view/the-courts-calculator.701658 accessed on 8 July 2019.

[82] 'Full restitution', that is that an injured party is, through the awarding of damages, restored to the state which would have prevailed had no injury been sustained.

[83] *Brincat and Others v. Malta*, Applications Nos. 60908/11, 62110/11, 62129/11, 62312/11, and 62338/11, ECHR 232 (2014), 24 July 2014.

ECtHR ordered the payment of non-pecuniary ('moral') damages to the applicants/victims. As Zammit comments:

> It was easily predictable that this could lead (…) to a divergence of approach between a case for damages against the government, against which a human rights action might always be made once moral damages were requested, and civil liability cases between private persons, in relation to whom a human rights remedy was not normally available.[84]

An important further development occurred in the case of *Agius v the Attorney General et*, which concerned the death of an inmate at Malta's main prison resulting from an incorrect administration of methadone to a drug addict. In this case, following the case being tried before the Civil Court, First Hall, and the Court of Appeal,[85] a Constitutional case was filed.[86] On appeal, the Constitutional Court[87] held that since Articles 1045 and 1046 of the Civil Code fall under the sub-title 'Of Torts and Quasi-Torts', it is clear that any prohibition of the award of moral or non-patrimonial damages could only apply to actions in tort or quasi-tort. The Constitutional Court's classification of the action in this case as originating from a breach of a contractual and/or legal (*ex lege*) relationship does evoke an uncomfortable future scenario in which non-patrimonial damage will only be compensated if the underlying relationship can be construed as contractual or legal, and not if it is understood as tortious.[88] The Constitutional Court also underlined that such awards should only be made once the convincing proof is brought that real emotional pain and suffering have been inflicted upon the victim and that this has not already been indirectly compensated under other headings (in the instant case non-patrimonal/moral damages were denied in view of the fact that the plaintiff was the heir of the father of the tort victim/deceased, was not financially dependent on him, and had moreover not produced any evidence that she enjoyed a particularly close relationship with the tort

---

[84] Zammit (n 73) 56.

[85] Civil Court, First Hall, 6 October 2010; Court of Appeal, 1 April 2014.

[86] Civil Court, First Hall (Constitutional Jurisdiction), 15 January 2015, Reference 33/2014.

[87] *Jane Agius v. the Attorney General, the Minister for the Interior and National Security and the Honourable Prime Minister, Constitutional Court*, 14 December 2015, Writ number 33/2014/1.

[88] Zammit (2018) (n 73) 61.

victim/deceased, sufficient to justify an additional award of moral damages to reflect pain and suffering caused by his death).

As aforementioned, in 2018, the Civil Code underwent some amendments, including the addition of a proviso to Article 1045(1), which reads as follows:

> Provided that in the case of damages arising from a criminal offence, other than an involuntary offence, and only in the case of crimes affecting the dignity of persons under Title VII of Part II of Book First of the Criminal Code and of wilful crimes against the person subject to a punishment of imprisonment of at least three years under Title VIII of Part II of Book First of the said Code, up to a maximum limit of ten thousand euro (€10,000) or up to such maximum limit as the Minister responsible for justice may by regulations establish both with regard to the maximum amount and about the method of computation depending on the case, the damage to be made good shall also include any *moral harm and, or psychological harm* caused to the claimant.[89] (my emphasis)

The assessment of Zammit, Head of the Department of Civil Law within the University of Malta, is that this recent enactment while introducing for the first time the explicit right of the plaintiff in an ordinary action in tort to recover moral and/or psychological damages, albeit within the parameters set out therein, may have (possibly, unintended) consequences insofar as the proviso may be interpreted to mean that moral and/or psychological damages may now only be (expressly) awarded within limits contemplated in the said proviso, but not in all other cases, e.g. where an involuntary offence causes the harm; thus foreclosing potential further judicial developments particularly in light of the effects of judgments by the Constitutional Court awarding moral damages in, for example, the asbestosis cases.[90]

5.4.2 Other Specific Branches of Maltese Law

An award of damages may be regulated by a specific branch of Maltese law outside the ambit of the Maltese Civil Code; namely: human rights cases,

---

[89] Added by Act XXXII.2018.15.

[90] Caruana Demajo, G., L. Quintano, D. Zammit (2018) XVIII. Malta, in Karner, Ernst and Steininger, Barbara C. (eds), *European Tort Law Yearbook*, Volume 7, Issue 1 (Dec 2018), p. 372.

the Media and Defamation Act,[91] the Enforcement of Intellectual Property Rights (Regulation) Act,[92] the Consumer Affairs Act,[93] the Promises of Marriage Law,[94] and, of course, the Data Protection Act 2018. For example, in proceedings instituted under the Media and Defamation Act, the Court may order the defendant to pay a sum not exceeding eleven thousand, six hundred and forty euro (€11,640) by way of *moral damages* in addition to actual damages; in actions for slander, the maximum amount to be awarded by way of moral damages is five thousand euro (€5000).

Intellectual Property Law

Damages in Maltese intellectual property cases are regulated by Article 12 of the Enforcement of Intellectual Property Rights (Regulation) Act[95] as follows:

(1) The Court shall on an application filed by the injured party, order any infringer who has, either knowingly or being reasonably expected to know, engaged in an infringing activity, to pay the rightholder damages commensurate with the actual prejudice suffered by the said rightholder as a result of the infringement.

(2) In setting the amount of damages due, the Court *shall* take into account all relevant aspects, including all the negative economic consequences that may have been suffered by the injured party including lost profits, as well as any unfair profits made by the infringer and, *where it deems appropriate*, other elements such as the *moral prejudice* caused to the rightholder by the infringement:

Provided that instead of the above method of calculation of damages, the Court may, *where it so considers appropriate*, choose to apply an alternative method of calculation involving the setting of a lump sum of damages payable which shall include elements such as at least the amount of royalties or fees which would have been due had the infringer requested authorisation to use the intellectual right in question.

(3) Where the Court is of the opinion that the infringer did not knowingly engage in infringing activity, it may order the recovery of profits or the

---

[91] Chapter 579 of the Laws of Malta.
[92] Chapter 488 of the Laws of Malta.
[93] Chapter 378 of the Laws of Malta.
[94] Chapter 5 of the Laws of Malta.
[95] Laws of Malta, chapter 488; transposing the provisions of Directive 2004/48/EC on the enforcement of intellectual property rights [2004] OJ L 157/45.

payment of damages, as may be pre-established in regulations made under the relevant legislation. (my emphasis)

Therefore, the Court has the discretion to award damages on an *arbitrio boni viri* basis under both Art.12(2) and under Art.12(2) proviso. However, it is not clear under which of these methods the Court has wider discretionary powers; in particular, it is not clear whether moral prejudice and/or similar elements are precluded from being included in the lump sum that can be awarded by the Court under the proviso to Article 12(2).[96]

Art.12(2) is one of the very few instances in Maltese law where moral prejudice is explicitly taken into consideration when liquidating damages. One of the first IP judgments to award damages invoking moral prejudice explicitly is the case *Air Malta P.L.C. vs Efly Company Limited*.[97] However, this was done on an *arbitrio boni viri* basis, and therefore no explanation of the methods of calculation in question was entertained by the Court.

In the case of *Av. Dottor Antoine Camilleri noe* (acting as special mandatory for and on behalf of foreign company Bacardi & Company Limited) *vs Patrick Cellars Limited*[98] the court—in a case concerning the 'exhaustion of rights'/trademark infringement by importing/commercialising goods in Malta which were not destined for the EU/EEA market—liquidated the damages caused to Bacardi, in terms of Article 12 of the Enforcement of Intellectual Property Rights (Regulation) Act, in the amount of fifty-two thousand six hundred and fifty euro (€52,650) in damages, including thirty thousand euro (€30,000) in other damages (particularly 'moral damages', which include reputational damage). The Court stated that it was applying Art.12(2)proviso and, having taken into consideration all the aspects of the case, awarding *arbitrio boni viri* the global amount of €30,000 in other damages.

In *Av. Dottor Antoine Camilleri noe* (acting as special mandatory for and on behalf of foreign company Nando's Limited) *vs Mirale and Lamare Limited*,[99] the court awarded ten thousand euro (€10,000), with interest

[96] C. Micallef Grimaud (2014) Damages in Maltese Intellectual Property Cases: A Brief Look at Article 12 of Chapter 488 of the Laws of Malta, Mamo TCV Advocates, 25 March 2014, https://www.mamotcv.com/resources/news/damages-in-maltese-intellectual-property-cases-a-brief-look-at-article-12-of-chapter488-of-the-laws-of-malta, visited 8 May 2019.

[97] *Air Malta PLC (C-2685) vs Efly Company Limited (C-46370)*—30 March 2010—First Hall, Civil Court.

[98] Civil Court, First Hall, 19 May 2015 (Application No. 406/2011).

[99] Civil Court, First Hall, 13 June 2019 (Application No. 853/2017).

running from the data of the filing of the case, in moral damages calculated based on *arbitrio boni viri* for the breach of rights suffered. The onus of conducting an assessment *arbitrio boni viri* is placed upon the judge as to the learned professional capable of delivering an amount based on equity. The author has been unable to trace any judgment of our courts which specifies in further detail how damages for 'moral prejudice' are calculated/quantified/liquidated in terms of Article 12 since in the case-law identified the Courts specifically entertained no further deliberations on this point.

Regarding Article 12(3), no such regulations for the recovery of profits or the payment of damages in cases where the infringer did not knowingly engage in infringing activity have been promulgated. Having said that, in all other cases (i.e. relating to Copyright, Trademarks, Patents and Designs etc.), the Maltese principles of Civil law (including tort) generally apply.[100]

Data Protection Law
The DPA 2018, Article 30(1), states as follows: 'Without prejudice to any other remedy available to him (…), a data subject may, where he believes that his rights under the GDPR or this Act have been infringed (…) by sworn application filed before the First Hall of the Civil Court, institute an action for an effective judicial remedy against the controller or processor concerned. (2) A data subject may also, by sworn application filed before the First Hall of the Civil Court, institute an action for damages against the controller or processor who processes personal data in contravention of the provisions of the GDPR or this Act.'

The DPA 2018 also explicitly provides in Article 30(3) that 'If in determining an action [for damages] the court finds that the controller or processor is liable for the damage caused pursuant to Article 82 of the [GDPR], the court shall determine the amount of damages, including, but not limited to, *moral damages* as the court may determine, due to the data subject' (authors' emphasis).

There are so far no decided cases awarding damages for intangible harm in the area of data protection law.

---

[100] Micallef Grimaud (n 99).

5.5   Representative Actions Pursuant to Article 80 GDPR

Malta has to the best of these authors' knowledge not introduced any legislative measures intended to facilitate representative actions pursuant to Article 80 GDPR. Neither have any such representative actions been brought in practice.

A 'representative action', defined as 'proceedings that are brought on behalf of a number of class members by a representative body', is possible according to the provisions of the Collective Proceedings Act,[101] enacted in 2012—*but* only with regard to an infringement of the Acts listed in Schedule A of the Act, i.e. the Competition Act,[102] and Articles 101 or 102 TFEU, the Consumer Affairs Act[103] and the Product Safety Act.[104] In a representative action, the Court shall approve a registered consumer association or a 'constituted body' to act as a class representative according to the terms of Article 12(1) of the Act. It would appear incongruous to the authors of this chapter if the DPA 2018 and the GDPR were not brought within the purview of this Act at the earliest opportunity.

The Malta IT Law Association (MITLA)[105] has reacted to certain developments at the local level, for example with regard to the government's announced plans to introduce public, smart CCTV surveillance cameras (with facial recognition technology) in selected locations in Malta to address "ant-social behaviour" hotspots.[106] MITLA has also pronounced

---

[101] Laws of Malta, chapter 520.
[102] Laws of Malta, chapter 379.
[103] Laws of Malta, chapter 378.
[104] Laws of Malta, chapter 427.
[105] MITLA is registered as a Voluntary Organisation (VO/1166) in terms of Article 3 of the Voluntary Organisations Act 2007 (Act No, XXII of 2007), Malta.
[106] MITLA (2017) 'Specific laws are required for mass-scale facial recognition applications', https://www.mitla.org.mt/specific-laws-required-mass-scale-facial-recognition-applications/ accessed on 17 July 2019. Reported in the news: Vella, Matthew (2017) 'IT experts warn of greater privacy risks with facial recognition CCTV: Plans for facial recognition CCTV in Paceville require new rules to safeguard fundamental rights, Malta IT law association says', MaltaToday, 7 December 2017, https://www.maltatoday.com.mt/news/national/82918/it_experts_warn_of_greater_privacy_risks_with_facial_recognition_cctv#. XS7f5i2Q1sM accessed on 17 July 2019; Vella, Matthew (2018) 'Facial recognition CCTV for Paceville and Marsa by 2019: The facial recognition software is expected to be deployed in Paceville and Marsa, after data protection concerns are addressed with the Information and Data Protection Commissioner', MaltaToday, 22 October 2018, https://www.maltatoday.com.mt/news/budget-2019/90331/facial_recognition_cctv_for_paceville_and_marsa_by_2019#.XS7gFi2Q1sM accessed on 17 July 2019. Cf. also: Zammit, Francois

itself on the matter of the erasure of criminal court judgements from the publicly accessible online judgments database (see above response to q. 7). Should the Collective Proceedings Act be suitably amended, in principle, MITLA should then qualify to bring a representative action in terms of Article 80(1) GDPR?

5.6   Other Involved National Regulatory Authorities

Malta has recently (2018) established a new authority—the Malta Digital Innovation Authority[107]—to regulate innovative technologies. However, the scope of this authority is limited to certifying the functionality of 'innovative technology arrangements' and does not extend to dealing with complaints relating to data protection. Any data protection issues in the application of any innovative technology arrangement would need to be referred to the Office of the IDPC.

It is understood that cooperation between the Office of the IDPC and other regulators has to date been informal and on an *ad hoc* basis.[108]

6   DATA PROCESSING FOR NATIONAL SECURITY PURPOSES

Personal data processing for 'national security' purposes is excluded from both the GDPR and the Law Enforcement Directive.

In Malta communications data is retained according to the provisions of S.L. 586.01 Processing of Personal Data (Electronic Communications Sector) Regulations.[109] Article 19(1) states that 'Data retained under this Part shall be disclosed only to the Police or to the Security Service, as the case may be, where such data is required for the purpose of the investigation, detection or prosecution of serious crime.'

(2019) 'Safe City Malta': Is Privacy the Real Crux of the Matter?', Isles of the Left, 16 January 2019, https://www.islesoftheleft.org/safe-city-malta-is-privacy-the-real-crux-of-the-matter/ accessed on 17 July 2019 expressing concern about potential uses of data collected from smart CCTV surveillance for social profiling and resultant discrimination.

[107] Established by the Malta Digital Innovation Authority Act, chapter 591, Laws of Malta, mdia.gov.mt.

[108] Discussion/interview held at the Office of the IDPC on 23 May 2019.

[109] Accessed at http://justiceservices.gov.mt/DownloadDocument.aspx?app=lom&itemid=11052&l=1.

The closest to a definition of the Security Service of Malta is that found in the Security Service Act,[110] Article 3, as follows:

(1) There shall continue to be a Security Service ... under the authority of the Minister.
(2) The function of the Service shall be to protect national security and, in particular, against threats from organised crime, espionage, terrorism and sabotage, the activities of agents of foreign powers and against actions intended to overthrow or undermine parliamentary democracy by political, industrial or violent means.
(3) It shall also be the function of the Service to act in the interests of— (a) the economic well-being of Malta; and (b) public safety, in particular, the prevention or detection of serious crime.

Subsidiary legislation 586.09 Restriction of the Data Protection (Obligations and Rights) Regulations,[111] Art. 4(4), provides: 'Any restriction to the rights of the data subject referred to in Article 23 of the GDPR shall only apply where such restrictions are a necessary measure required: (a) for the safeguarding and maintaining of *national security*, public security, defence and the international relations of Malta; ...' (authors' emphasis).

It is unclear whether Malta's national authorities accept the application of the EU Charter to data retention for national security purposes as the issue has never really been a controversial matter in this country.

7   EXAMPLES

7.1   *Surveillance and Interception of Telecommunications*

Malta's compliance with Article 9 of Convention is far from being satisfactory since the current set of safeguards and remedies as provided by Maltese law are inadequate in the light of developments of modern information and communication technologies. The provisions on oversight of surveillance in Malta were already quite weak in the Security Service Act enacted when public use of the Internet was still in its infancy. It is understood that the Government of Malta is (In October 2020) at an advanced

---

[110] Laws of Malta, Chapter 391.
[111] Accessed at http://justiceservices.gov.mt/DownloadDocument.aspx?app=lom&itemid=12845&l=1.

stage of drafting comprehensive legislation to replace Chapter 391. At the time of writing, it is not yet clear as to the extent to which the reforms in this part of the law which is not covered by EU law will meet the same standards set by the reforms in other EU member states such as the Netherlands, France, Belgium etc. Nor is it clear as to whether they would meet or exceed the protections envisaged in a set of detailed recommendations 'which should tighten safeguards and avoid the current potential for conflicts of interest, especially where the role of Ministers and the Prime Minister is concerned'. The latter was communicated to the Government of Malta in December 2019 and again in January 2020 by the UN Special Rapporteur on the right to privacy.[112] This call for reform was partially motivated by the revelation in the media that the former Prime Minister of Malta chief of staff, Keith Schembri, was present for Malta Security Service (MSS) meetings including that in which Yorgen Fenech, a powerful local businessman, was shown to be the main suspect in the assassination of Daphne Caruana Galizia,[113] a local journalist. The latter may have been about to reveal incriminating evidence of corruption within or very close to the government.[114] Schembri and Fenech were friends, with the latter having been reported to have footed some part of the bill when the former was abroad to undergo cancer treatment.[115] In other words, Schembri was privy to details on the MSS' investigation that was pointing at his close friend Fenech as one of the main suspects in the investigation on the Daphne Caruana Galizia assassination. Meanwhile, Fenech,

[112] 'Malta: UN expert recommends broad changes to surveillance laws', at https://unric. org/it/malta-un-expert-recommends-broad-changes-to-surveillance-laws/. The Special Rapporteur's communication to the Government is available at https://spcommreports. ohchr.org/TMResultsBase/DownLoadPublicCommunicationFile?gId=25001.

[113] 'Keith Schembri was privy to Security Service details on Yorgen Fenech as main suspect', MaltaToday, 28 November 2019, at https://www.maltatoday.com.mt/news/national/98922/keith_schembri_was_privy_to_security_service_details_on_yorgen_fenech_as_main_suspect#.X04hKC2w0cg.

[114] "Had my mother published, Electrogas would have gone into liquidation'—Matthew Caruana Galizia', Newsbook, 28 August 2020, at https://newsbook.com.mt/en/had-my-mother-published-electrogas-would-have-gone-into-liquidation-matthew-caruana-galizia/.

[115] '€24,000 Mayo clinic bill Fenech paid for Keith Schembri, MaltaToday', 22 December 2019, at https://www.maltatoday.com.mt/news/national/99382/24000_mayo_clinic_bill_fenech_paid:for_keith_schembri#.X04lJy2w0cg.

currently under arrest, claimed during police investigations that Schembri was his co-conspirator.[116]

7.2   Police Surveillance During 2019 Protests

In the context of reports from various media organisations[117] that several plainclothes policemen were seen in strategic positions taking pictures and video footage of people during the civil protests occurring in Malta during the period October—December 2019, the Malta IT Law Association (MITLA) issued a statement[118] calling upon the Information and Data Protection Commissioner to look into the matter to ensure that any processing of so-called 'special categories of personal data' carried out by the Police is carried out in accordance with applicable laws, and in particular, the Data Protection (Processing of Personal Data by Competent Authorities for the Purposes of the Prevention, Investigation, Detection or Prosecution of Criminal Offences or the Execution of Criminal Penalties) Regulations,[119] which transposes EU Directive 2016/680,[120] and in full respect of the fundamental rights and freedoms of the protestors. No formal outcomes have been published regarding this matter.

---

[116] 'As it happened: 'Keith Schembri wanted Daphne dead,' Fenech told police', Times of Malta, 27 August 2020, at https://timesofmalta.com/articles/view/live-blog-police-inspector-to-testify-about-yorgen-fenech.814473.

[117] See for example, 'Police fail to explain why they photographed demonstrators', at https://timesofmalta.com/articles/view/police-fail-to-explain-why-they-photographed-demonstrators.754549.

[118] 'Police Surveillance During Protests May be Unlawful', 4 December 2019, at https://www.mitla.org.mt/wp-content/uploads/2019/12/MITLA-POLICE-SURVEILLANCE-STATEMENT.pdf.

[119] Subsidiary Legislation 586.08 of the Laws of Malta (S.L. 586.08), http://www.justice-services.gov.mt/DownloadDocument.aspx?app=lom&itemid=12840&l=1.

[120] Directive (EU) 2016/680 of 27 April 2016 on the protection of natural persons with regard to the processing of personal data by competent authorities for the purposes of the prevention, investigation, detection or prosecution of criminal offences or the execution of criminal penalties, and on the free movement of such data, and repealing Council Framework Decision 2008/977/JHA. OJ L 119, 4.5.2016, p. 89–131. ELI: https://eur-lex.europa.eu/eli/dir/2016/680/oj.

7.3   Police Access to Speed Cameras Operated by the Transport Authority

It has been reported that the police have signed an MoU with Transport Malta about having direct access to road cameras.[121] 'Home Affairs Minister said the cameras were useful for monitoring traffic as well as fighting crime.'

The Office of the IDPC carried out an investigation. It was reported in the local news that "The investigation was conducted both at Transport Malta and the Police and it was concluded that, contrary to what has been reported in the media, the processing of personal data subject to the MoU was in line with the applicable data protection legal framework."[122]

7.4   The Proposal by the Government of Malta to Deploy Smart CCTV Surveillance Cameras in Public Spaces

Government's proposal to introduce smart CCTV surveillance cameras in places accessible to the public considered to be 'problem areas' was met with controversy, causing the Government to backtrack from its initial announcement that the cameras to be deployed would have 'advanced facial recognition capability' to the ostensibly less intrusive 'advanced video surveillance'.[123] The proposed system garnered a critical reaction from the UN Special Rapporteur on the Right to Privacy. It motivated a letter sent to the European Commission by a local sociologist, Michael Briguglio.[124] In overview, the limits to intrusions of privacy and data protection rights of data subjects set out in European privacy, and data protection law was underlined; it is not known whether any further practical

---

[121] Police to have access to Transport Malta road cameras: 250 more cameras planned, at https://timesofmalta.com/articles/view/police-to-have-access-to-transport-malta-road-cameras.734560.

[122] 'Police access to road CCTV is lawful—IDPC', Newsbook, 13 January 2020, at https://newsbook.com.mt/en/police-access-to-road-cctv-is-lawful-idpc/.

[123] Rollback on facial recognition CCTV: no legal justification for intrusive technology, MaltaToday, 26 November 2018, at https://www.maltatoday.com.mt/news/national/91196/rollback_facial_recognition_cctv_malta_intrusive_technology#.X09xaC2w0ch.

[124] 'Brussels reply on Safe City suggests facial recognition CCTV impossible without proper justification', MaltaToday, 5 April 2019, https://www.maltatoday.com.mt/news/europe-2019/94121/brussels_reply_on_safe_city_suggests_facial_recognition_cctv_impossible_without_proper_justification#.X09xmS2w0ch.

steps forward on the project have been taken since—the matter has not featured again in public debate since.

7.5   Data Processing for Research Purposes Under the Auspices of the University of Malta

As aforementioned, the 'research ethics committee of an institution recognised by the Commissioner' for the purposes of DPA Article 7 is the University Research Ethics Committee, and in particular its sub-committee on data protection (UREC-DP). The University has published a Research Code of Practice providing 'guiding principles and standards of good practice in research across all subject disciplines and areas of study in the University'[125]; It applies to all those undertaking research on the University's premises using its facilities, or on behalf of the University, including staff, students, visiting or affiliate staff, associates, contractors and consultants.[126] It has also published the Research Ethics Review Procedures which apply 'to all UM staff, students, and anyone else researching under its auspices.'[127] UREC may also consider requests for ethics and data protection review by researchers external to the UM, against payment.[128] In brief, the researcher is required to complete a self-assessment exercise on research ethics and data protection (REDP). Depending on the outcome of this self-assessment, the researcher may be further required to submit an application for REDP review to their Faculty Research Ethics Committee (FREC). If the proposed research involves 'special categories of personal data' as defined in the GDPR, the FREC reviews the application and makes a recommendation to UREC. The role of UREC-DP includes liaising with the IDPC in terms of DPA Section 7 to obtain any necessary authorisation required for research proposals that have been referred to it.[129] UREC-DP is also tasked with arbitrating in those cases where researchers do not agree with FREC decisions on data protection matters not related to special categories of personal data.

[125] Research Code of Practice https://www.um.edu.mt/__data/assets/pdf_file/0011/338942/ResearchCodeofPractice.pdf.
[126] Ibid.
[127] Research Ethics Review Procedures https://www.um.edu.mt/__data/assets/pdf_file/0006/338901/ReserachEthicsReviewProcedures.pdf.
[128] Ibid.
[129] One of the authors sits on UREC and UREC-DP, and acts as a reviewer on such applications that are submitted to UREC by the FRECs.

7.6   Blockchain Applications

Researchers at UM are engaged in an ongoing pilot project on using blockchain technology to manage dynamic consent for research purposes in the context of the biobank.[130] In the words of the project team, 'Dwarna' is 'a web portal for 'dynamic consent' that acts as a hub connecting the different stakeholders of the Malta Biobank: biobank managers, researchers, research partners, and the general public. The portal stores research partners' consent in a blockchain to create an immutable audit trail of research partners' consent changes. Dwarna's structure also presents a solution to the European Union's General Data Protection Regulation's right to erasure—a right that is seemingly incompatible with the blockchain model. Dwarna's transparent structure increases trustworthiness in the biobanking process by giving research partners more control over which research studies they participate in, by facilitating the withdrawal of consent and by making it possible to request that the biospecimen and associated data are destroyed.'[131] One of the authors of this paper was engaged as a legal consultant for the carrying out of a Data Protection Impact Assessment (DPIA) for this project.

7.7   Digital Contact-Tracing

Malta has deployed a digital contact tracing application, 'COVID Alert Malta', to help fight against the spread of Covid-19. The digital contact tracing solution that the government has deployed follows the DP-3T, Decentralized Privacy-Preserving Proximity Tracing, model.[132] One of the authors of this paper was engaged by the local authorities as an external legal consultant to aid the exercise of carrying out a DPIA. The DPIA should eventually be published and made publicly accessible.

---

[130] See Mamo, Nicholas, Gilliam M Martin, Maria Desira, Bridget Ellul, Jean-Paul Ebejer, 'Dwarna: A Blockchain Solution for Dynamic Consent in Biobanking', *European Journal of Human Genetics*, Vol. 28, 2020, pp. 609–626.

[131] Ibid.

[132] DP3T https://github.com/DP-3T/documents.

8   CONCLUSION

Malta had participated in the Council of Europe's Committee of Experts on Data Protection since 1984, and during 1993–1996 a comprehensive Information Practices Act was drafted by a Working Group led by the then Minister of Justice and including the Attorney-General, the Deputy Attorney General and a domain expert. Yet, it took the best part of twenty years before Malta finally enacted a Data Protection Law in 2003. The change in Government of 1996–1998 and other factors meant that privacy and data protection never made it to the highest point of political priorities. The political will to introduce the most minimalist of data protection laws that could be deemed to meet the minimum standards of the *acquis communautaire* only materialised the year before Malta acceded to the EU in 2004. Thanks to its membership of the EU, Malta is now obliged to respect the high standards set in the GDPR like every other EU member state. Since it is a Directive and not a Regulation, the Police Directive may have afforded the Maltese Parliament more wriggle room when it comes to transposition. Yet, it seems to have been imported lock, stock and barrel into Maltese law. On the other hand, the coming into force of the Police Directive in May 2018 is too recent to enable a fair determination of whether Malta's implementation of this Directive meets the expectations of its drafters.

Privacy advocates in Malta are, in autumn 2020, looking forward to two important opportunities: the repeal and replacement of the Security Service Act and the much-anticipated Constitutional Convention. The former presents an opportunity to regulate matters of surveillance for national security purposes which lie outside the scope of GDPR or the Police Directive, and a blueprint[133] already exists to act as a springboard for discussion. Reform of Malta's Constitution would finally help privacy to reach par with other fundamental human rights, and again, concrete proposals have been made, one of which has been reproduced in this paper. One can only hope that in a few years' time, one can look back with satisfaction at lessons well learned rather than yet more opportunities squandered.

[133] See note 620 *supra*.

CONCLUSION

Malta has been a member of the European Union for over fifteen years. From the above chapters, one can say that more or less European Union law has fully been aligned with the Maltese legal order. Generally speaking the implementation and enforcement of EU law in Malta has been a success. Improvement can come if the state invests more in legal resources for the civil service including the judiciary and the office of the Attorney General/State Advocate as well as the University. Maltese lawyers cannot keep up to date unless they have access to the various legal resources that are mushrooming in Europe, which are making the use of comparative law more accessible and more widespread. While the transposition and implementation have generally been a success, one of the most notable failures in the integration has been the lack of use of Article 267 TFEU by the Maltese courts—the preliminary reference procedure. The reasons could be various, and it is beyond the scope of this book, though it is widely acknowledged that the law courts in Malta are among the least efficient and least accountable institutions on the island who are plagued by the rule of law issues.[1] However, leaving this drawback aside, Malta has been very successful in the implementation and enforcement of EU law. Malta has proved that small size in itself does not matter as Malta has generally

[1] See Case C-896/19 *Repubblika v Prim Ministru*.

I. Sammut, J. Agranovska (eds.), *The Implementation and Enforcement of European Union Law in Small Member States*, https://doi.org/10.1007/978-3-030-66115-1

performed much better than the Member States who have had more experience and are larger and so have more resources. The above chapters while giving a snapshot of how EU law is implemented and enforced in Malta, prove that small states and a mixed jurisdiction are also good ingredients to accept and integrate EU law into the national legal order. Malta can serve as a microcosm for other present or future Member States who are also looking at improving their reception of EU law.